MODELS COVERED 1962-1978
Road - Motocross - Trials - Enduro

Cota 123	Texas	King Scorpion
Cappra 125-MX	250 Trail	Enduro 250
Cota 123 Trail	Impala-Cross 250	Rapita 250
Cappra 125 VA	Sport 250	Cappra 250-Five
Cota 172	Cota 247	Cappra 250-GP
Enduro	Cota 247 Trail	Cappra 250-MX
Impala-Cross 175	LaCross 66/67	Cappra 250-VR
Impala-Sport	Scorpion 250	Cappra 250 V-75
Impala	Cappra 250	Cappra 360-GP
Commando 175	King Scorpion Automix	Cappra 360-DS
Kenya		

CONTENTS

CHAPTER ONE

GENERAL INFORMATION 1

    Introduction   Expendable supplies
    Service hints   Safety first
    Tools

CHAPTER TWO

ENGINE, TRANSMISSION, AND CLUTCH 4

    Operating principles   Primary drive gear
    Periodic engine service   Shifter
    Preparation for engine disassembly   Kickstarter
    Cylinder and cylinder head   Crankcase halves
    Piston, piston pin, and   Transmission
       piston rings   Crankshaft
    Crankcase covers   Bearings
    Engine sprocket   Oil seals
    Magneto   Automix pump
    Clutch

CHAPTER THREE

ELECTRICAL SYSTEM 51

    Magneto ignition system   Spark plug
    Electronic ignition system   Battery
    Rectifier   Lights

CHAPTER FOUR

CARBURETION 66

Operation
Carburetor overhaul frequency
Amal monobloc carburetor
Amal concentric carburetor
Bing carburetor

Amal Mark II carburetor
Adjustment
Modification
Miscellaneous carburetor problems

CHAPTER FIVE

CHASSIS SERVICE 93

Frame
Handlebar
Front forks
Wheels and tires
Brakes

Shock absorbers
Swinging arm
Exhaust system
Drive chain
Rear sprocket

CHAPTER SIX

PERIODIC SERVICE AND MAINTENANCE 111

CHAPTER SEVEN

TROUBLESHOOTING 112

Operating requirements
Starting difficulties
Poor idling
Misfiring
Flat spots
Power loss
Overheating
Backfiring

Piston seizure
Excessive vibration
Clutch slip or drag
Poor handling
Brake problems
Lighting problems
Troubleshooting guide

CHAPTER EIGHT

SPECIFICATIONS 117

INDEX 127

FLOYD CLYMER - 2025 EDITION
MONTESA
WORKSHOP MANUAL
ALL MODELS
125cc - 175cc - 250cc - 360cc
ROAD - MOTOCROSS
TRIALS - ENDURO
1962 - 1978

A Floyd Clymer Publication - 2025 VelocePress.com

PREFACE

TRADEMARKS & COPYRIGHT

Montesa® has been a subsidiary of Montesa Honda S.A. since 1982 and this publication is not sponsored by or endorsed by the trademark owner. We recognize that some words, model names and designations, for example, mentioned herein are the property of the trademark holder. We use them for identification purposes only. This is not an official publication however; it may include non-copyright works that pre-date the Honda acquisition of the trademark.

INTRODUCTION

Welcome to the world of digital publishing ~ the book you now hold in your hand was printed using the latest state of the art digital technology. The advent of print-on-demand has forever changed the publishing process, never has information been so accessible and it is our hope that this book serves your informational needs for years to come. If this is your first exposure to digital publishing, we hope that you are pleased with the results. Many more titles of interest to the classic automobile and motorcycle enthusiast, collector and restorer are available via our website at www.VelocePress.com. We hope that you find this title as interesting as we do.

NOTE FROM THE PUBLISHER

The information presented is true and complete to the best of our knowledge. All recommendations are made without any guarantees on the part of the author or the publisher, who also disclaim all liability incurred with the use of this information.

INFORMATION ON THE USE OF THIS PUBLICATION

This manual is an invaluable resource for those interested in performing their own maintenance. However, in today's information age we are constantly subject to changes in common practice, new technology, availability of improved materials and increased awareness of chemical toxicity. As such, it is advised that the user consult with an experienced professional prior to undertaking any procedure described herein. While every care has been taken to ensure correctness of information, it is obviously not possible to guarantee complete freedom from errors or omissions or to accept liability arising from such errors or omissions. Therefore, any individual that uses the information contained within, or elects to perform or participate in do-it-yourself repairs or modifications acknowledges that there is a risk factor involved and that the publisher or its associates cannot be held responsible for personal injury or property damage resulting from the use of the information or the outcome of such procedures.

WARNING!

One final word of advice, this publication is intended to be used as a reference guide, and when in doubt the reader should consult with a qualified technician.

CHAPTER ONE

GENERAL INFORMATION

INTRODUCTION

This book was written to help owners service and repair Montesa motorcycles. The information applies to all 123cc through 360cc models.

SERVICE HINTS

Most of the service procedures covered are straightforward, and can be performed by anyone reasonably handy with tools. It is suggested, however, that you consider your own capabilities before attempting any operation involving major disassembly of the engine. Some operations, for example, require the use of a press. It would be wiser to have those performed by a shop equipped for such work, rather than to try to do the job yourself with makeshift equipment. Some procedures require precision measurements. Unless you have the skills and equipment to make these, it would be better to have a motorcycle shop make them for you.

Repairs are faster and much easier if your machine is clean before you begin work. There are special cleaners for washing the engine and related parts. Just brush or spray on the cleaning solution, let it stand, then rinse it away with a garden hose. Clean all oily or greasy parts with cleaning solvent as you remove them. *Never use gasoline as a cleaning agent.* Gasoline presents an extreme fire hazard. Be sure to work in a well ventilated area when you use cleaning solvent. Keep a fire extinguisher, rated for gasoline fires, handy just in case.

Special tools are required for some service procedures. These may be purchased at Montesa dealers. If you are on good terms with the dealer's service department, you may be able to borrow his.

Much of the labor charge for repairs made by dealers is for removal and disassembly of other parts to reach the defective one. It is frequently possible to do all of this yourself, then take the affected subassembly in for repair.

Once you decide to tackle the job yourself, read the entire section in this manual which pertains to it. Study the illustrations and the text until you have a good idea of what's involved. If special tools are required, make arrangements to get them before you start. It is frustrating to get partly into a job and then find that you are unable to complete it.

TOOLS

For proper servicing, you will need an assortment of ordinary hand tools. As a minimum, these include:

1. Combination wrenches
2. Socket wrenches
3. Plastic mallet
4. Small hammer
5. Snap ring pliers

6. Phillips screwdrivers
7. Pliers
8. Slot screwdrivers
9. Feeler gauges
10. Spark plug gauge
11. Spark plug wrench
12. Dial indicator

A tool kit, widely available and suitable for most minor servicing is shown in **Figure 1**.

Electrical system servicing requires a voltmeter, ohmmeter or other device for determining continuity, and a hydrometer for battery-equipped machines. The hydrometer is inexpensive, and should be part of every motorcyclist's tool kit.

EXPENDABLE SUPPLIES

Certain expendable supplies are also required. These include grease, oil, gasket cement, wiping rags, cleaning solvent, and distilled water. Cleaning solvent is available at many service stations. Distilled water, required for the battery, is available at every supermarket. It is sold for use in steam irons, and is quite inexpensive.

SAFETY FIRST

Professional motorcycle mechanics can work for years and never sustain a serious injury. If you observe a few rules of common sense and safety, you can enjoy many safe hours servicing your own machine. You can also hurt yourself or damage the bike if you ignore these rules.

1. Never use gasoline as a cleaning solvent.
2. Never smoke or use a torch in the vicinity of flammable liquids such as cleaning solvent in open containers.
3. Never smoke or use a torch in an area where batteries are charging. Highly explosive hydrogen gas is formed during the charging process.
4. If welding or brazing is required on the machine, remove the fuel tank to a safe distance, at least 50 feet away.
5. Be sure to use the proper size wrenches for nut turning.
6. If a nut is tight, think for a moment what would happen to your hand should the wrench slip. Be guided accordingly.
7. Keep your work area clean and uncluttered.
8. Wear safety goggles in all operations involving drilling, grinding, or use of a chisel.
9. Never use worn tools.
10. Keep a fire extinguisher handy and be sure it's rated for gasoline and electrical fires.

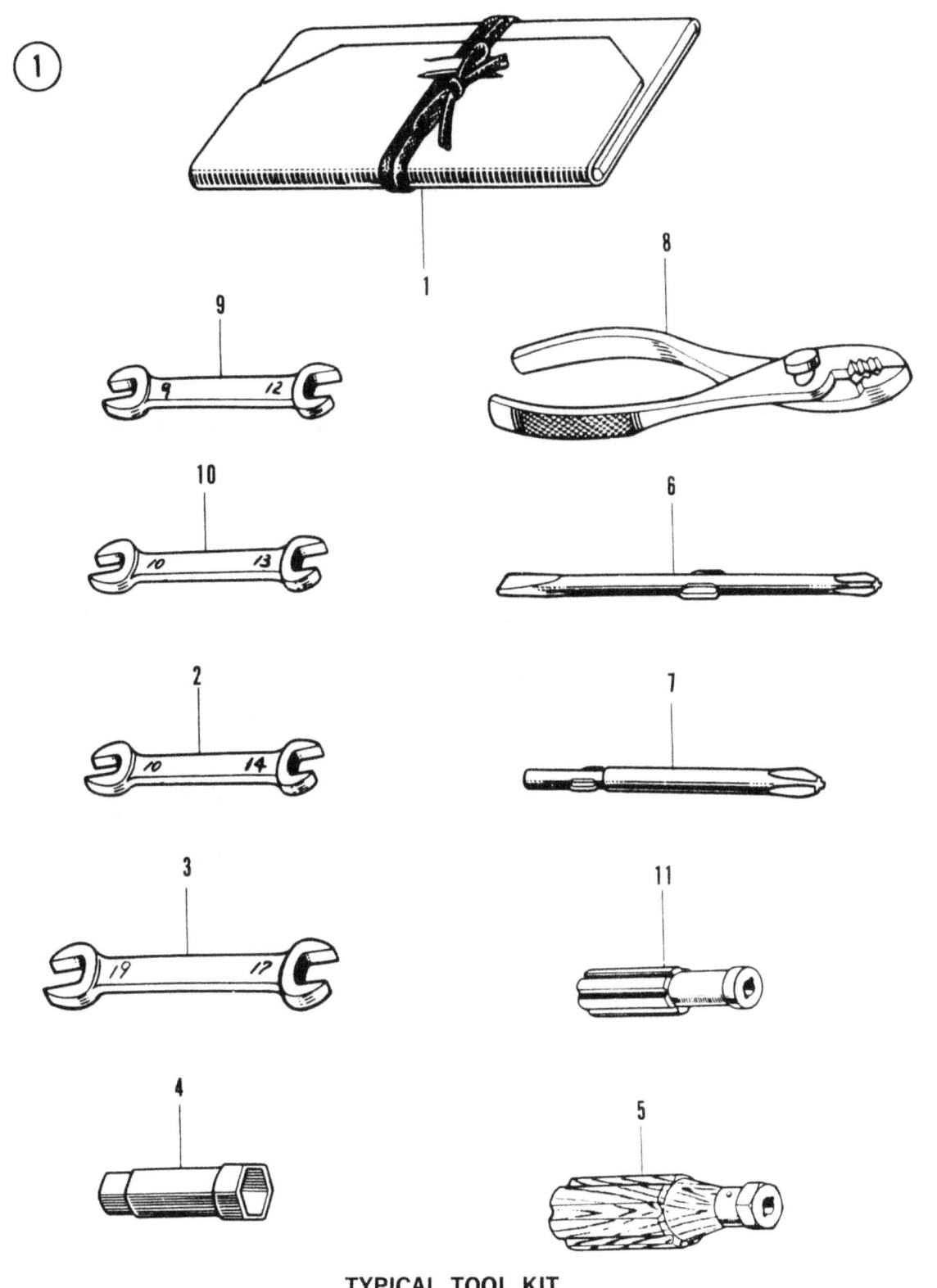

TYPICAL TOOL KIT

1. Tool bag
2. 10 x 14mm open-end wrench
3. 17 x 19mm open-end wrench
4. Spark plug wrench
5. Screwdriver handle
6. No. 2 Phillips and slotted screwdriver
7. No. 3 Phillips screwdriver
8. 135mm pliers
9. 9 x 12mm open-end wrench
10. 10 x 13mm open-end wrench
11. Screwdriver handle

CHAPTER TWO

ENGINE, TRANSMISSION, AND CLUTCH

This chapter describes removal, disassembly, service, and reassembly of the engine, transmission, and clutch. It is suggested that the engine be serviced without removing it from the chassis except for overhaul of the crankshaft assembly, transmission, gearshift mechanism, or bearings. Operating principles of piston port 2-stroke engines are also discussed in this chapter.

OPERATING PRINCIPLES

Figures 1 through 4 illustrate operating principles of 2-stroke engines. During this discussion, assume that the crankshaft is rotating counterclockwise. In **Figure 1**, as the piston travels downward, a scavenging port (A) between the crankcase and the cylinder is uncovered. The exhaust gases leave the cylinder through the exhaust port (B), which is also opened by the downward movement of the piston. A fresh fuel/air charge, which has previously been compressed slightly, travels from the crankcase (C) to the cylinder through the scavenging port (A) as the port opens. Since the incoming charge is under pressure, it rushes into the cylinder quickly and helps to expel the exhaust gases from the previous cycle.

Figure 2 illustrates the next phase of the cycle. As the crankshaft continues to rotate, the

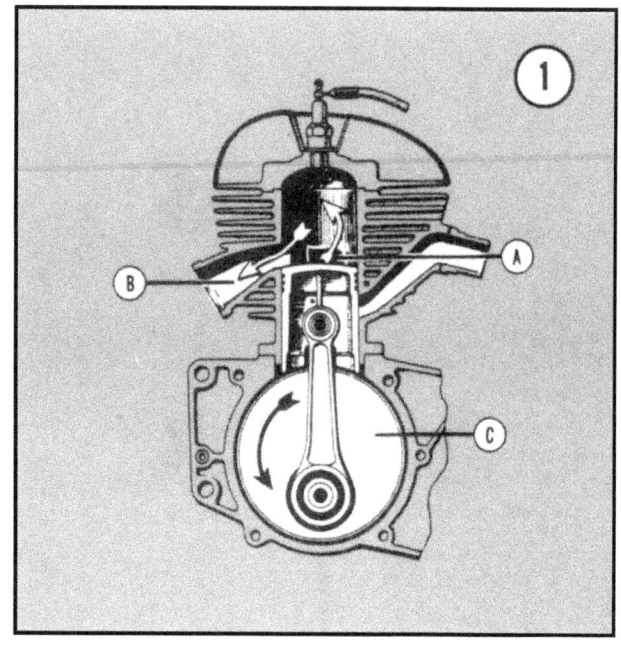

piston moves upward, closing the exhaust and scavenging ports. As the piston continues upward, the air/fuel mixture in the cylinder is compressed. Notice also that a low pressure area is created in the crankcase at the same time. Further upward movement of the piston uncovers the intake port (D). A fresh fuel/air charge is then drawn into the crankcase through the intake port because of the low pressure created by the upward piston movement.

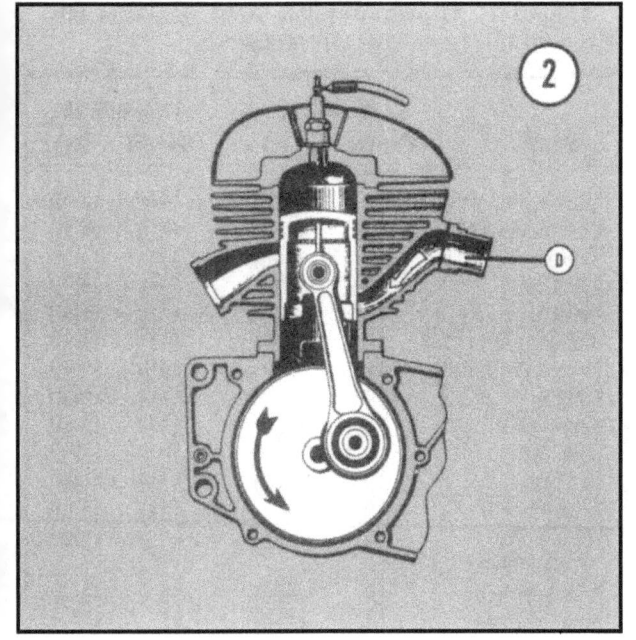

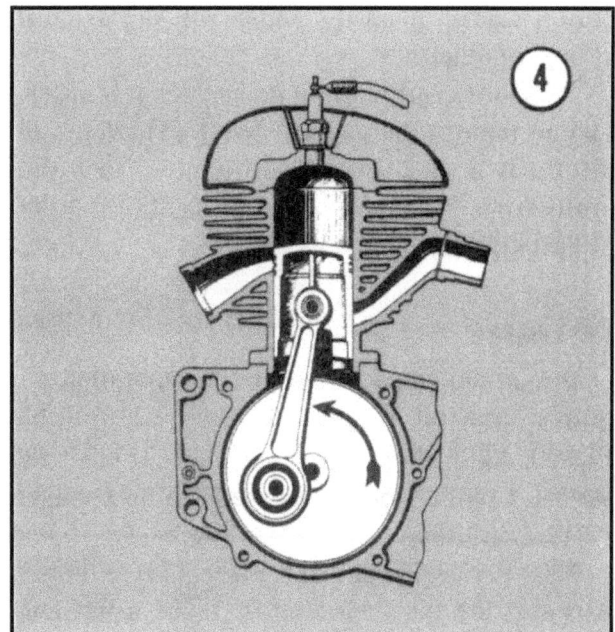

The third phase is shown in **Figure 3**. As the piston approaches top dead center, the spark plug fires, igniting the compressed mixture. The piston is then driven downward by the expanding gases.

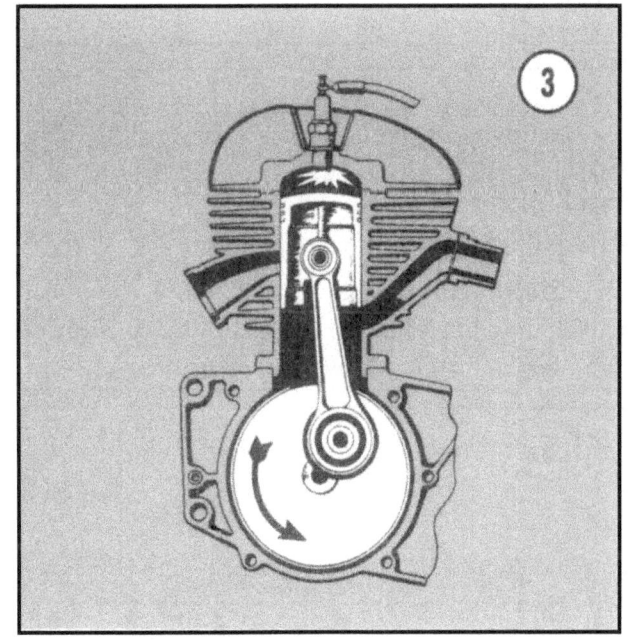

When the top of the piston uncovers the exhaust port, the fourth phase begins as shown in **Figure 4**. The exhaust gases leave the cylinder through the exhaust port. As the piston continues downward, the intake port is closed and the mixture in the crankcase is compressed in preparation for the next cycle.

It can be seen from the foregoing discussion that every downward stroke of the piston is a power stroke.

PERIODIC ENGINE SERVICE

To maintain peak operating efficiency, certain maintenance services should be performed periodically on the engine and its accessories. These services are described in following paragraphs.

Air Cleaner

The air cleaner removes dust and abrasive particles from the air before they enter the engine. Should an appreciable quantity of dirt get in, rapid wear of pistons, rings, and cylinders will result. Air passages in the carburetor may also become clogged.

If the air cleaner becomes clogged, engine air intake is hampered, thereby reducing engine efficiency, power, and gas mileage. Therefore, the air cleaner must be inspected and cleaned at regular intervals.

Carbon Removal

Two-stroke engines are particularly susceptible to carbon formation. Deposits within the combustion chamber result in an increase in compression ratio, which can cause overheating, preignition, and possible engine damage. Exhaust ports, exhaust pipes, and mufflers also collect carbon deposits, which rob the exhaust system of efficiency.

To remove carbon from the engine, it is necessary to remove the cylinder head, cylinder, and piston. It is good practice to remove such deposits from the engine about every 2,000 miles (3,200 kilometers).

Oil Change

Proper clutch and transmission operation requires clean oil. Change oil every 1,500 miles (2,400 kilometers) for machines ridden on streets. Competition models require oil changes every 2 or 3 races.

Start the engine and run it for a few minutes to warm the oil, then stop it. Place a flat pan beneath the engine and remove clutch and transmission drain plugs. Removal of both filler plugs will permit faster draining.

> NOTE: *Some models are equipped with only one drain plug; the clutch and the transmission share a common oil supply.*

Tighten both drain plugs securely upon installation.

Table 1 lists proper transmission and clutch oil quantities for the various models. Use SAE 20 oil in the clutch and SAE 90 oil in the transmission.

PREPARATION FOR ENGINE DISASSEMBLY

1. Drain the oil from the clutch and transmission. Warm the engine first if possible.
2. Thoroughly clean the engine exterior of dirt, oil, and foreign materials, using one of the cleaners formulated for the purpose.
3. Turn the fuel petcock to OFF. Disconnect the fuel line at the carburetor.
4. Remove the exhaust pipe at the cylinder.
5. Remove the air inlet tube or air filter at the carburetor.
6. Disconnect the clutch cable at the engine and the throttle cable at the carburetor.
7. Remove the spark plug cable and spark plug.
8. Remove kickstarter and gear change levers.

Table 1 TRANSMISSION AND CLUTCH OIL QUANTITIES

Model	Clutch Ounces	(cc)	Transmission Ounces	(cc)
Impala, Impala Sport	10	(300)	13½	(400)
Commando 175	10	(300)	13½	(400)
Kenya	10	(300)	13½	(400)
250 Trial	11¾	(350)	13½	(400)
Texas	10	(300)	13½	(400)
Impala Cross (175)	10	(300)	13½	(400)
Impala Cross (250)	10	(300)	13½	(400)
Enduro	10	(300)	13½	(400)
Sport (250)	10	(300)	13½	(400)
Cota 247	6¾	(200)	10	(300)
La Cross	10	(300)	13½	(400)
Scorpion 250	10	(300)	13½	(400)
Cappra 250 (all models)	10	(300)	11	(330)
King Scorpion	10	(300)	11	(330)
King Scorpion (Automix)	10	(300)	11	(330)
Cappra 360 GP/DS	10	(300)	11	(330)
Cappra 125	10	(300)	11	(330)
Cota 123	Transmission and clutch		30½	(900)
Cota 123 Trail	Transmission and clutch		30½	(900)
Cappra 125 VA	Transmission and clutch		30½	(900)
Cota 172	Transmission and clutch		20	(600)
Cota 247 Trail	6¾	(200)	10	(300)
Enduro 250	10	(300)	11	(330)
Rapita 250	10	(300)	11	(330)
Cappra 250 V-75	10	(300)	11	(330)

9. Remove the right crankcase cover (left cover on Cota 123, Cota 123 Trail, Cota 172 and Cappra 125 VA).

10. Disconnect the master link, then remove the drive chain. It is good practice to reconnect the chain ends after removal. Be sure to connect the master link as shown in **Figure 5**.

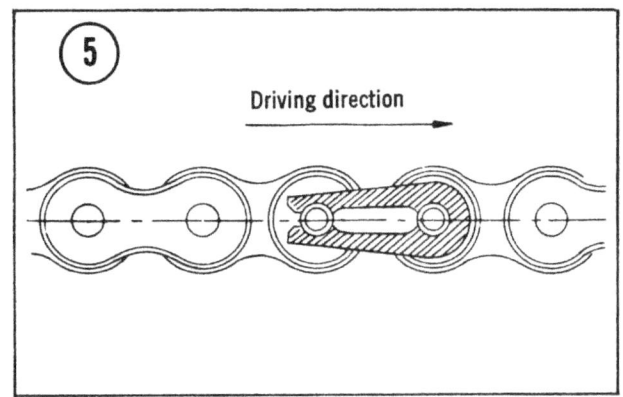

11. Disconnect all wiring from the magneto.
12. Remove the engine mount bolts, then lift the engine from the frame.

13. Reverse the removal procedure to install the engine. Be sure to check the following items before starting.
   a. Transmission oil level
   b. Clutch oil level
   c. Clutch adjustment
   d. Throttle cable adjustment
   e. Drive chain adjustment
   f. Engine mounting bolts
   g. Ignition timing

CYLINDER AND CYLINDER HEAD

Cylinders are cast from lightweight aluminum alloy, with cast iron sleeves. Note that the cylinder sleeve is of sufficient thickness to permit boring and honing after long usage or a piston seizure.

Cylinder Head Removal and Installation

To avoid possible distortion of the cylinder head, allow the engine to cool before removal. To remove cylinder head, proceed as follows:
1. Remove the spark plug.
2. Remove the cylinder head nuts (**Figure 6**). If there are bolts in the cylinder head, remove them also. Lift the cylinder head from the cylinder. Should it not come off easily, tap it lightly with a rubber mallet. Do not pry it off for removal; doing so may cause damage to the sealing surface.

Reverse the removal procedure to install the cylinder head. Tighten the nuts in a criss-cross manner. Torque nuts as listed in **Table 2**.

Table 2 CYLINDER HEAD AND BARREL TORQUE

Model	Cylinder Fixing Nut Torque		Cylinder Head Fixing Nut Torque	
	Ft.-lb.	(mkg)	Ft.-lb.	(mkg)
250 Trail	18	(2.5)	25	(3.5)
Cota 247	18	(2.5)	25	(3.5)
King Scorpion	18	(2.5)	25	(3.5)
Cappra 250	18	(2.5)	25	(3.5)
Cappra 250 VR	18	(2.5)	25	(3.5)
Cota 123	18	(2.5)	25	(3.5)
Cota 123 Trail	18	(2.5)	25	(3.5)
Cappra 125 VA	18	(2.5)	25	(3.5)
Cota 172	18	(2.5)	25	(3.5)
Cota 247 Trail	18	(2.5)	25	(3.5)
Enduro 250	18	(2.5)	25	(3.5)
Rapita 250	18	(2.5)	25	(3.5)
Cappra 250 V-75	18	(2.5)	25	(3.5)
All other models	18	(2.5)	15	(2.1)

Carbon Removal (Combustion Chamber)

Carbon deposits in the combustion chamber result in an increase in compression ratio and can cause preignition, overheating, and excessive fuel consumption. To remove these deposits, scrape them off with the rounded end of a hacksaw blade or a screwdriver, as shown in **Figure 7**. Be careful that you do not damage the sealing surface.

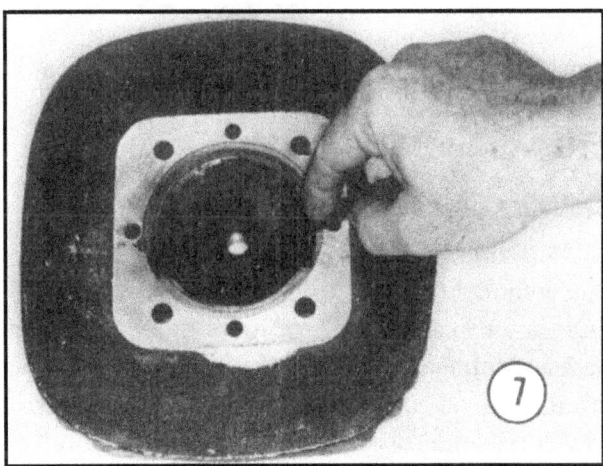

Cylinder Removal

Some cylinders are attached only by thrustuds. Others are attached with additional bolts. Remove these bolts, if installed. Note that washers are installed under the bolt heads. Tap the cylinder around the exhaust port lightly with a plastic mallet, then pull it away from the crankcase (**Figure 8**). Stuff clean rags into the

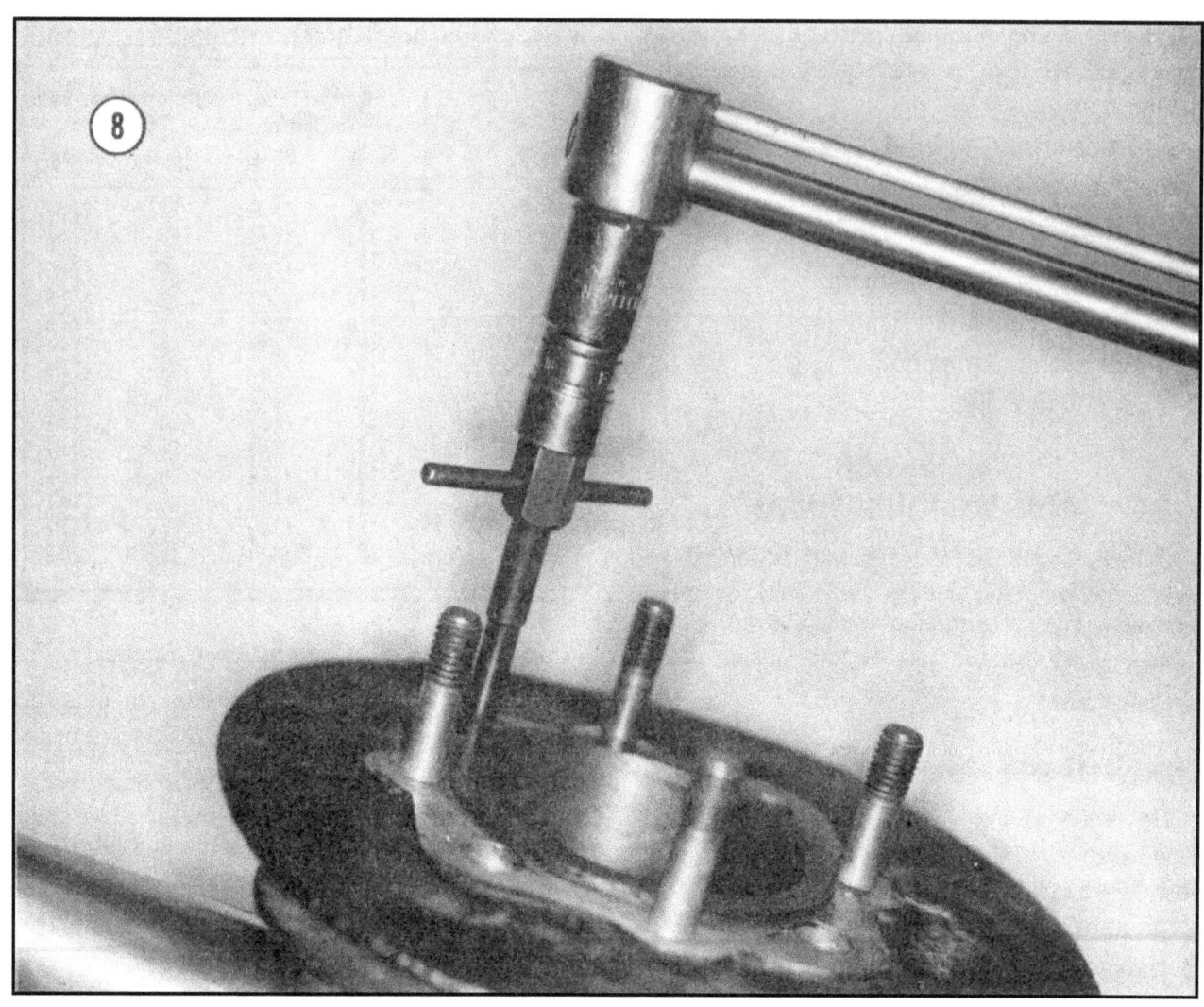

crankcase opening to prevent entry of any foreign material.

Cylinder Inspection

Measure cylinder wall wear at 3 depths within the cylinder, using a cylinder gauge or inside micrometer, as shown in **Figure 9**. Position the instrument parallel and then at right angles to the crankshaft at each depth. If any measurement exceeds standard bore by 0.006 in. (0.15mm), or if the difference between any 2 measurements exceeds 0.002 in. (0.05mm), rebore and hone the cylinder to the next oversize, or replace the cylinder. Pistons are available in oversizes of 0.01 in. (0.25mm) and 0.02 in. (0.50mm). After boring and honing, the difference between maximum and minimum diameters must not be more than 0.0004 in. (0.01mm). Standard cylinder diameters are listed in **Table 3**. All dimensions are plus or minus 0.0002 in. (0.005mm).

Carbon Removal (Cylinder)

Scrape the carbon deposits from around the cylinder exhaust port. The rounded end of a hacksaw blade is a suitable tool for carbon removal.

Cylinder Installation

Be sure that each piston ring end gap is aligned with the locating pin in the ring groove. Lubricate the piston and cylinder, then insert the piston into the lower end of the cylinder. It will be necessary to compress each piston ring as it goes into the cylinder. **Figure 10** illustrates this operation. Always use a new cylinder base gasket upon reassembly. Tighten cylinder nuts to the torque figures shown in Table 2.

Cylinder Sleeve Replacement

Montesa cylinders are fitted with replaceable cast iron sleeves. After long usage or a piston

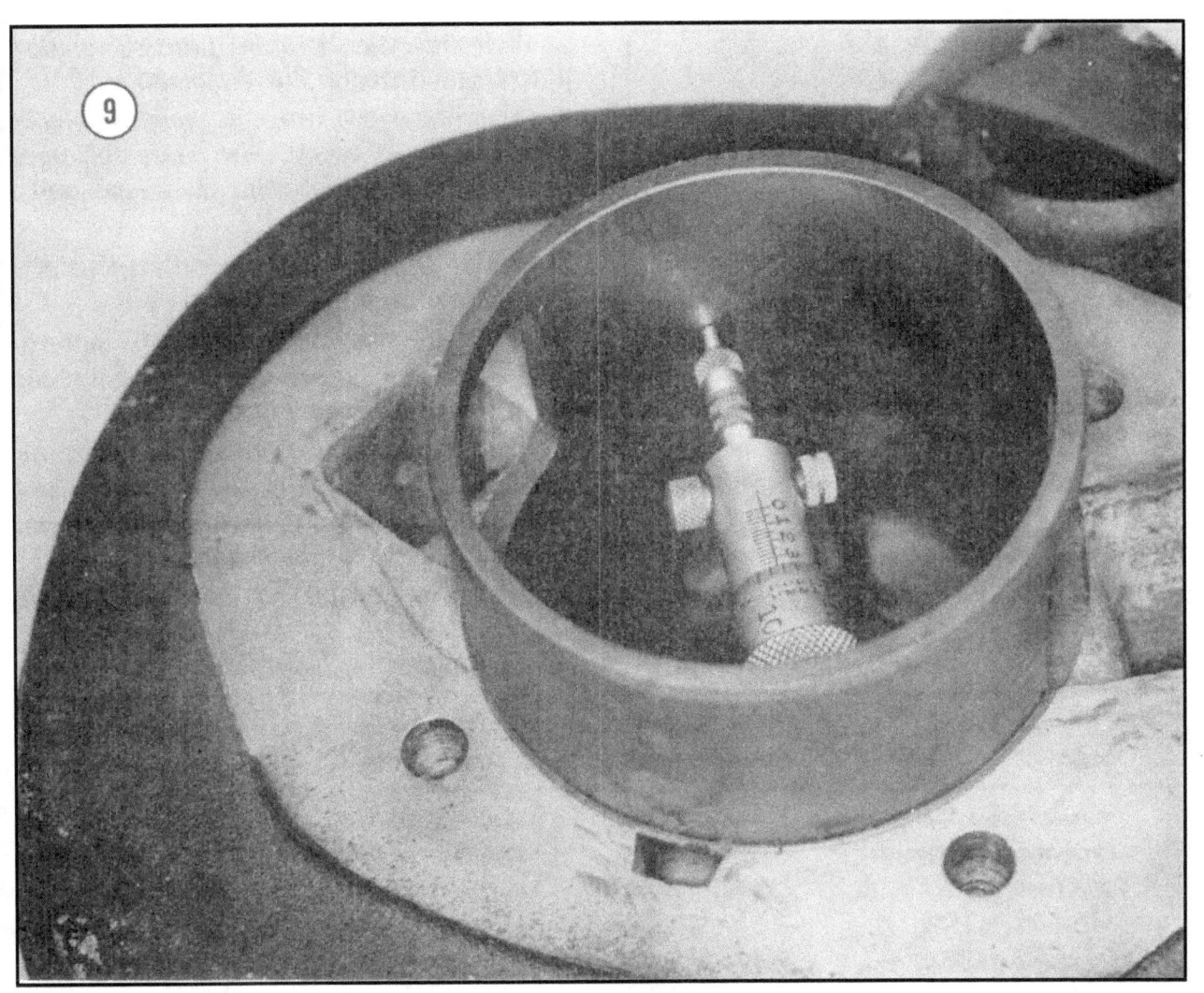

Table 3   CYLINDER BORE DIAMETER

Model	Diameter Inches	(Millimeters)	Model	Diameter Inches	(Millimeters)
Impala Sport	2.3988	(60.93)	Cappra 250 VR	2.758	(70.05)
Impala	2.3988	(60.93)	King Scorpion	2.8563	(72.55)
Commando 175	2.3988	(60.93)	(Except Automix)		
Kenya	2.3988	(60.93)	King Scorpion (Automix)	2.758	(70.05)
250 Trial	2.8563	(72.55)	Cappra 360 GP/DS	3.0724	(78.04)
Impala Cross (175)	2.3988	(60.93)	Cappra 125 MX	2.0276	(51.50)
Texas	2.3988	(60.93)	Cota 123	2.1263	(54.01)
Impala Cross (250)	2.8541	(72.49)	Cota 123 Trail	2.1263	(54.01)
Enduro	2.3988	(60.93)	Cappra 125 VA	2.1263	(54.01)
Sport 250	2.8563	(72.55)	Cota 172	2.3988	(60.93)
Cota 247	2.8563	(72.55)	Cota 247 Trail	2.8563	(72.55)
La Cross	2.8568	(72.56)	Enduro 250	2.758	(70.05)
Scorpion 250	2.8563	(72.55)	Rapita 250	2.758	(70.05)
Cappra 250 (Except VR)	2.8568	(72.56)	Cappra 250 V-75	2.758	(70.05)

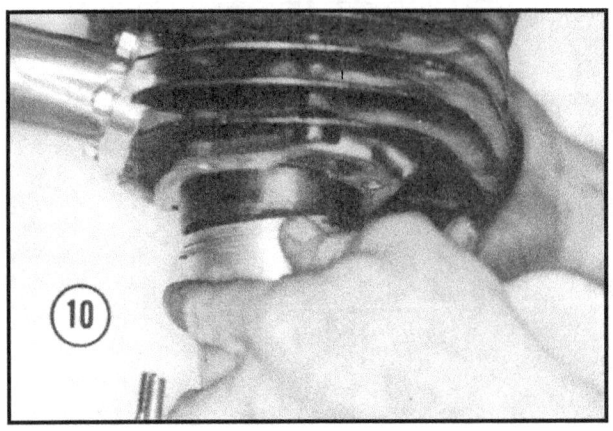

seizure, the cylinder liner may be bored and honed to accommodate an oversize piston.

To replace cylinder sleeve, proceed as follows:

1. Preheat a furnace of adequate size to approximately 1,100°F (600°C).

2. Place the cylinder in the furnace and allow it to remain there for 3 to 4 minutes.

3. Start the sleeve from its bore by tapping with a piece of wood, then grasp the upper portion of the sleeve with pliers and pull it completely free.

4. With the cylinder hot, insert the new sleeve, taking care that all ports align properly.

5. Using a suitable press, maintain approximately 75 lb. (35 kg) pressure on the sleeve until the entire assembly cools.

6. Bore and hone the cylinder assembly to the desired size. Standard, first, and second oversizes are listed in **Table 4**. All measurements are plus or minus 0.0002 in. (0.005mm).

After boring and honing, smooth all ports and

Table 4   STANDARD AND OVERSIZE CYLINDER BORE DIAMETERS

Model	Standard Inches (mm)	1st Oversize Inches (mm)	2nd Oversize Inches (mm)
Impala, Impala Sport	2.3988 (60.93)	2.4086 (61.18)	2.4185 (61.43)
Commando 175, Kenya	2.3988 (60.93)	2.4086 (61.18)	2.4185 (61.43)
250 Trial	2.8563 (72.55)	2.8661 (72.80)	2.8760 (72.05)
Impala Cross (175)	2.3988 (60.93)	2.4086 (61.18)	2.4185 (61.43)
Impala Cross (250)	2.8541 (72.49)	2.8640 (72.75)	2.8738 (73.00)
Enduro	2.3988 (60.93)	2.4086 (61.18)	2.4185 (61.43)
Sport 250	2.8563 (72.55)	2.8661 (72.80)	2.8760 (73.05)
Cota 247	2.8563 (72.55)	2.8661 (72.80)	2.8760 (73.05)
La Cross	2.8568 (72.56)	2.8667 (72.81)	2.8765 (73.06)
Scorpion 250	2.8563 (72.55)	2.8661 (72.80)	2.8760 (73.05)
Cappra 250 (all models except VR)	2.8568 (72.56)	2.8667 (72.81)	2.8765 (73.06)
Cappra 250 VR	2.758 (70.05)	2.768 (70.30)	2.778 (70.55)
King Scorpion (Except Automix)	2.8563 (72.55)	2.8661 (72.80)	2.8760 (73.05)
King Scorpion Automix	2.758 (70.05)	2.768 (70.30)	2.778 (70.55)
Texas	2.3988 (60.93)	2.4086 (61.18)	2.4185 (61.43)
Cappra 360 GP/DS	3.0724 (78.04)	3.0822 (78.29)	3.0921 (78.54)
Cappra 125 MX	2.0276 (51.50)	2.0374 (51.75)	2.0473 (52.00)
Cota 123	2.1263 (54.01)	2.1362 (54.26)	2.1460 (54.51)
Cota 123 Trail	2.1263 (54.01)	2.1362 (54.26)	2.1460 (54.51)
Cappra 125 VA	2.1263 (54.01)	2.1362 (54.26)	2.1460 (54.51)
Cota 172	2.3988 (60.93)	2.4086 (61.18)	2.4185 (61.43)
Cota 247 Trail	2.8563 (72.55)	2.8661 (72.80)	2.8760 (73.05)
Enduro 250	2.758 (70.05)	2.768 (70.30)	2.778 (70.55)
Rapita 250	2.758 (70.05)	2.768 (70.30)	2.778 (70.55)
Cappra 250 V-75	2.758 (70.05)	2.768 (70.30)	2.778 (70.55)

thoroughly clean the cylinder assembly to prevent entry of any possible traces of abrasive particles into the engine.

PISTON, PISTON PIN, AND PISTON RINGS

Montesa pistons are made from aluminum alloy. Each is fitted with 2 piston rings. All service operations on the piston and connecting rod upper end may be accomplished without engine removal.

Piston Pin

Cover the crankcase opening to prevent any parts or foreign material from entering. Remove the clips at each end of the piston pin with needle nose pliers (**Figure 11**), then use a drift and a small hammer to tap the piston pin from its bore. Hold the piston firmly so that no excessive force is applied to the connecting rod. On machines with loose needle bearings, take care that no bearings are lost. **Figure 12** illustrates a slotted section of a discarded cylinder sleeve used to hold the piston in position as the piston pin is driven out. A shortened piece of an old piston pin between the drift and the piston pin to be removed will prevent loss of needle bearings when the piston is removed (**Figure 13**).

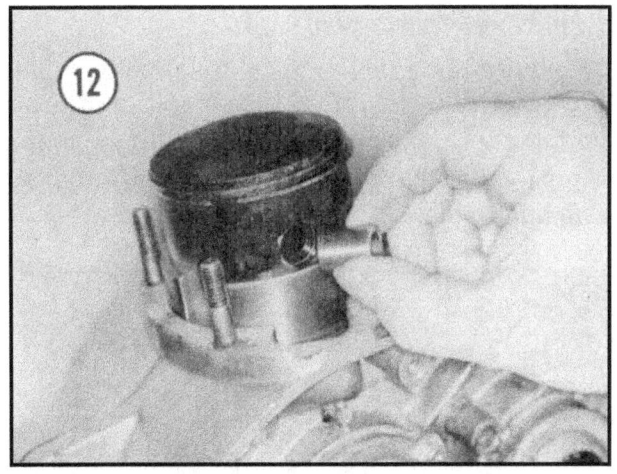

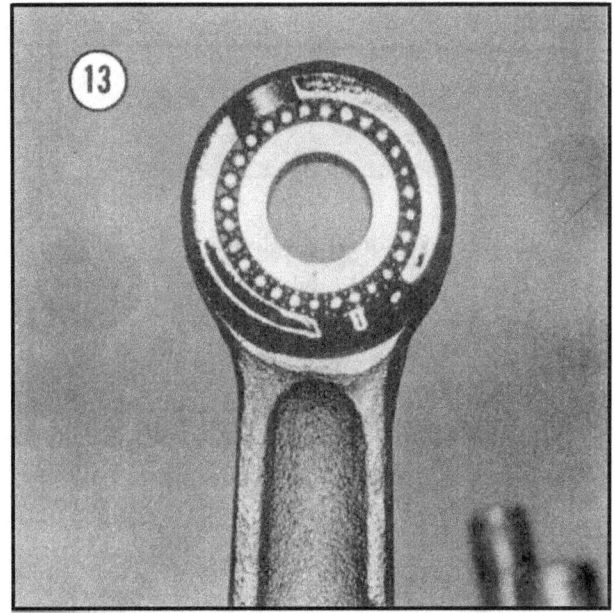

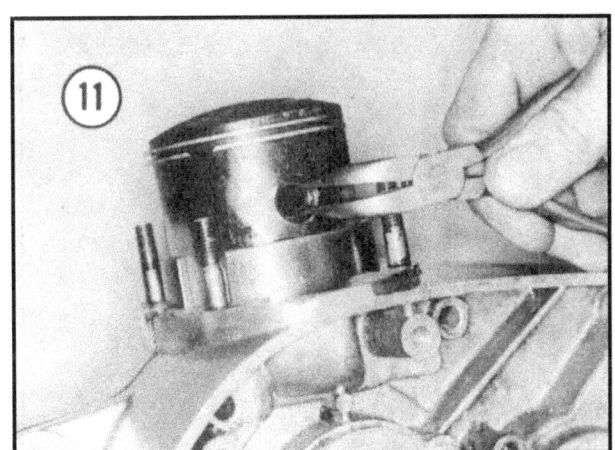

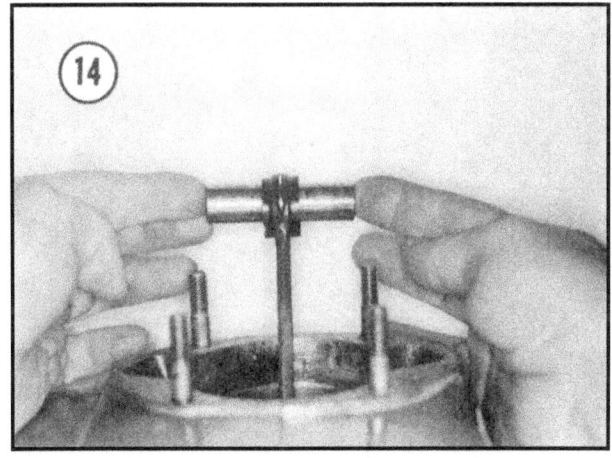

Check each needle bearing for cracks, and if any exist, replace all bearings. Examine the piston pin for scratches or wear. To check bearings for wear, insert them into the end of the connecting rod, then insert a new piston pin, as shown in **Figure 14**. Replace the bearings and/or the rod if clearance is excessive. Typical clearance for new parts is 0.00012-0.00086 in. (0.003-0.022mm). Any clearance over 0.0018 in. (0.045mm) should be considered excessive.

Piston Ring Replacement

Remove the piston rings by spreading the top ring with a thumb on each end, as shown in **Figure 15**. Then remove the ring from the top of the piston. Repeat the procedure for the remaining ring.

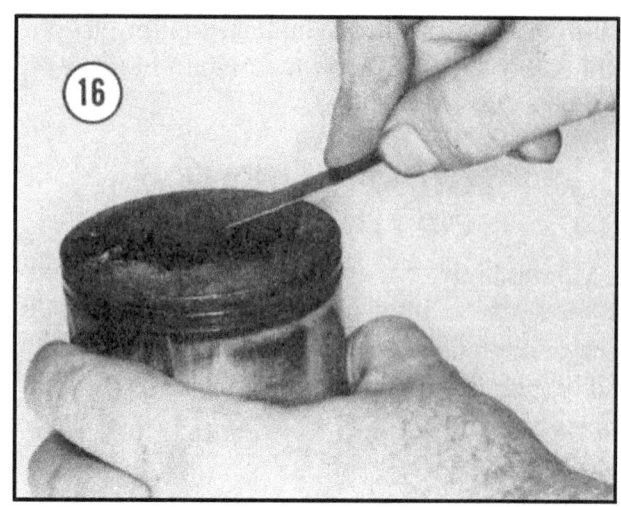

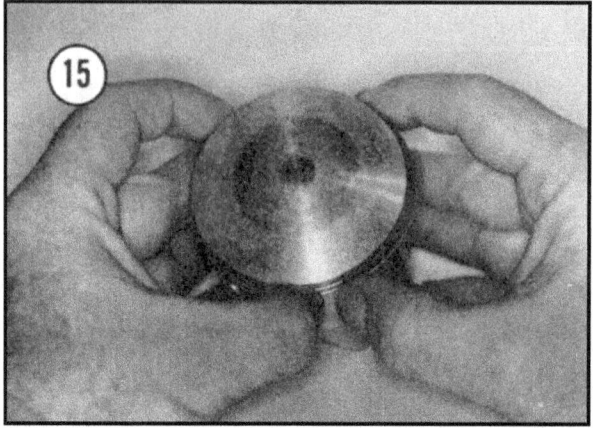

Scrape the carbon from the head of the piston (**Figure 16**). Then clean all carbon and gum from the piston ring grooves using a broken piston ring or a ring groove cleaning tool. Any deposits left in the grooves will cause the rings to stick, thereby causing gas blow-by and loss of power.

Measure each ring for wear as shown in **Figure 17**. Insert the ring 0.2 in. (5mm) into the cylinder, then measure piston ring gap with a feeler gauge. To ensure that the ring is squarely in the cylinder, push it into position with the head of the piston. Standard gap for all but 360cc models is 0.0078-0.0137 in. (0.20-0.35mm). On 360cc models, piston ring gap should be 0.0118-0.0177 in. (0.30-0.45mm). Any gap of 0.04 in. (1.0mm) should be considered excessive. Replace both rings in that event.

To check the fit of the piston ring in its groove, slip the outer surface of the ring into the groove next to the locating pin, then roll the ring completely around the piston. If any binding occurs, determine and correct the cause before proceeding. Then measure clearance between each ring and its groove at several places around the piston, as shown in **Figure 18**. Clearance greater than 0.0067 in. (0.07mm) should be considered excessive.

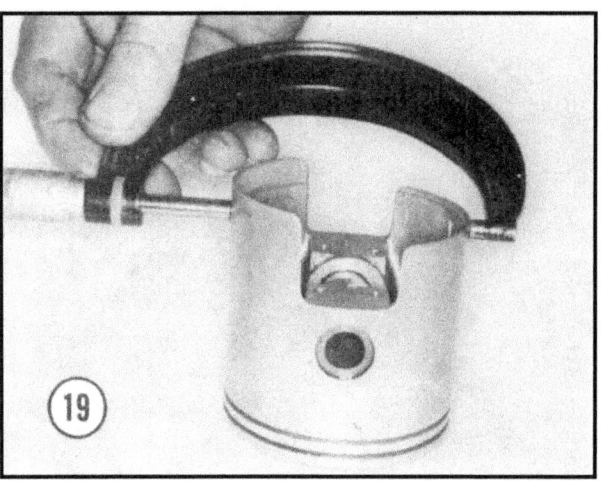

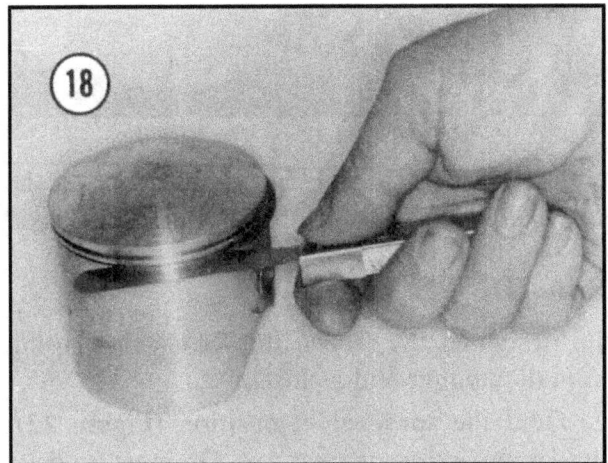

When you replace the rings, install the lower one first. Be sure that the rings are installed so that the U-shape notch formed by the ends of each ring aligns with the locating pin in each piston groove. Upper and lower rings are interchangeable, except in the case where there is one chrome plated ring. Chrome plated rings go on top. Spread the rings carefully with your thumbs, just enough to slip them over the piston.

Piston Clearance—
Checking and Correcting

Piston clearance is the difference between the maximum piston diameter and the minimum cylinder diameter. Measure the outside diameter of the piston skirt (**Figure 19**) at right angles to the piston pin. The measurement should be made just about at the bottom of the piston. Proper piston clearances are listed in **Table 5**.

A piston showing signs of seizure will result in noise, loss of power, and damage to the cylinder wall. If such a piston is reused without correction, another seizure will develop. To correct this condition, lightly smooth the affected area with No. 400 emery paper or a fine oilstone (**Figure 20**). Replace the piston if it is deeply scratched.

Table 5   PISTON TO CYLINDER CLEARANCE

Model	Inch	(Millimeter)
Impala Sport	0.0012	(0.030)
Impala	0.0012	(0.030)
Commando 175	0.0012	(0.030)
Kenya	0.0012	(0.030)
250 Trial	0.0033	(0.085)
Impala Cross (175)	0.0012	(0.030)
Impala Cross (250)	0.0010	(0.025)
Enduro	0.0012	(0.030)
Sport 250	0.0033	(0.085)
Cota 247	0.0012	(0.030)
La Cross	0.0039	(0.099)
Scorpion 250	0.0033	(0.085)
Cappra 250 (except VR)	0.0039	(0.099)
Cappra 250 VR	0.0027	(0.070)
King Scorpion (except Automix)	0.0014	(0.035)
King Scorpion Automix	0.0024	(0.060)
Cappra 360	0.0033	(0.085)
Cappra 125 MX	0.0019	(0.048)
Cota 123	0.0017	(0.045)
Texas	0.0012	(0.030)
Cota 123 Trail	0.0017	(0.045)
Cappra 125 VA	0.0022	(0.058)
Cota 172	0.0012	(0.030)
Cota 247 Trail	0.0012	(0.030)
Enduro 250	0.0024	(0.060)
Rapita 250	0.0024	(0.060)
Cappra 250 V-75	0.0027	(0.070)

Piston Installation

Install the piston with the longer skirt toward the front of the machine. Always use new piston pin retaining clips.

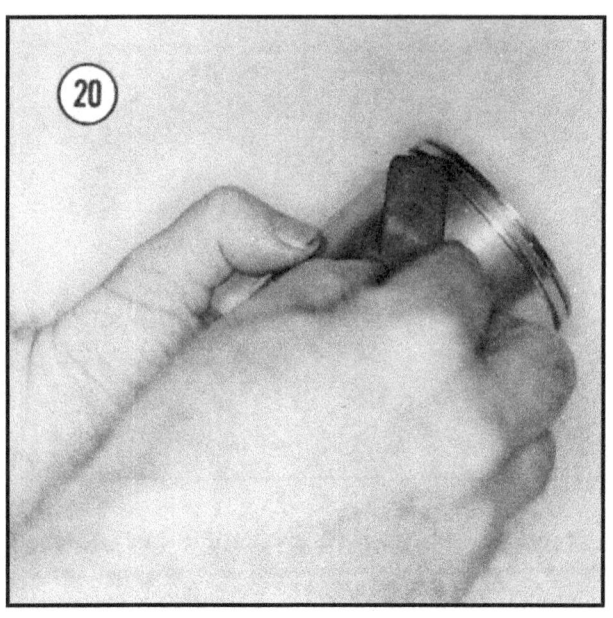

CRANKCASE COVERS

Under the crankcase covers are the magneto, clutch, flywheel, primary reduction gears, and external parts of the kickstarter and shifter. These parts may be serviced without removing the engine.

To remove the crankcase covers, proceed as follows:

1. Remove the drain and filler plugs from the clutch cover, then allow the oil to drain.
2. Remove kickstarter and gear change pedals, if necessary.
3. Remove the crankcase cover attaching screws (**Figure 21**). Note that all screws are of equal length.

Cover Inspection

Examine the sealing surface of the cover for any damage. If the sealing surface is damaged, oil will leak. Do not remove the oil seals from the kickstarter or gearshift shafts unless they are damaged or leaking.

Cover Installation

Reverse removal procedure to install cover. Always use a new gasket upon installation.

ENGINE SPROCKET

The engine sprocket is subject to wear and abrasion from sand and dust, which tend to

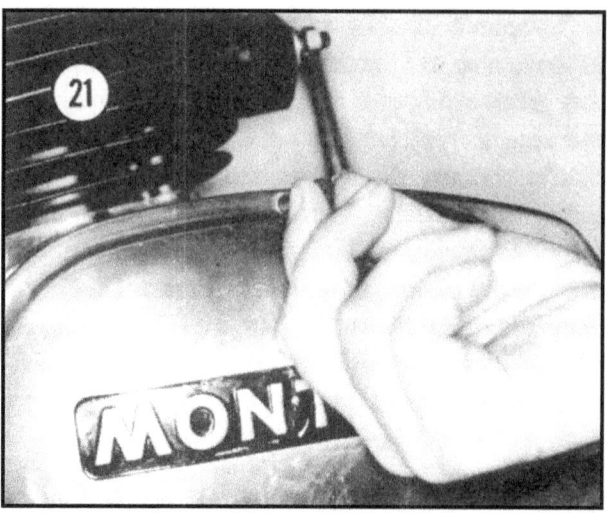

collect on the sprocket. To minimize wear, the sprocket is made from abrasion resistant steel.

Removal

1. Straighten the tab on the lockwasher, using a small hammer and a chisel.
2. Hold the sprocket in position (**Figure 22**), then remove the sprocket nut. On most models, this nut has a left-hand thread.

3. Install a sprocket puller (**Figure 23**), then remove the sprocket.
4. Pull out the shaft key (**Figure 24**).

Inspection

A worn sprocket results in excessive chain noise, and will shorten the life of the chain. Replace the sprocket if it shows any defects. **Figure 25** compares worn and serviceable sprockets.

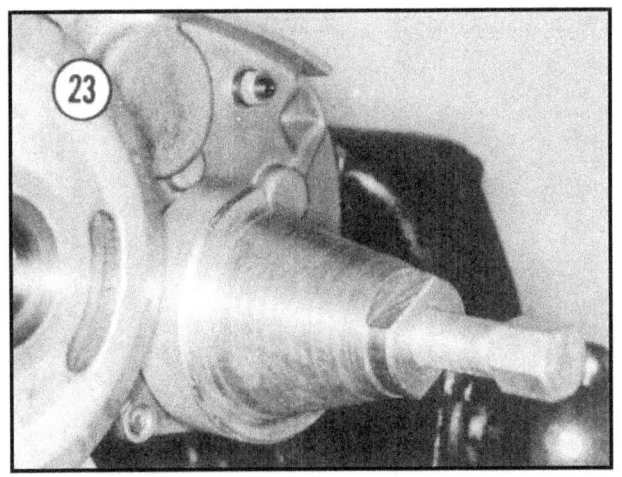

Installation

Reverse the removal procedure to install the sprocket. Use a new lockwasher, and be sure to bend up the tab.

MAGNETO

Each machine is equipped with a flywheel magneto as the source of electrical system power. Removal and installation only are discussed in this section. For details of magneto troubleshooting and service, refer to Chapter Three.

Removal

1. Hold the flywheel in position, remove the attaching nut (**Figure 26**), then pry out the lockwasher with a small screwdriver. Note that the flywheel nut has a left-hand thread, and that a special left-hand lockwasher is used.

2. Install the flywheel puller (**Figure 27**). Turn puller screw clockwise to remove flywheel.

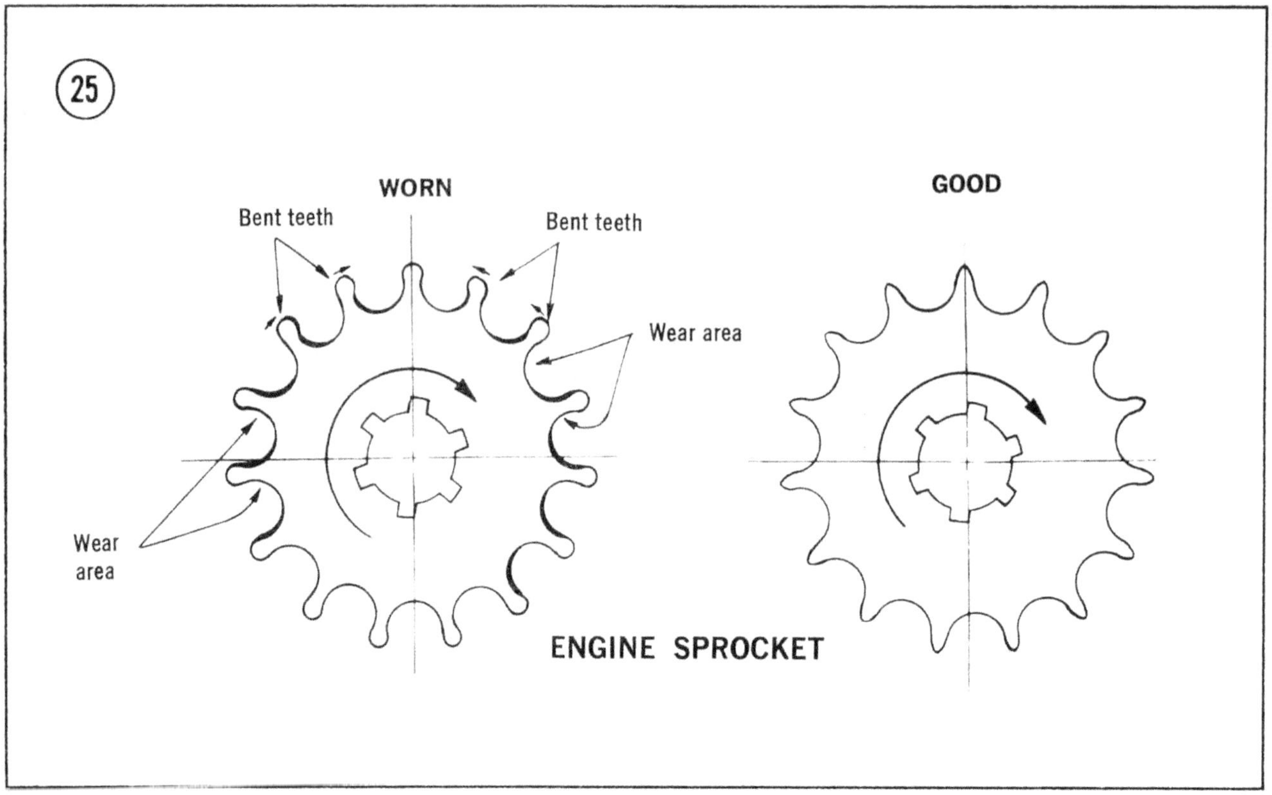

25
WORN
GOOD
Bent teeth
Bent teeth
Wear area
Wear
area
ENGINE SPROCKET

26

27

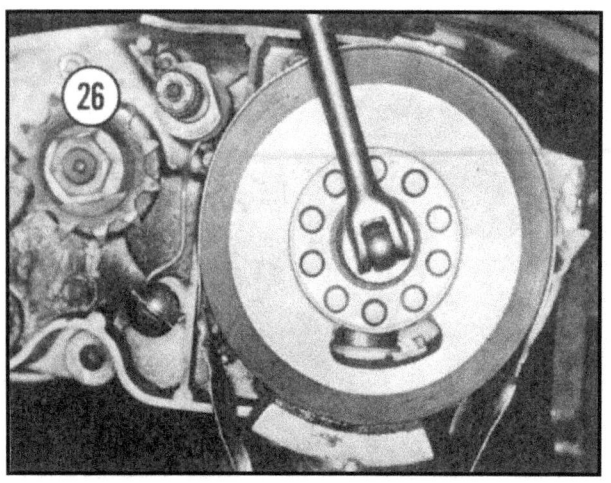

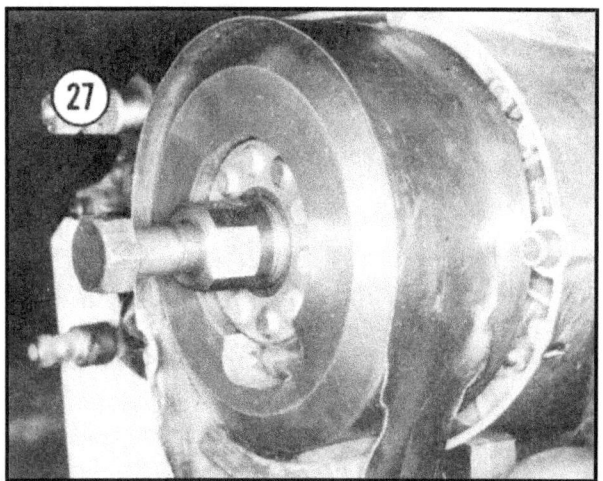

3. Remove the 3 screws which attach the stator plate (**Figure 28**).

Installation

Reverse the removal procedure to install the magneto. Be sure that no metallic particles cling to the flywheel magneto. Torque the retaining nut to 72 ft.-lb. (10 mkg). Don't forget to adjust ignition timing.

Auxiliary Flywheel

Some models are equipped with an auxiliary flywheel on the clutch side of the engine. To remove this flywheel, proceed as follows:

1. Cut and discard the lock wire (**Figure 29**).
2. Remove the flywheel retaining nut.
3. Install the flywheel puller (**Figure 30**), then turn the puller screw clockwise to remove the flywheel (**Figure 31**).
4. Pull out the shaft key.

Reverse the removal procedure to install the auxiliary flywheel. Be sure to put in a new lock wire. Consider the turning direction of the retaining nut as you install the lock wire.

28

29

CLUTCH

Montesa clutches feature multiple steel discs in an oil bath. Service procedures for all models are similar.

Removal

1. Pull out the 3-pronged release crown (**Figure 32**).

2. Flatten the lock tab, then remove the retaining nut and lock tab (**Figure 33**). Note the location of the shoulder on the nut.

3. Pull the entire pack of clutch plates from the clutch housing (**Figure 34**).

4. Pull off the grooved bushing (**Figure 35**).

5. Remove the clutch housing (**Figure 36**).

6. Remove the spacer (**Figure 37**). Note the thickness of this spacer. There is a similar spacer on the same shaft on some models; the thinner of the two is closer to the outside of the engine.

Inspection

Inspect the gear teeth on the clutch housing for nicks, burrs, or excessive wear. Minor damage to the teeth may be smoothed with an oilstone; if not, replace the clutch housing.

Check the clutch housing center bearing for smooth operation. This bearing may be replaced, if necessary. To do so, remove the snap ring and thrust washer, then press out bearing.

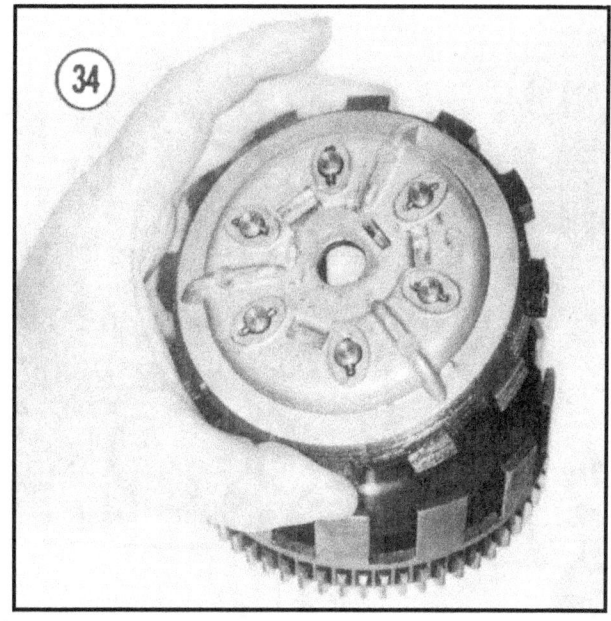

Examine the brass push piece (**Figure 38**). Replace it in the event of excessive wear. Upon reassembly, note that the chamfer goes toward the clutch release lever, as shown in the illustration.

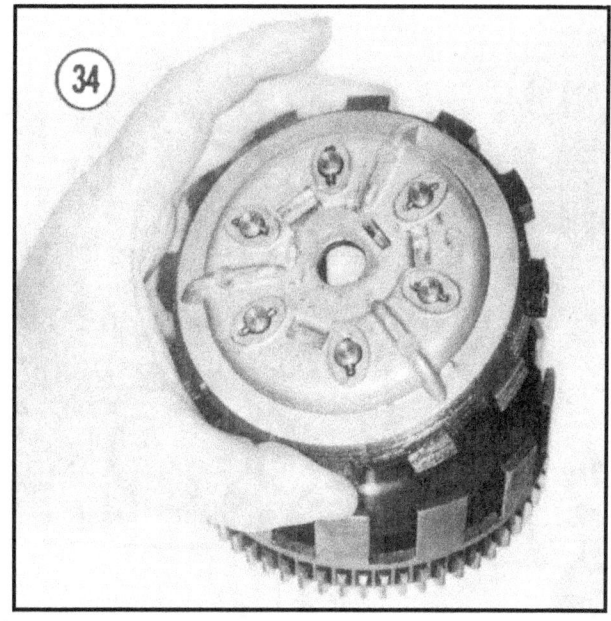

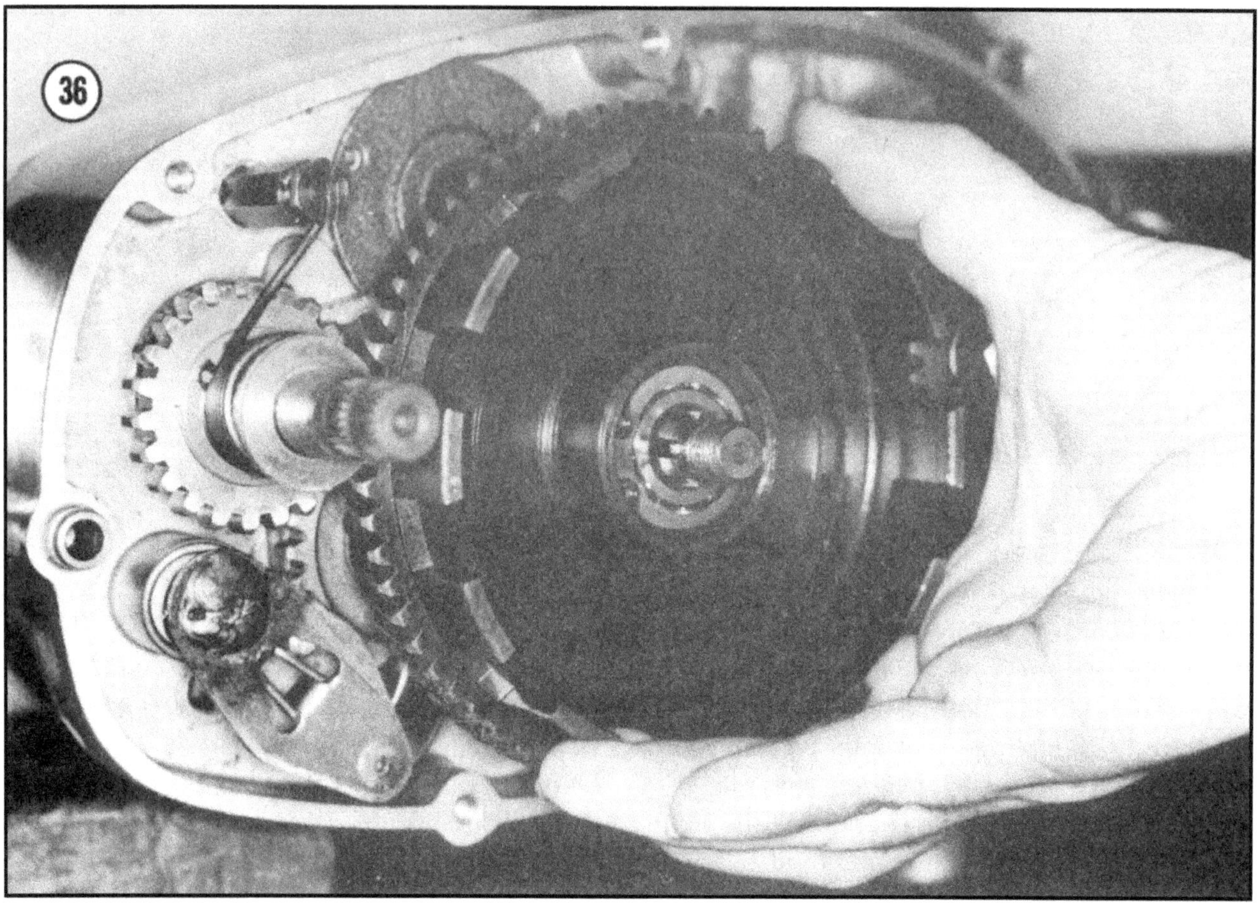
36

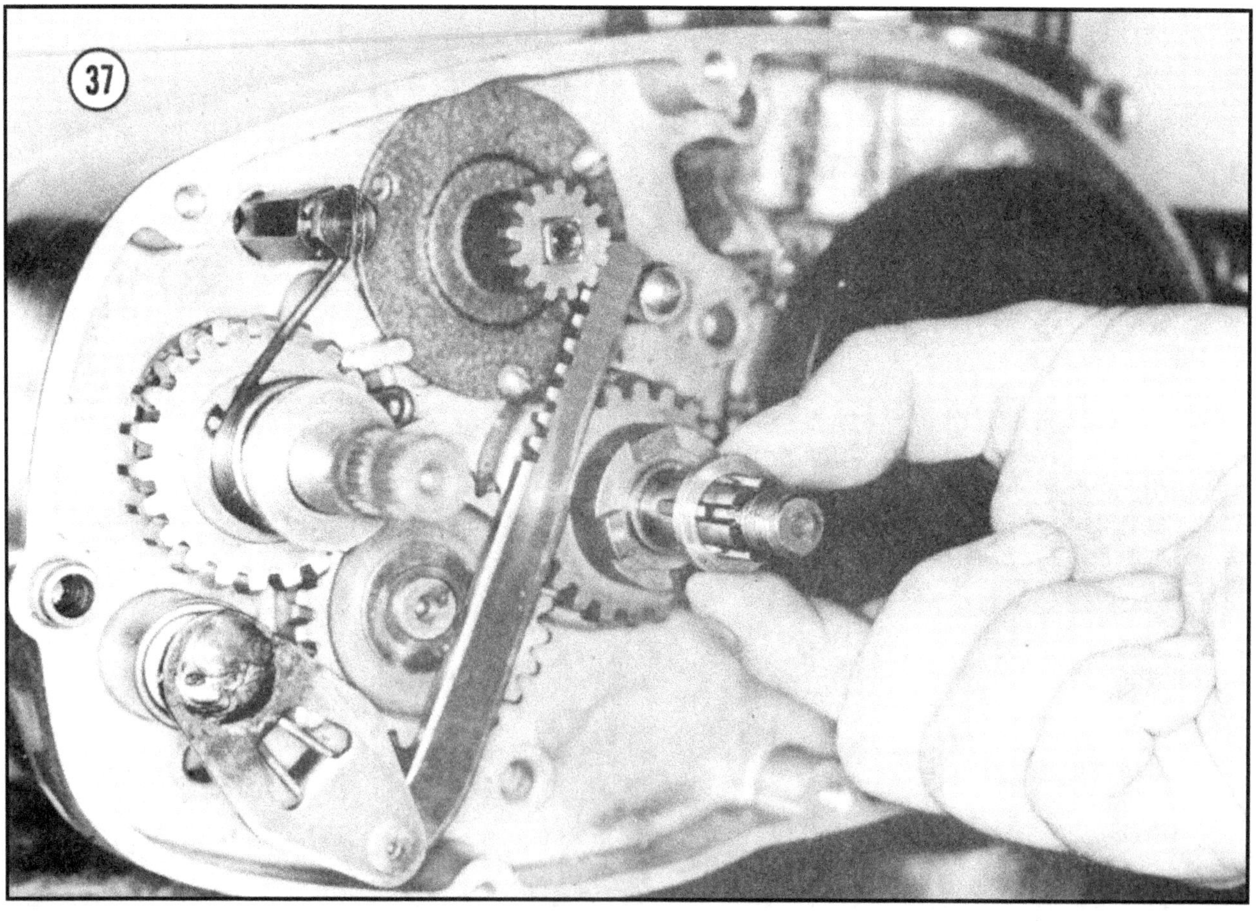
37

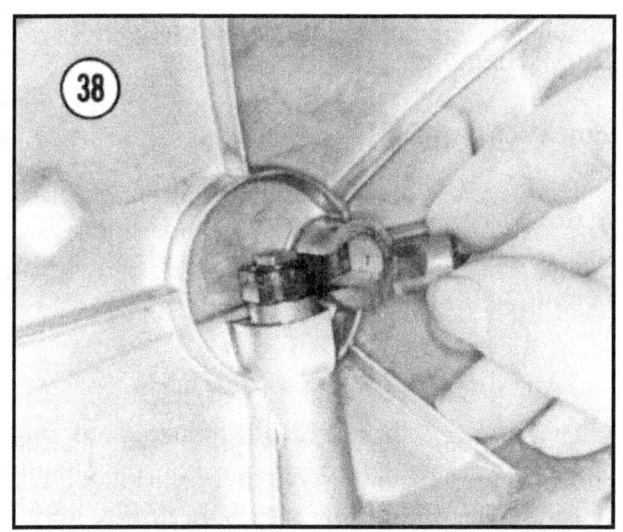

1. Mount the clutch disc pack in a suitable holding fixture, as shown in **Figure 39**.

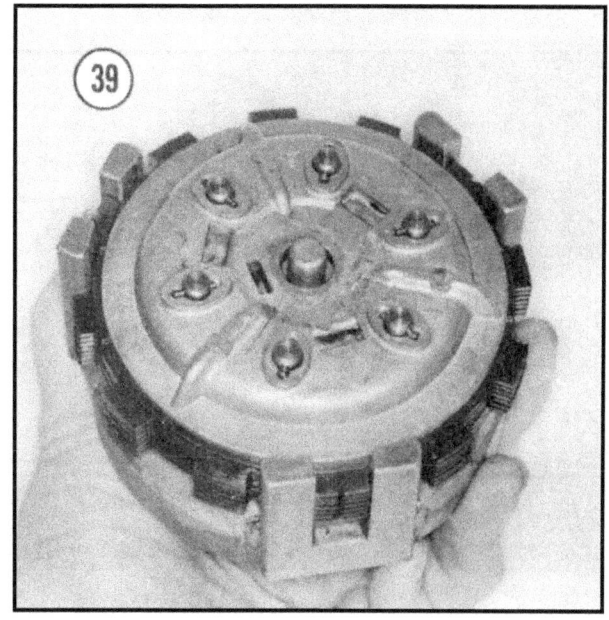

Clutch Disc Replacement

CAUTION
If the package of clutch discs is disassembled for any reason, do not mix up the order in which they were assembled. Install new discs in the same order as they are received from the factory.

2. Mount the assembly in a press, then apply pressure to the spring plate until the retaining pins may be removed (**Figure 40**).

3. Slowly release pressure until the assembly is free of the press.

4. Remove the spring plate (**Figure 41**).

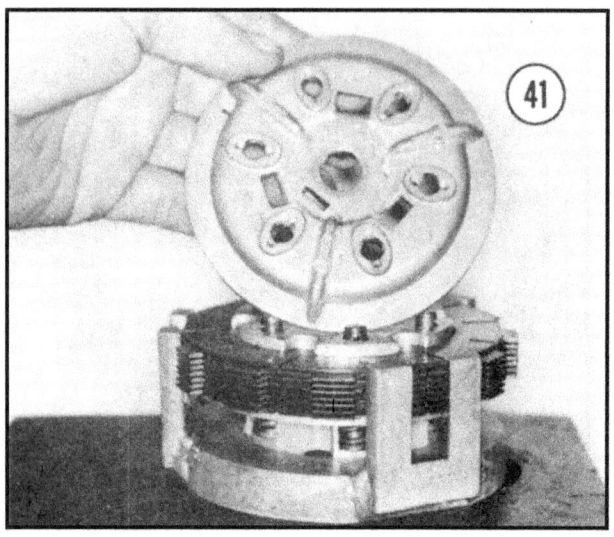

5. Remove the clutch discs.

6. Remove the springs, if necessary.

7. Reverse the disassembly procedure to install new clutch plates.

8. Tighten retaining nut to approximately 15 ft.-lb. (2 mkg).

Clutch Adjustment

Rotate the clutch adjustment nut as required to provide approximately 0.08 in. (2mm) free play at the clutch lever (**Figure 42**). Tighten the locknut after adjustment.

PRIMARY DRIVE GEAR

The primary drive gear is mounted on the end of the crankshaft. Together with the clutch housing gear, the primary gear performs initial reduction.

Removal

1. Remove the retaining nut. An impact wrench will make this operation easier. If no impact wrench is available, use a flywheel holding tool to prevent the crankshaft from turning.

2. Use a suitable gear puller (**Figure 43**) to remove the primary pinion.

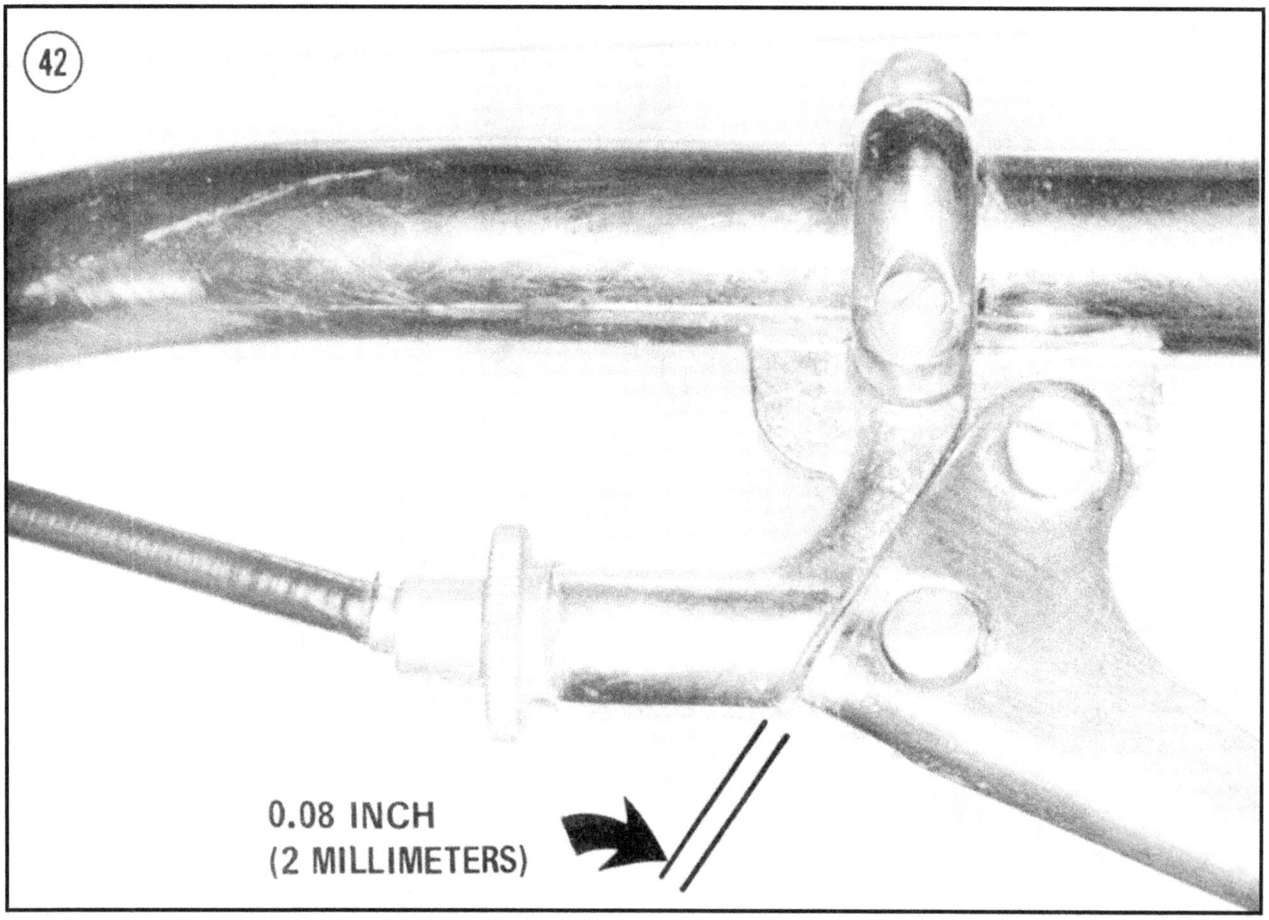

CAUTION
Do not use a torch or try to pry the primary pinion from its shaft. Such efforts will only result in damage to the crankshaft.

3. On some models, the primary pinion is integral with the auxiliary flywheel. Tapped holes in the auxiliary flywheel permit use of a puller (**Figure 44**).

Inspection

Check the gear teeth for burrs, nicks, or scratches. If any small defects are found, smooth the gear teeth with an oilstone. Replace the gear if the oilstone doesn't clean up the defects.

Installation

Reverse the removal procedure to install the primary pinion. Pay particular care to the following points:
1. Clean the tapered end of the crankshaft and the tapered bore in the gear with alcohol before assembly.
2. Tighten retaining nut to 72 ft.-lb. (10 mkg).

SHIFTER

There are 2 types of shifters. Type 1 transmits shift pedal motion to the transmission through a pawl and sector gear mechanism under the left crankcase cover. Type 2 shifter components are under the right crankcase cover. In this shifter, motion of the gearshift pedal is transmitted through a rack and pinion to the transmission.

Type 1 Disassembly

1. Remove shifter detent plunger (**Figure 45**).

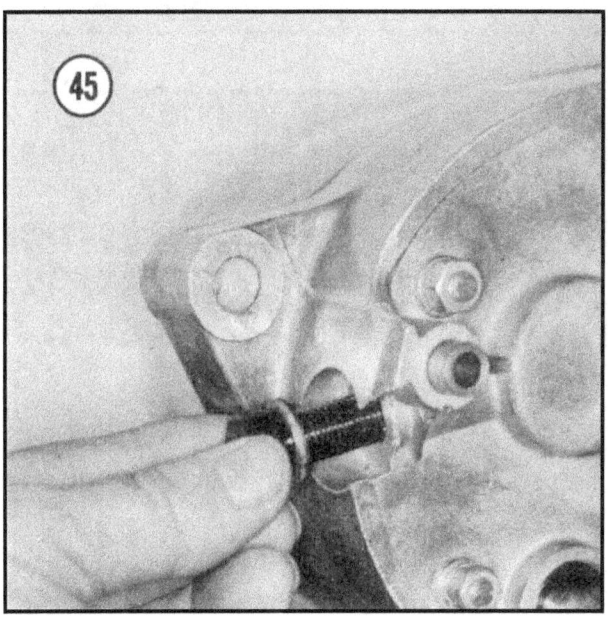

2. Remove the shifter return spring assembly (**Figure 46**).
3. Remove both shifter pawls (**Figure 47**). Note that they are under spring pressure; don't let them fly away.
4. Remove the sector gear.
5. Remove the adjusting cam (**Figure 48**) after first removing its retaining nut.
6. Remove the stop plate (**Figure 49**).

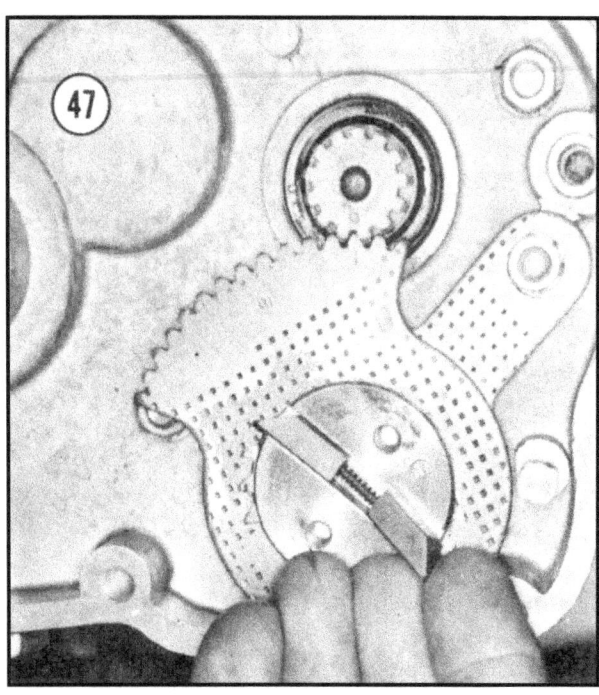

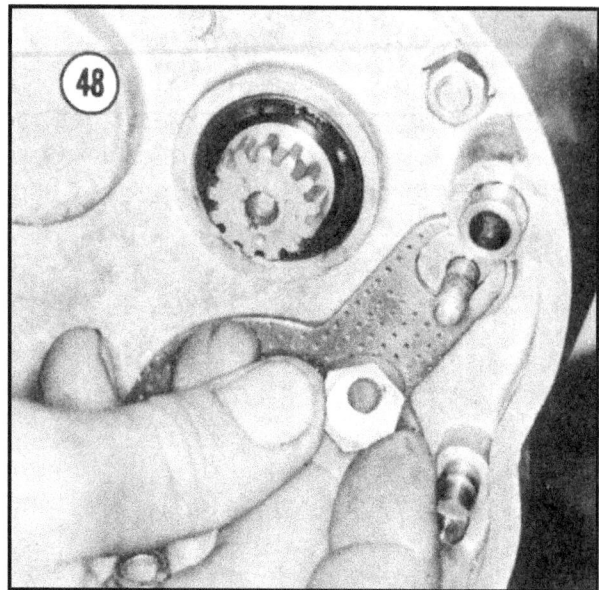

Type 1 Inspection

Examine all parts for wear. Pay close attention to the internal teeth on the sector gear and to the detents on the stop plate. Be sure that the return spring is not fatigued or broken.

Type 1 Reassembly

Reverse the removal procedure to reassemble and install the shifter. Note the following points:
1. Be sure that transmission gears are in neutral.
2. The lateral groove in the end of the gearshift pedal shaft is not centered. **Figure 50** illustrates correct position for this groove during assembly.

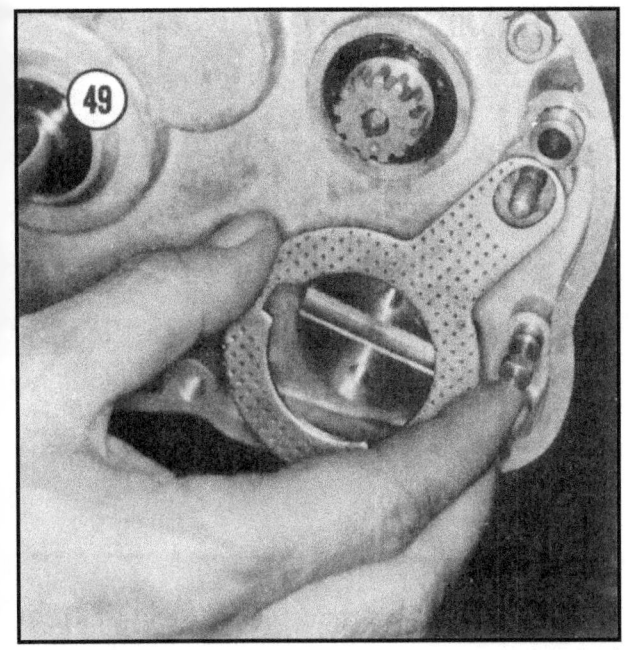

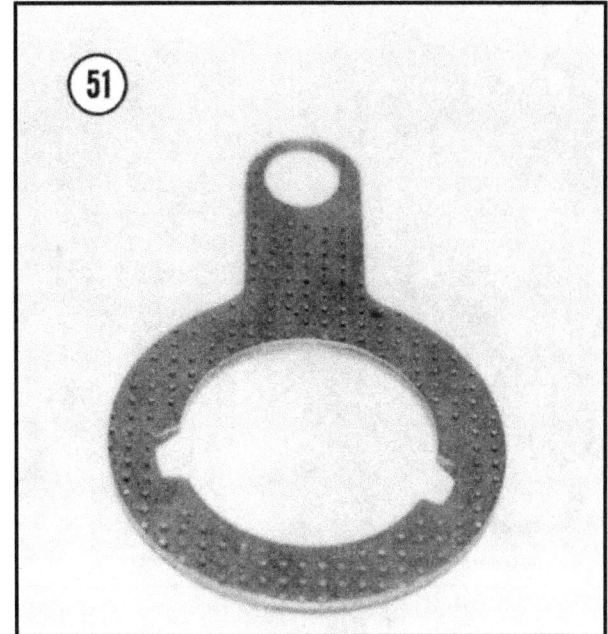

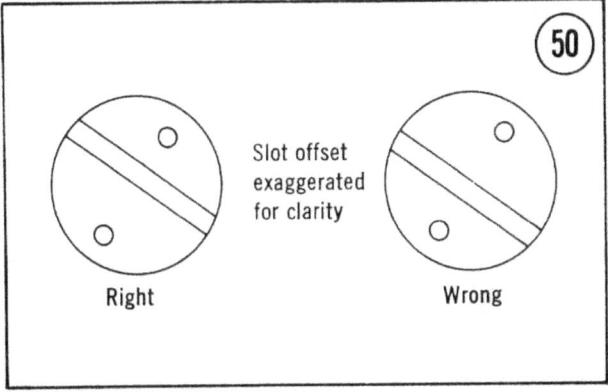

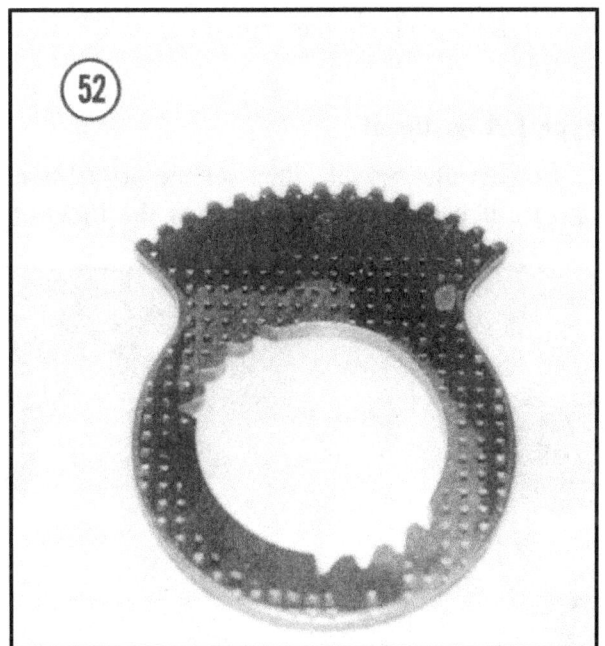

3. It is possible to install both the stop plate and sector gear backward. **Figure 51** illustrates the correct way to install the stop plate. Note that the detent on the left is slightly higher than that on the right. With the sector gear installed properly, the internal detents on the left will be higher than those on the right (**Figure 52**).

4. If the return spring assembly was disassembled, there is an easy way to install the spring. Hold the base plate and spring as shown in **Figure 53**. Then twist the spring 180 degrees away from you (**Figure 54**). Finally, move the spring around in front of the base plate, then install the center spring guide and cover. The cover is staked on.

5. There is a stamped mark on the third tooth from the right on the sector gear. Align this mark with the punched mark on the shift cam gear (**Figure 55**).

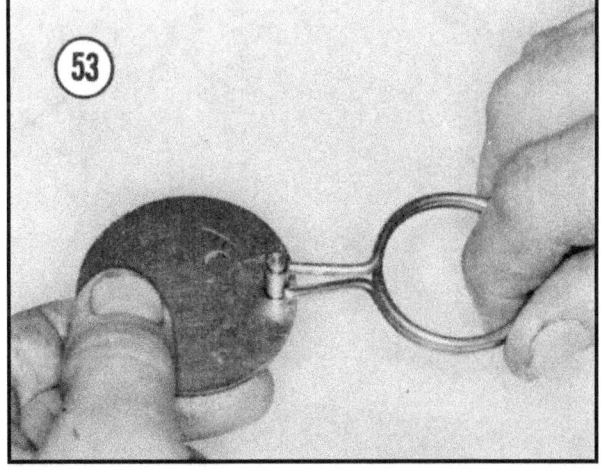

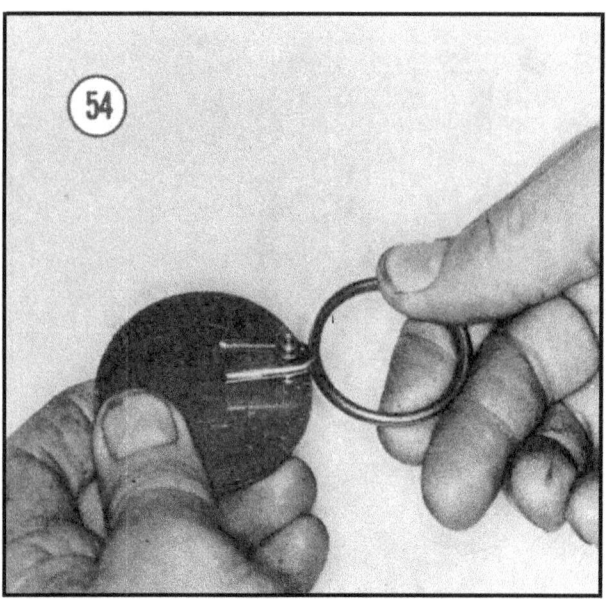

2. Operate the gearshift pedal through all gears. If any gear fails to engage properly, go back to first gear.

3. Rotate the transmission input shaft slightly, then again try to engage each gear. Continue with Steps 2 and 3 until it is possible to engage all gears. Leave the transmission input shaft in this position.

4. Loosen the locknut, then turn the adjusting cam so that when the indexing plunger bottoms in each detent, the shift pawl engages its stop.

5. Tighten the adjusting cam locknut.

6. Start either of the return spring assembly retaining screws, then move the gearshift pedal as required to align the remaining screw with its hole.

Type 2 Disassembly

1. Remove shifter detent screw (**Figure 56**).
2. Using a small magnet, pull out the detent ball (**Figure 57**).
3. Remove the shift cam pinion (**Figure 58**), after removing its retainer.
4. Remove the snap ring and retaining washer from the left end of the shifter shaft, then pull out the shaft (**Figure 59**).

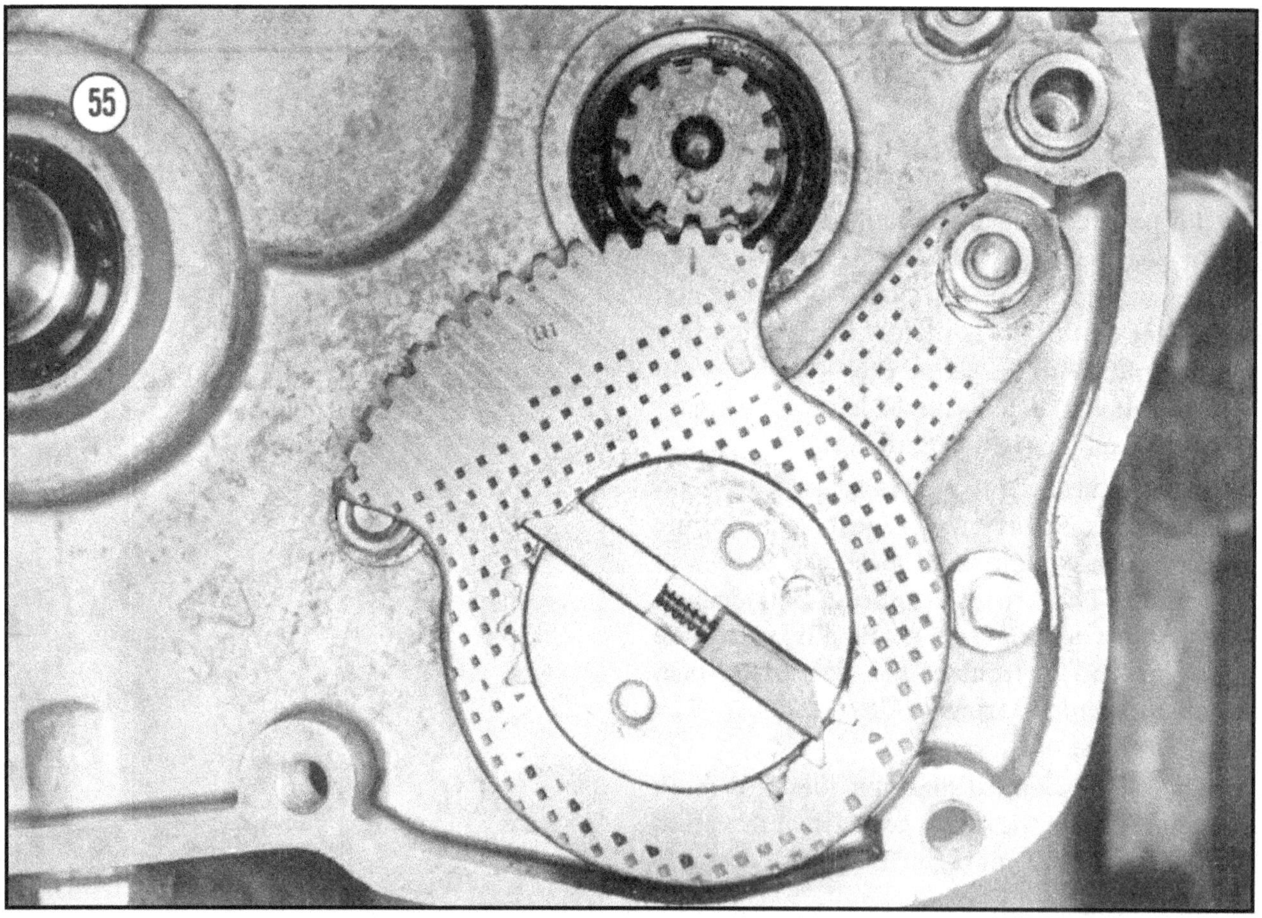

Type 1 Adjustment

1. Loosen the locknut, then set the adjustment cam to its center position. Tighten the locknut.

27

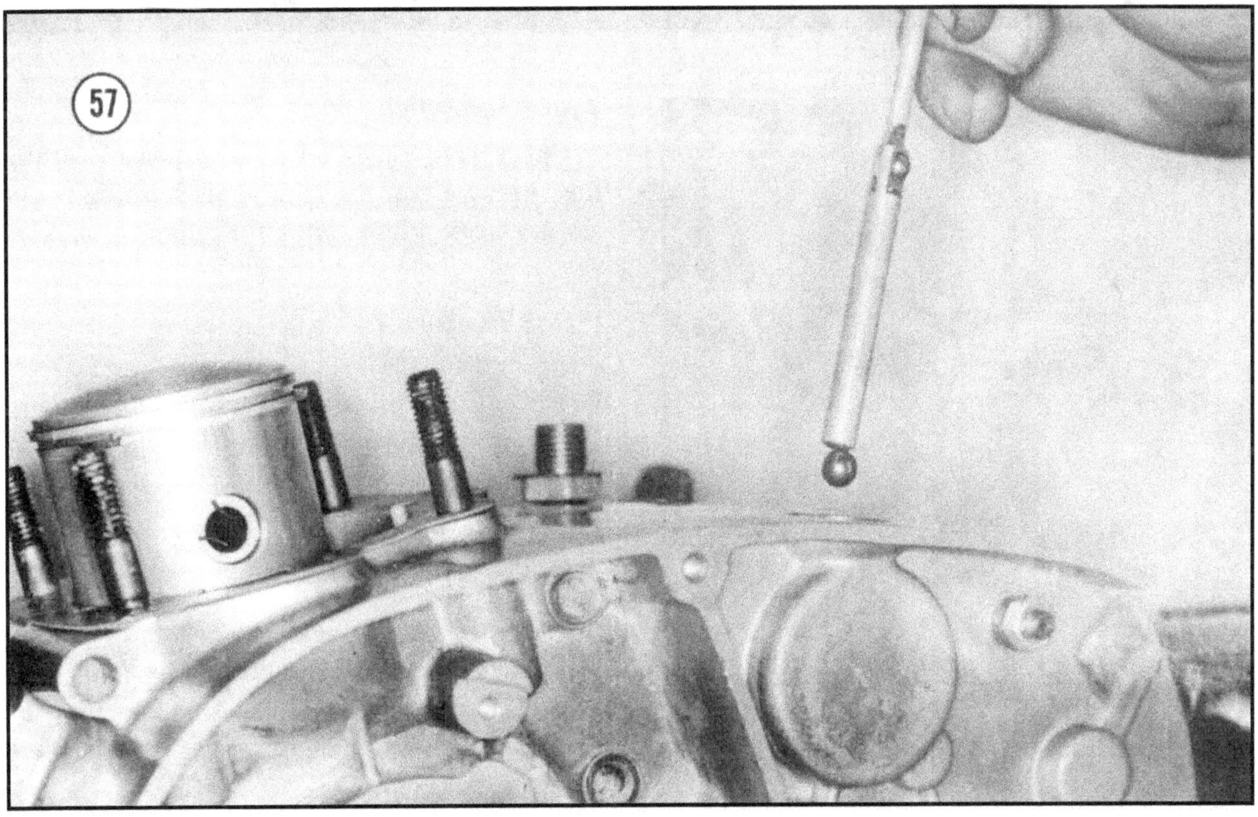

5. Remove the shift pawl cover (**Figure 60**). Don't lose the 2 pawls.

Type 2 Inspection

Check both pawls for wear, especially at the tips. Be sure that the rack guide bushing is not worn. Check return spring for fatigue or cracks.

Type 2 Reassembly

Reverse the disassembly procedure to reassemble the shifter. **Figure 61** illustrates the correct position of the pawls before installation. Observe the following points:

1. Transmission gears must be in neutral for assembly.

2. Turn the square shaft each way until it stops, then leave it in approximately mid-position.

3. Install the pinion on the shaft so that the punched mark on the pinion aligns with the mark on the rack (**Figure 62**).

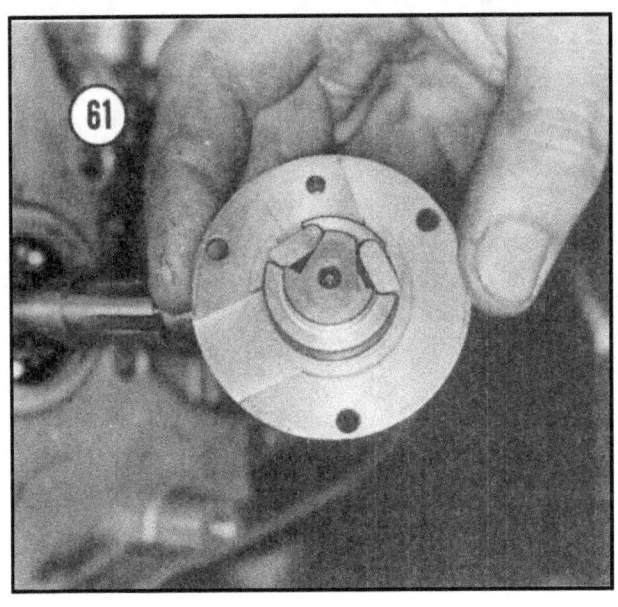

KICKSTARTER

There are 2 types of kickstarter mechanisms. All Type 1 kickstarter components are contained within the crankcase halves. Service procedures on Type 1 kickstarters are described in the transmission section. Type 2 kickstarters are accessible for service by removing the right crankcase cover.

Type 2 Disassembly

1. Unhook the return spring from the spring post (**Figure 63**).
2. Pull out the kick gear assembly (**Figure 64**).
3. Pull the clutch gear from its shaft (**Figure 65**).

4. Remove the spacer (**Figure 66**). Do not confuse this spacer with that previously removed.

5. Remove the snap ring and retaining washer, then pull the kickstarter idle gear from its shaft (**Figure 67**).

6. To disassemble the kick gear assembly, remove the outer thrust washer, spring guide, spring, and snap ring.

Type 2 Inspection

Be sure that the kick gear slides smoothly along its splines. Be sure that the return spring is not fatigued or broken. Examine each gear for worn, burred, or broken teeth.

Type 2 Reassembly

Reverse the removal procedure to reassemble and install the kickstarter. **Figure 68** illustrates the proper position for kick gear guide and stop.

CRANKCASE HALVES

Crankcases on all models split into left and right halves without special tools.

Disassembly

1. Remove all bolts and nuts which hold the two crankcase halves together. Note that there are O-rings under each bolt head. On machines with Type 2 kickstarters, the kickstarter spring post is also a crankcase bolt, and must be removed.

> NOTE: *Do not remove the nut just above and to the left of the kickstarter shaft.*

2. Examine the shifter shaft carefully. If there are any burrs on it as a result of being rubbed by the chain, grind them smooth before proceeding.

3. Place the engine in a horizontal position with the magneto side downward.

4. Hold the crankcase half which is uppermost while a helper with a wooden or rawhide mallet alternately strikes the end of the transmission input shaft and the lower end of the crankshaft. Do not attempt to pry the 2 halves apart.

32

CAUTION
There are end play adjustment shims installed at the ends of the crankshaft, transmission shafts, and shift cam. Carefully remove and tag them, so that they may be returned to their proper locations.

Inspection

Examine the mating surfaces of the crankcase halves carefully. Any nicks or scratches, as from tools used to pry the halves apart, will result in oil leakage. Crankcase halves must be replaced in pairs.

Reassembly

Reverse the disassembly procedure to reassemble the crankcase halves. Note the following points:

1. Insert crankcase bolts with their heads on the clutch side of the engine. Note that there is an O-ring under the head of each bolt. This O-ring must be in perfect condition to prevent oil leakage.

2. Note that one crankcase bolt has a flat washer under the head; its location is shown by the arrow in **Figure 69**. This bolt must not protrude so far on the opposite side that it contacts the magneto stator plate. There is also a washer under the nut on the other side.

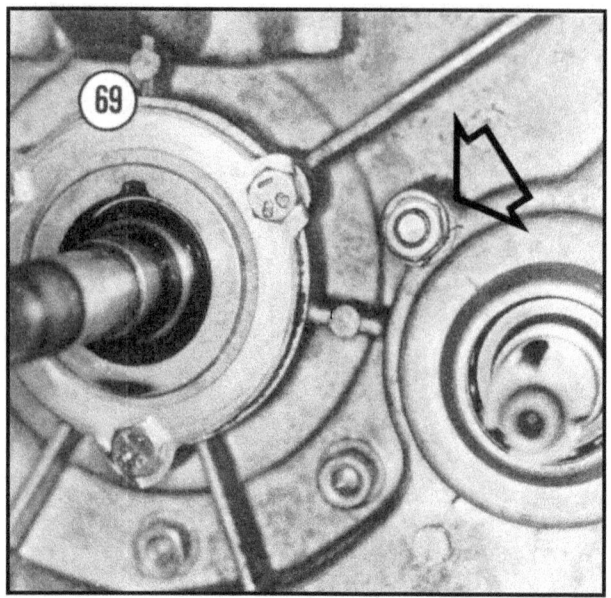

3. End play of transmission shafts, shifter cam, and crankshafts must be adjusted under any of the following conditions. Refer to the applicable sections.

    a. Crankcase gasket of different thickness is installed
    b. Transmission gears were replaced
    c. Crankcase halves were replaced
    d. Crankshaft was replaced or overhauled
    e. Shifter cam was replaced
    f. Bearings replaced

4. Remove shaft oil seals before assembling the crankcase halves.

TRANSMISSION

Montesa bikes are equipped variously with 4-, 5-, or 6-speed transmissions. Although disassembly and service procedures are described only for 5- and 6-speed transmissions, service of 4-speed transmissions should present no difficulty.

> NOTE: *During transmission disassembly, be sure to carefully note the removal order and location of each small part as it is removed.*

5-Speed Disassembly

1. Remove shifter detent plunger if it was not removed previously. Note the spacer under the bolt head.

2. Remove the kickstarter gear (**Figure 70**) after removing its spacer.

3. Lift the entire transmission, together with the shifter cam, as an assembly from the right crankcase half (**Figure 71**).

4. Shift forks may be removed, if necessary, by cutting the safety wire, then unscrewing each guide pin.

5. Individual gears may then be removed from their shafts, if necessary.

6. **Figure 72** illustrates the input shaft assembly. Gears are, from left to right, 5th (sliding), 4th, 3rd, 2nd, and 1st. Gears on the output shaft are shown in **Figure 73**. They are, from left to right, 5th, 4th, 3rd, 2nd, and 1st.

7. Remove the snap ring and washer, then pull out the shifter shaft.

5-Speed Inspection

1. Examine each shift fork for binding or evidence of rubbing on one side. Measure clearance between each shift fork and the groove on its associated gear. Typical standard clearance is 0.002-0.01 in. (0.05-0.25mm). Any clearance over 0.025 in. (0.6mm) should be considered excessive. Replace any shift fork which shows burrs or other damage.

2. Any burrs, pits, or roughness on the gear teeth will cause wear on the mating gear. Replace any gear with such defects. Examine its mating gear carefully and replace it if there is any doubt about its condition. It may be possible to smooth minor burrs with an oilstone.

3. Examine the ratchet teeth on the kickstarter gear. If these teeth are worn or broken, the kickstarter mechanism will slip.

4. Examine the teeth on the dog clutches. Worn or broken teeth can result in missed shifts.

5-Speed Reassembly

Reverse the disassembly procedure to reassemble and install the transmission. Observe the following points:

1. There are 3 different lengths of dowel pins along which the movable members slide. On the output shaft the pins for the sliding member between the 1st and 2nd gear are 0.827 in.

70

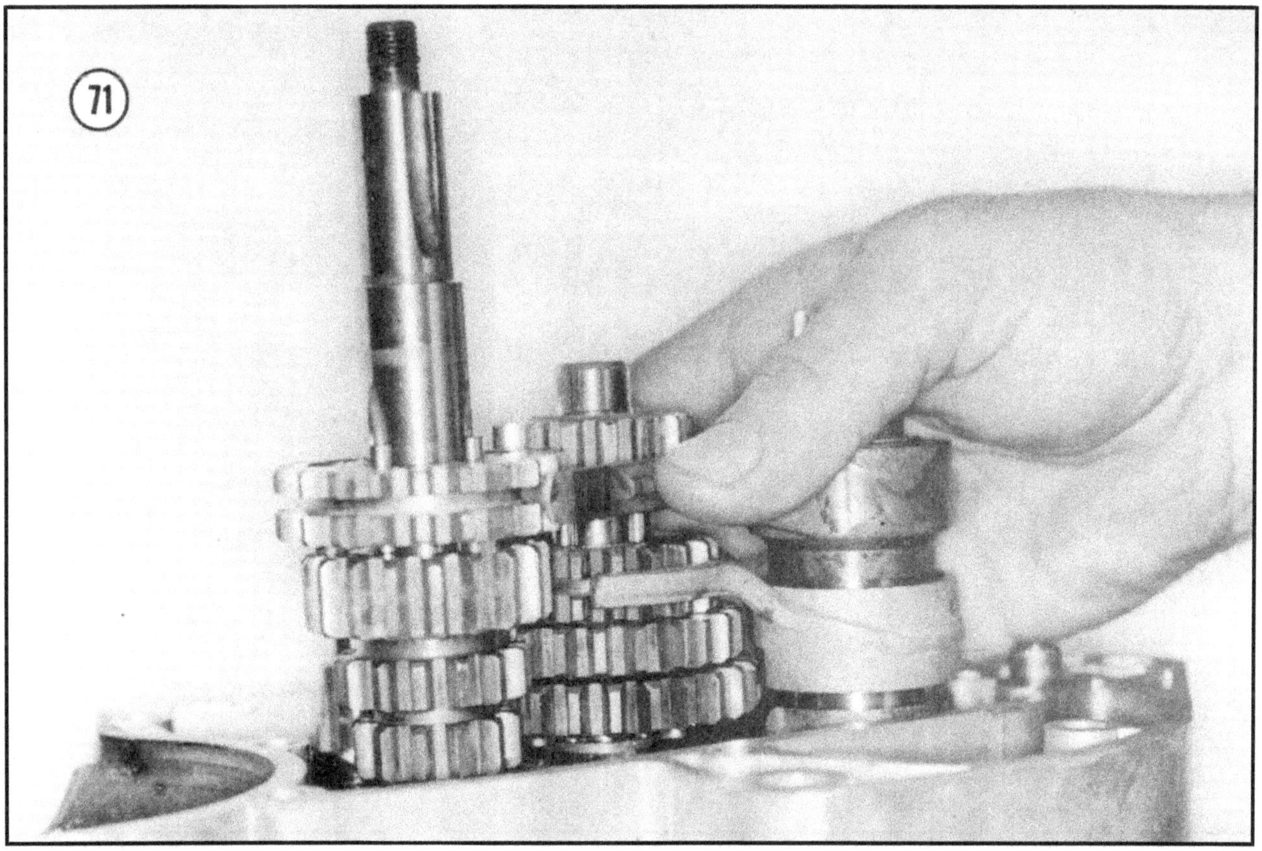

71

35

(72)

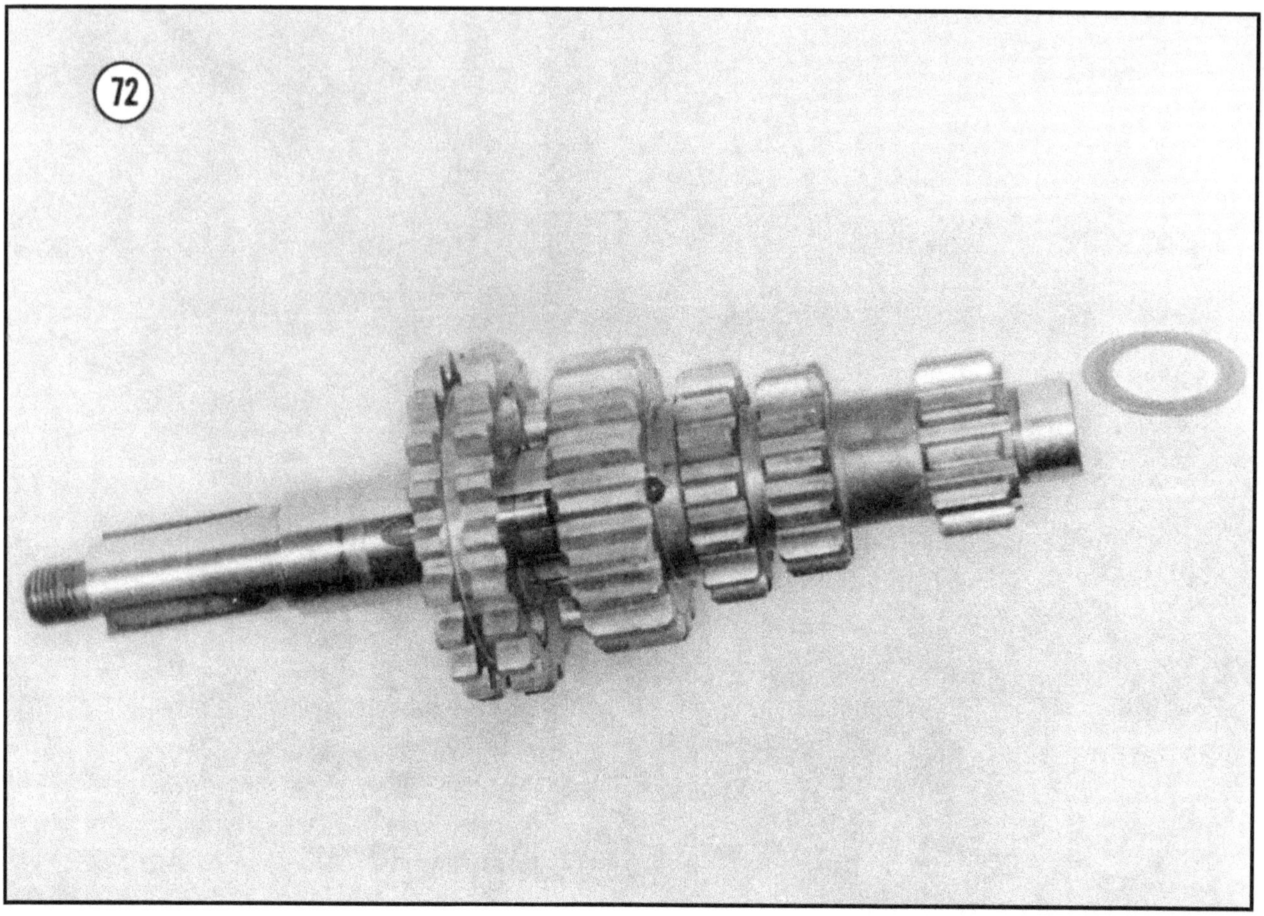

(73)

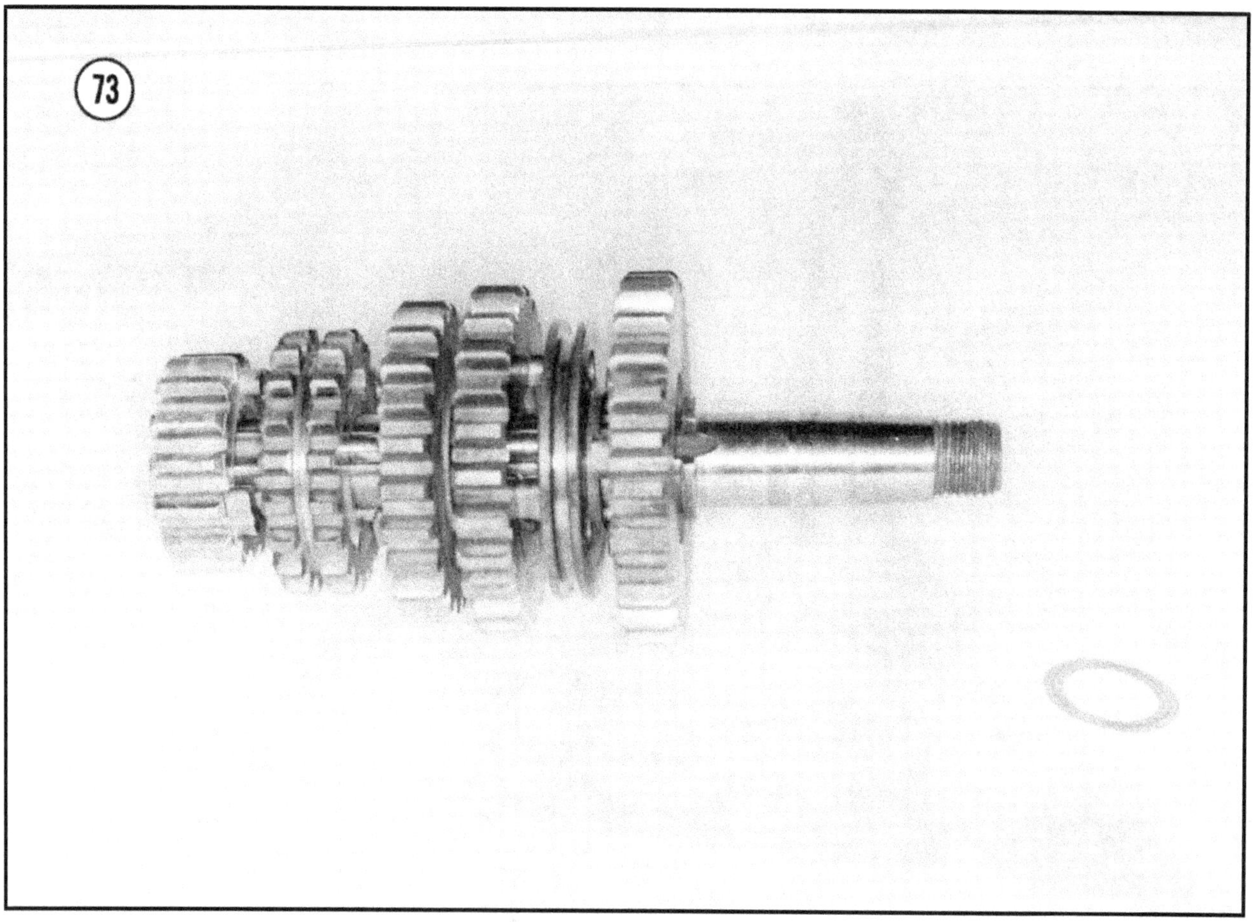

(21.0mm) long. The other sliding member on the output shaft is 4th gear; its pins are 0.957 in. (24.3mm) long. Pins for the sliding gear on the input shaft are 0.761 in. (19.3mm) long.

2. Rotate the shifter shaft fully clockwise (**Figure 74**).

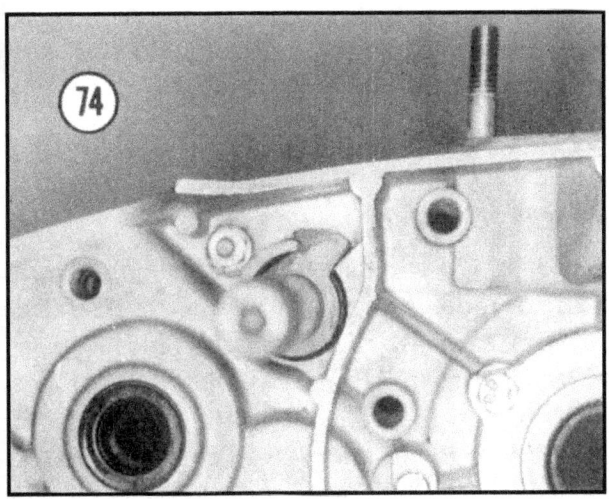

3. Slide the ratchet on the shifter shaft so that the raised portion on the ratchet circumference is approximately centered on guide (**Figure 75**).

4. Rotate the shaft clockwise, until the raised portion on the ratchet can be slipped under the guide (**Figure 76**).

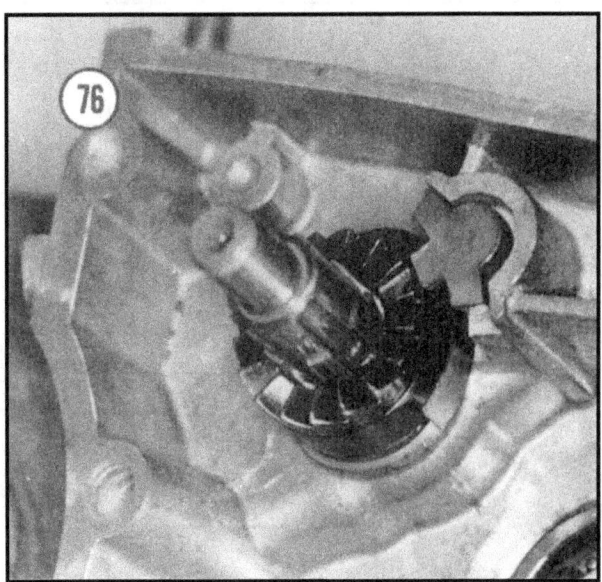

5. Install end play adjustment shims into the right crankcase half. Use grease to hold them in place during installation.

6. Assemble the transmission and shifter as a unit (**Figure 77**), then install the assembly into the right crankcase half (**Figure 78**).

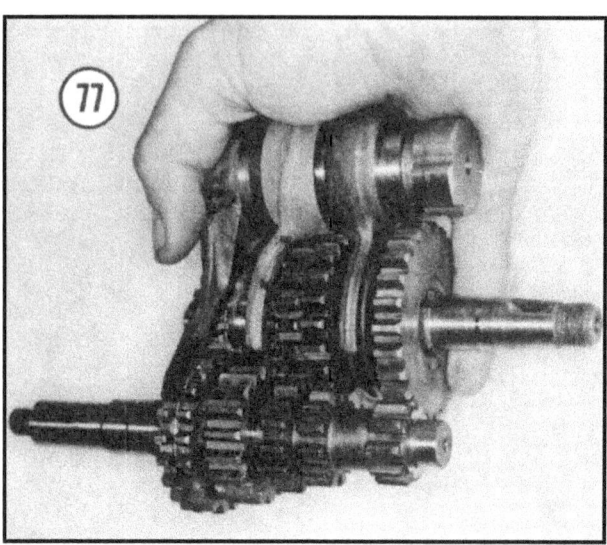

7. Install the kickstarter gear with the ratchet teeth facing the kickstarter ratchet (**Figure 79**). Don't forget the kickstarter gear washer (**Figure 80**).

6-Speed Disassembly

1. Remove shifter detent bolt, spring, and ball, if they were not removed previously.

2. Lift the entire transmission assembly, together with the shifter cam and forks, from the left crankcase. **Figure 81** illustrates the transmission removed. Gears are, from left to right, 2nd, 6th, 3rd, 4th, 5th, and 1st.

3. Slide each shift fork from the shift fork guide rail (**Figure 82**).

6-Speed Inspection

1. Examine each shift fork for bending or evidence of rubbing on one side. Measure clearance between each shift fork and the groove on its associated gear. Typical standard clearance is 0.002-0.01 in. (0.05-0.25mm). Any clearance over 0.025 in. (0.6mm) should be considered excessive. Replace any shift fork which shows burrs or other damage.

2. Any burrs, pits, or roughness on the gear teeth will cause wear on the mating gear. Replace

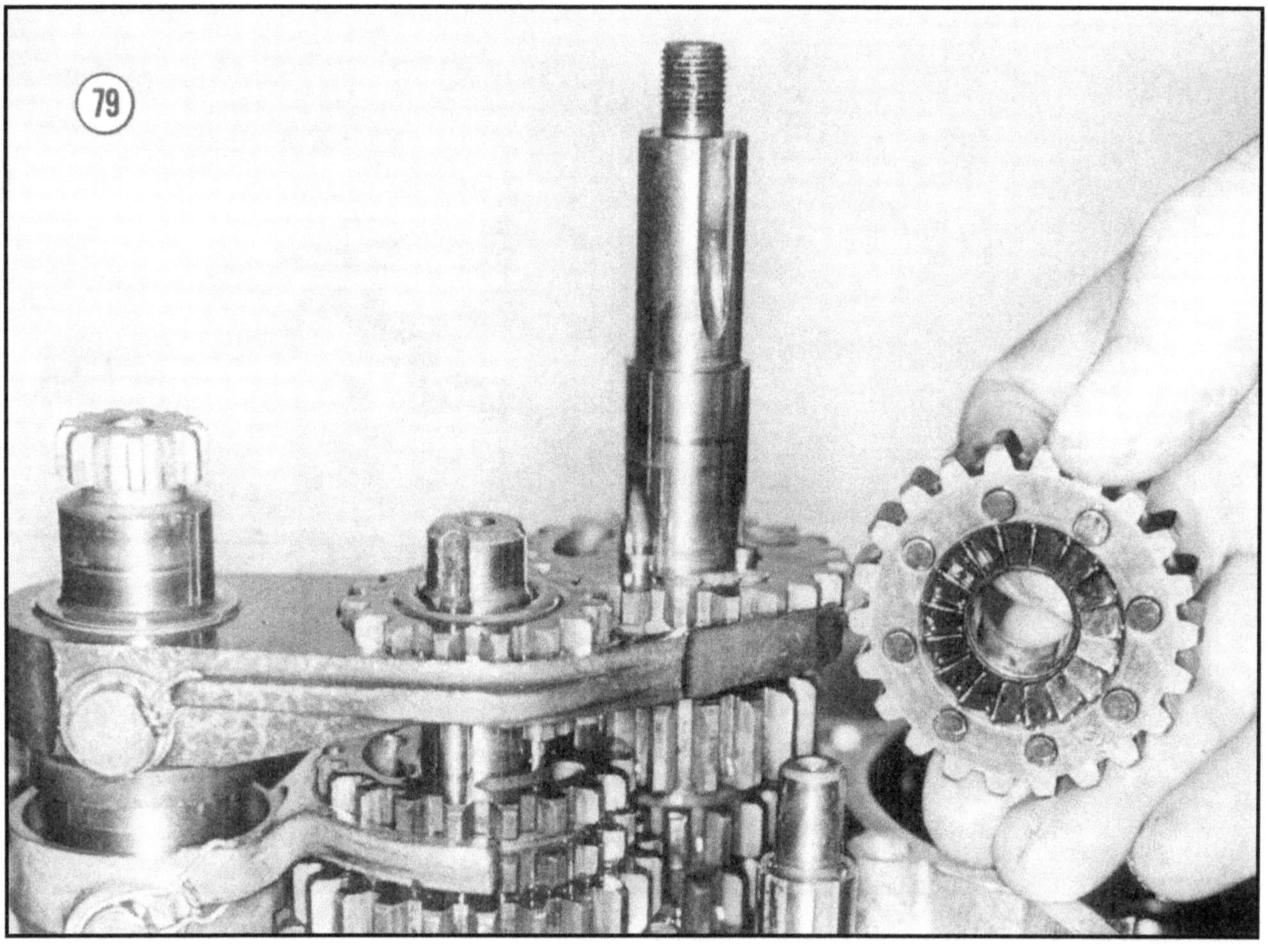

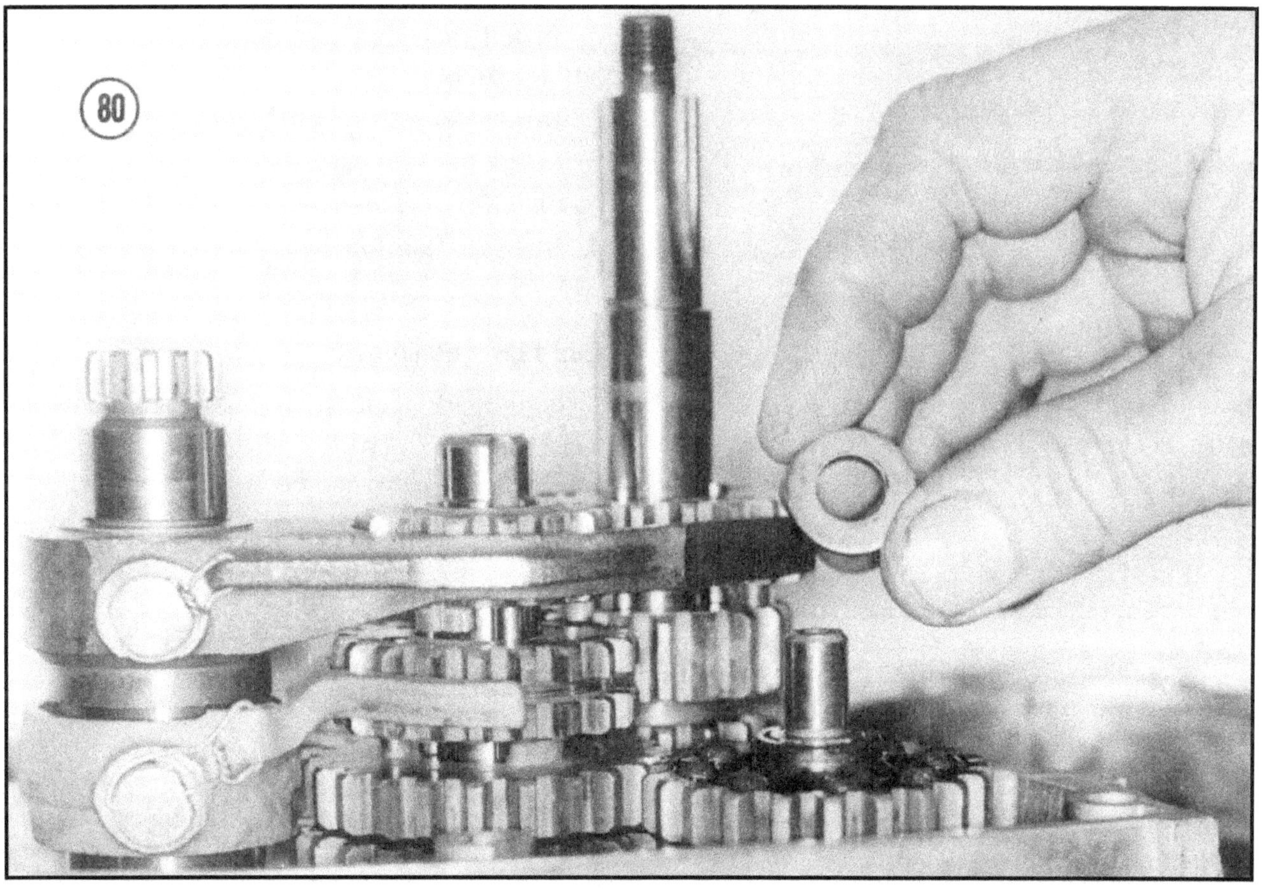

39

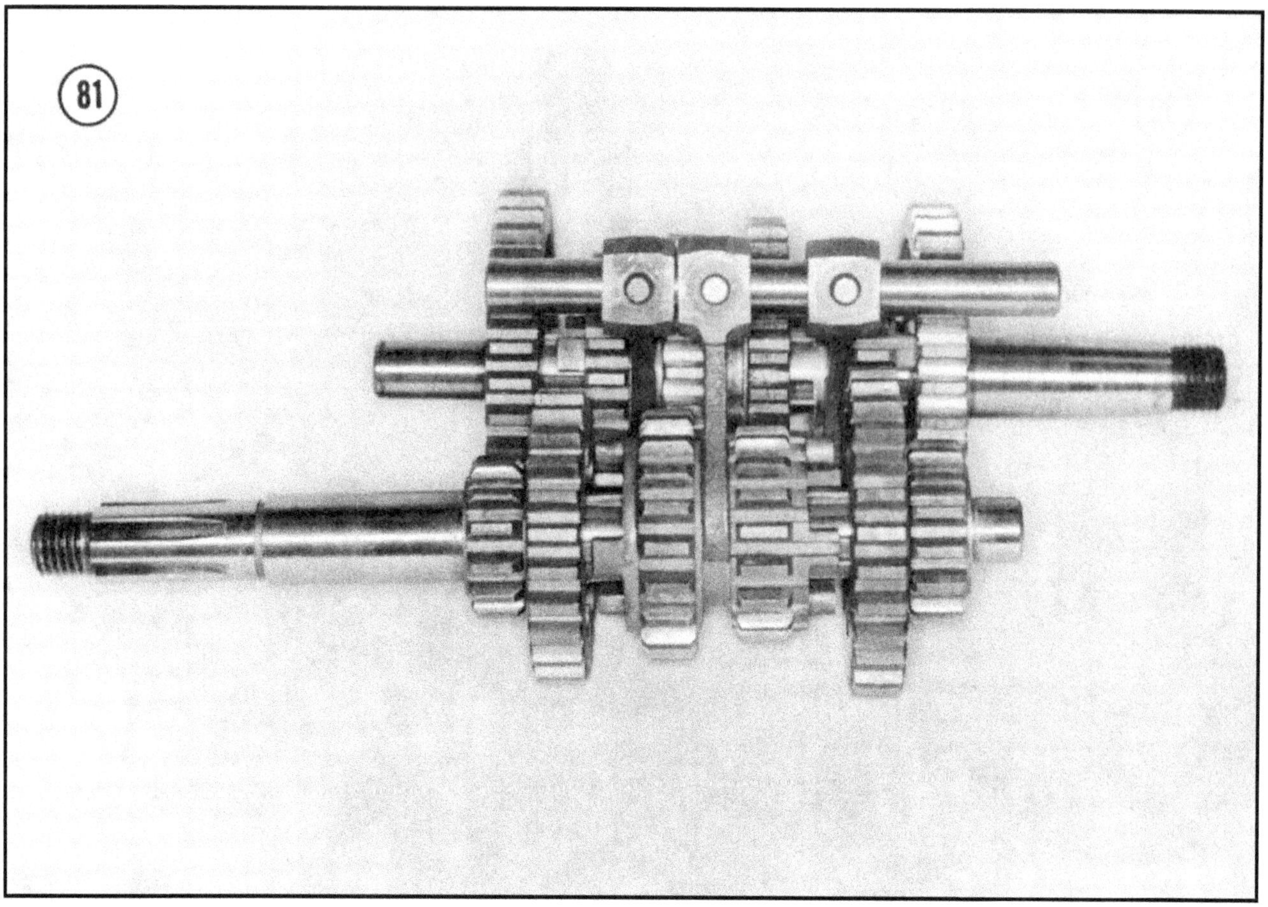

any gear showing such defects. Examine the mating gear carefully and replace it also if there is any doubt about its condition. It may be possible to smooth minor burrs with an oilstone.

3. Examine the teeth on the dog clutches. Worn teeth can result in missed shifts.

6-Speed Reassembly

1. Install the input and output shafts into the left crankcase.
2. Install the shift forks (**Figure 83**).
3. Install the shift cam, then work the guide pin on each shift fork into its groove in the shift cam.
4. Install the shift fork guide rail (**Figure 84**).

End Play Adjustment

Transmission shafts and shift drums must have the proper end play if they are to function properly. To adjust end play, proceed as follows.

1. Measure and record the width of each transmission shaft assembly (**Figure 85**). Call this measurement "dimension A."
2. Using a setup similar to that shown in **Figure 86**, determine and record the distance between the mating surfaces on each crankcase mating surface and the bearing inner races. Call these measurements "dimensions B and C."
3. Measure and record the thickness of the gasket to be used.

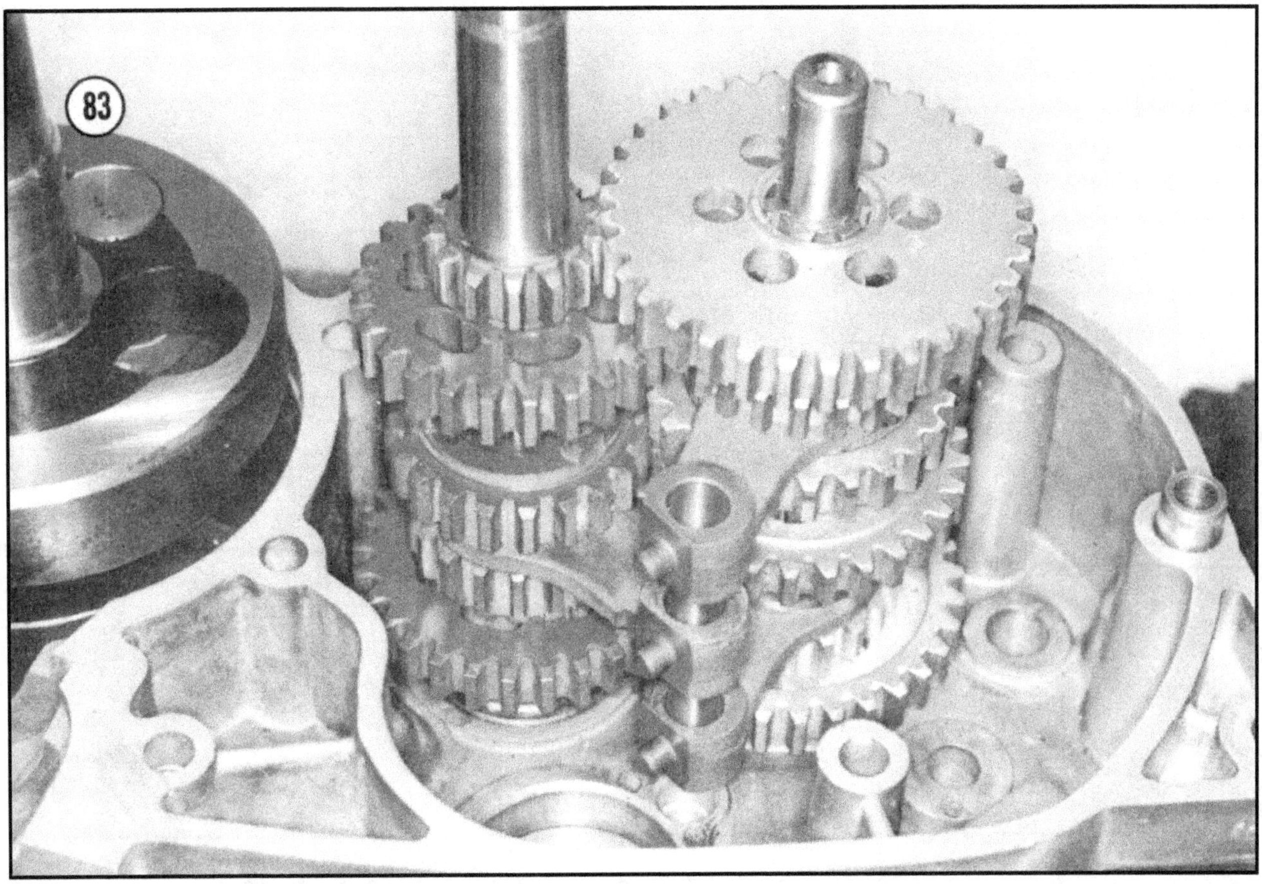
83

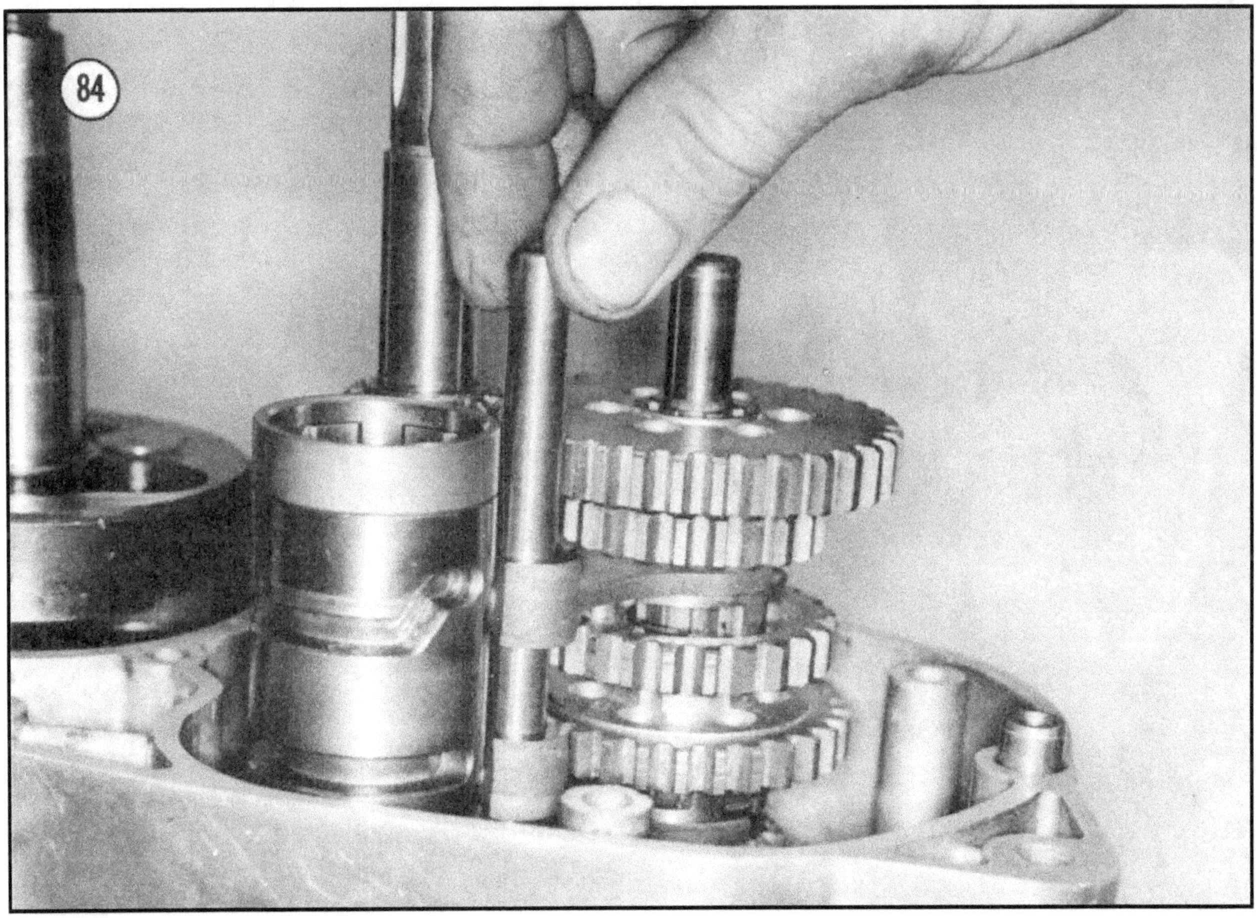
84

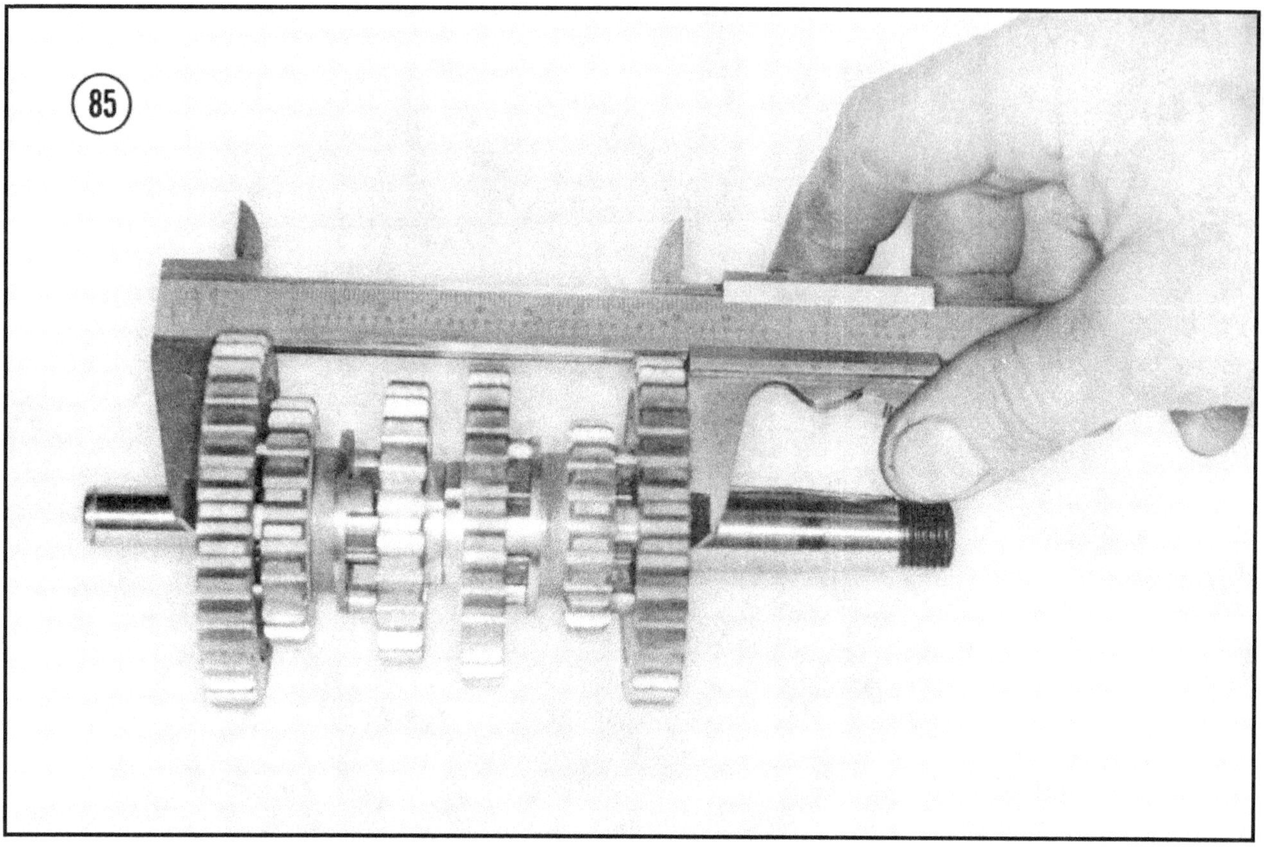

42

4. Sample calculation:

Width of gear assembly	3.696	(dimension A)
Depth to bearing	2.630	
Less thickness of parallels	−0.737	
	1.893	(dimension B)
Depth to bearing	2.540	
Less thickness of parallels	−0.737	
	1.803	(dimension C)

Add:
Dimension B	1.893	
Dimension C	1.803	
Gasket	0.024	
	3.720	(dimension D)

Subtract the width of the transmission shaft (dimension A) from the distance between bearings (dimension D) to determine unadjusted end play.

3.720	(dimension D)
−3.696	(dimension A)
0.024	(unadjusted end play)

Desired end play is 0.004-0.008 in. (0.1-0.2mm). Therefore, to determine total shim thickness for that shaft, subtract desired end play (0.006 in. for example) from total unadjusted end play (0.024 in.).

0.024	(unadjusted end play)
−0.006	(desired end play)
0.018	(total shims required)

Add shims totaling 0.018 in. to the shaft in question.

5. Repeat the procedure for the remaining transmission shaft.

6. Determine and adjust shift cam end play in a similar manner, with one exception. Distribute shims on each end of the cam so that with the gears in neutral, there will be an equal distance between both sides of the sliding members in the transmission and the members which they engage.

7. After the crankcase halves are assembled, check both transmission shafts for free rotation. There should be barely perceptible end play in each shaft.

CRANKSHAFT

The crankshaft operates under conditions of high stress. Dimensional tolerances are critical. It is necessary to locate and correct crankshaft defects early to prevent more serious trouble later.

Crankshaft Removal

When the crankcase halves are split, the crankshaft will remain in one half because it is a shrink fit in the drive end bearing. To remove the bearing, first remove all oil seals, then heat the crankcase half on a hot plate to approximately 300-350°F (150-180°C), then pull out the crankshaft and bearing. Note the location of any spacers under the bearing.

Crankshaft Inspection

Measure crankshaft alignment as shown in **Figure 87**. Mount the crankshaft in a lathe, V-blocks, or other suitable centering device. Rotate the crankshaft through a complete revolution and measure runout at each end as shown by the dial gauge. Repair or replace the crankshaft if runout exceeds 0.0012 in. (0.035mm).

If the dial gauge shows misalignment on both ends at the same angular position of the crankshaft, crank wheels are not parallel. Correct this condition by squeezing them together with a vise or driving them apart with a wedge, as required. Misalignment at different angular positions is an indication that the 2 crank wheels are not on the same center. Tap the crank wheels with a brass or lead mallet to align them. Recheck alignment after each adjustment.

Measure big end bearing radial play. Radial play should not exceed 0.0035 in. (0.09mm). In the event that no suitable equipment is available for making this measurement, repair or replace the crankshaft if there is any perceptible looseness in the lower end bearing.

Measure the lower end side play (**Figure 88**). Cappra 125 VA, Enduro 250, Cappra V-75 and Cappra 250 VR engines (from engine No. 73M 6001 onward) are fitted with connecting rod lower end washers that are slightly smaller in overall diameter than the inside of the connecting rod's bearing surface. These smaller

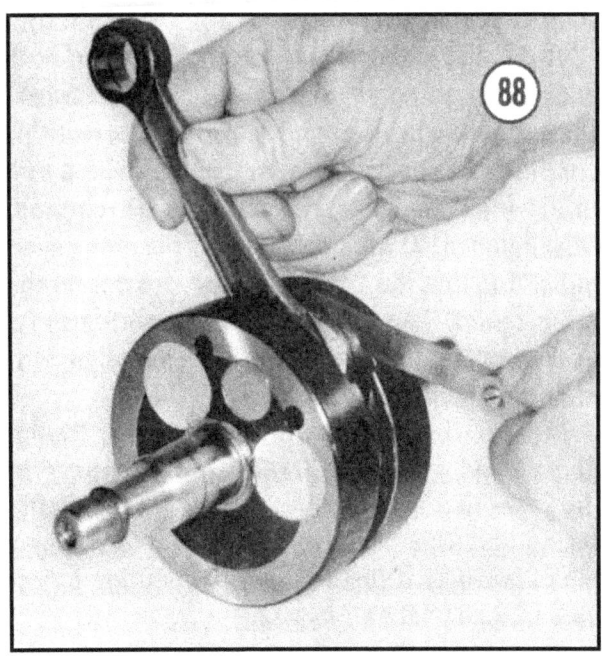

Table 6. The clearance should be measured from the side of the connecting rod itself to the inner faces of the crankshaft on the Enduro 250, Cappra 125 VA, Cappra VR and V-75 engines. The clearance is measured from the spacer washers to the inner faces of the crankshaft on all other models.

Crankshaft Overhaul

1. Measure the width of the crankshaft assembly (**Figure 89**). Record this dimension for use when reassembling the crankshaft.
2. Mount the crankshaft assembly in a suitable press jig (**Figure 90**) so that the entire upper crank wheel is supported.
3. Press out the crankpin from the upper crank wheel (**Figure 91**).
4. Remove the connecting rod and bearings.
5. Turn the remaining crank wheel over. Then press out the crankpin (**Figure 92**).
6. Examine each crank wheel for burrs or other damage.

washers allow the rod movement to be controlled by the piston. Two washers must be inserted between the upper end of the connecting rod and the piston, one washer on each side of the connecting rod. The lower end side play is listed in

Table 6 CLEARANCE BETWEEN ROD AND CRANKSHAFT

Model	Maximum Play Inch	(Millimeter)
Texas	0.012	(0.30)
Impala Sport	0.012	(0.30)
Impala	0.006	(0.15)
Commando 175	0.006	(0.15)
Kenya	0.006	(0.15)
250 Trial	0.012	(0.30)
Impala Cross (175)	0.019	(0.50)
Impala Cross (250)	0.012	(0.30)
Enduro	0.012	(0.30)
Sport 250	0.019	(0.50)
Cota 247	0.012	(0.30)
La Cross	0.019	(0.50)
Scorpion 250	0.019	(0.50)
Cappra 250 (except VR)	0.019	(0.50)
Cappra 250 VR	0.078	(2.00)
King Scorpion (except Automix)	0.019	(0.50)
King Scorpion Automix	0.012	(0.30)
Cappra 360 GP/DS	0.019	(0.50)
Cota 123	0.012	(0.30)
Cappra 125 MX	0.019	(0.50)
Cota 123 Trail	0.019	(0.50)
Cappra 125 VA	0.078	(2.00)
Cota 172	0.019	(0.50)
Cota 247 Trail	0.019	(0.50)
Enduro 250	0.078	(2.00)
Rapita 250	0.019	(0.50)
Cappra 250 V-75	0.078	(2.00)

Note: On Cappra 250 VR engines fitted with V-75 connecting rod bearings and spacers use dimensions shown. On VR (prior to No. 73 M 6001) engines with original bearings the clearance should be 0.019 inches (0.50mm).

7. Lubricate the crankpin hole in each crank wheel, and also the new crankpin. White grease is a suitable lubricant.

8. Press the new crankpin into one crank wheel (**Figure 93**). Be very careful that the crankpin is started squarely into its hole.

9. Install the new bearings and connecting rod (**Figure 94**). There is no front or back side on the connecting rod; it fits either way.

10. Align the remaining crank wheel carefully, then press until lower end side clearance is as specified in Table 6. A feeler gauge of appropriate thickness inserted between the connecting rod and crank wheel makes an excellent stop. It will slip out easily when pressure is removed from the assembly.

11. Measure width of the assembled crankshaft. It should be the same as was determined earlier in Step 1.

BEARINGS

The crankshaft and both transmission shafts rotate on ball bearings. Always check bearing condition when the engine is disassembled.

Removal

If any bearing is to be replaced, first remove all oil seals from the crankcase half. Then heat the crankcase half on a hot plate until the bearings fall out. Note that there are shims behind the crankshaft bearings.

Inspection

Since the bearings are a shrink fit in the crankcase, they are made with a slight clearance between the balls and races. Therefore, it is impossible to judge wear by checking clearance.

To check the bearing, first clean it thoroughly in solvent, dry it, then lubricate it with light oil. Spin the bearing (**Figure 95**), and check for abnormal noise or roughness as it coasts down. Do not spin a dry bearing.

Crankshaft bearings in 2-stroke engines are particularly susceptible to damage resulting from dirt. **Figure 96** shows a bearing which failed after the machine was operated only a short distance without an air filter.

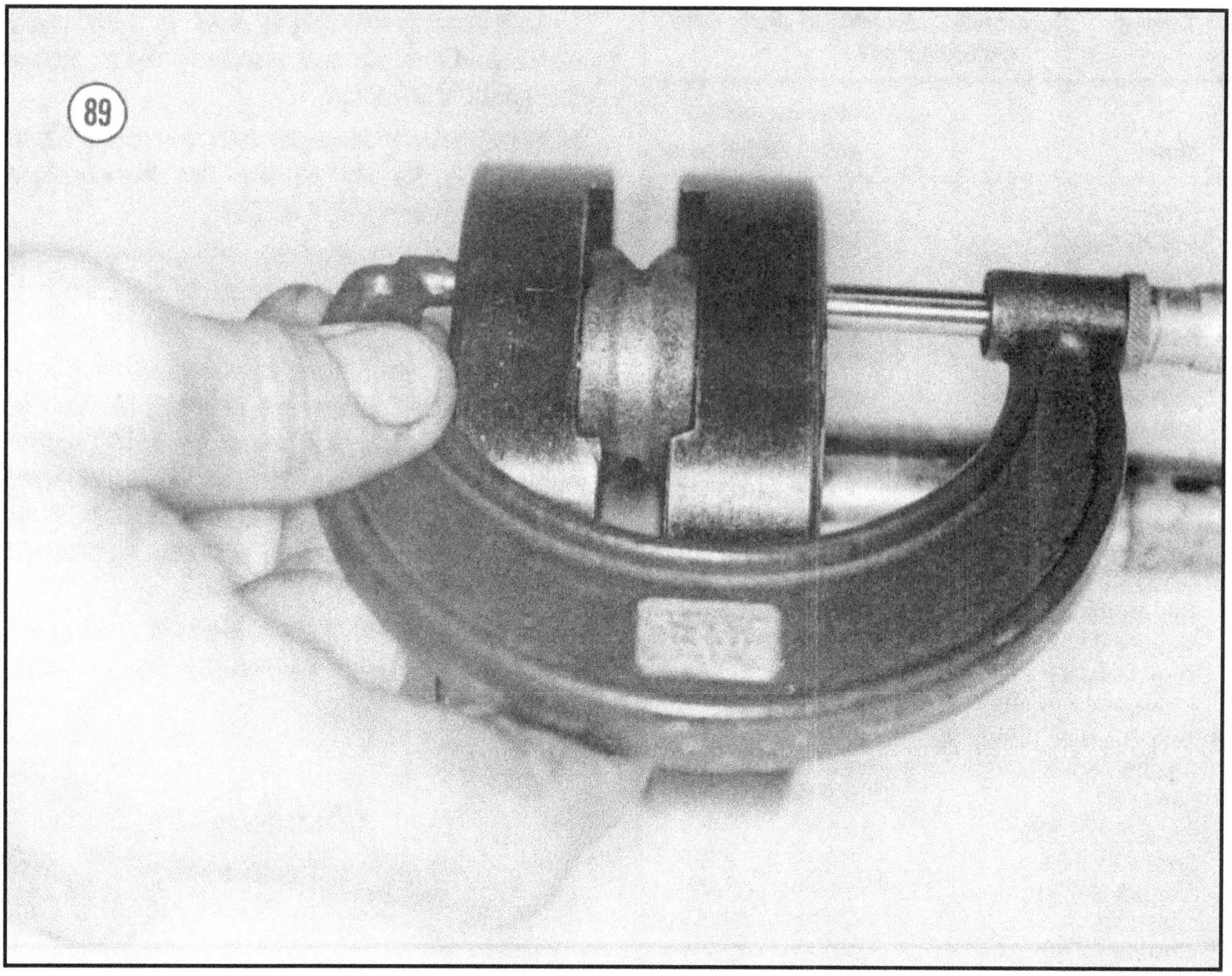

(92)

(93)

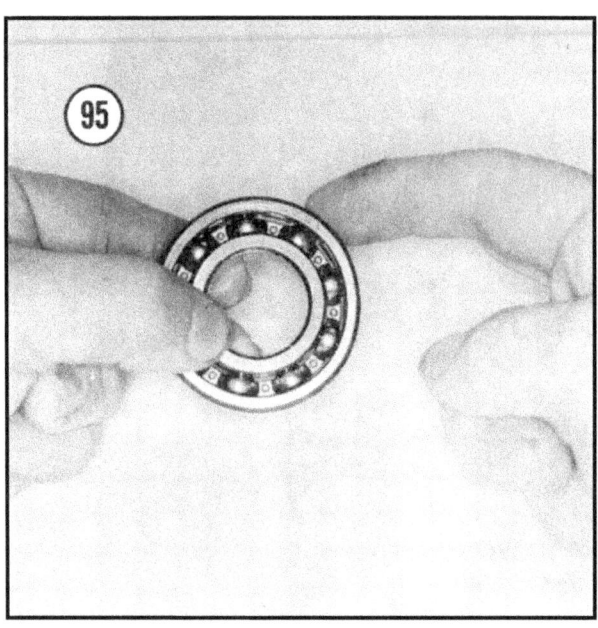

Bearing Installation

Reverse the removal procedures to install the bearings. Observe the following points:

1. Be sure that the hole for each bearing is perfectly clean before installation.
2. The transmission input shaft bearing on the clutch side must also absorb thrust loads from the clutch. The inner race of this bearing is greater in diameter on one side. The wider side of this bearing should be installed toward the inside of the transmission. All other bearings fit either way.
3. Do not use a torch for heating the crankcase halves.

OIL SEALS

Oil seals perform several important functions. In addition to retaining oil within the engine, they also prevent entry of foreign material. Crankshaft oil seals also retain primary compression pressure within the crankcase. It is good practice to replace all oil seals every time the engine is disassembled.

To remove oil seals, it is only necessary to pry them out with a screwdriver. Remove retainers from crankcase oil seals first.

Lubricate oil seal lips before installation. Place an oil seal installation sleeve over shaft

(96)

(**Figure 97**), then tap the seal into position with a seal driver (**Figure 98**).

AUTOMIX PUMP

Late King Scorpion and Rapita 250 models are equipped with an engine-driven oil pump, which meters lubricating oil into the engine induction tract. Oil pump outlet is controlled not only by engine speed, but also by throttle position, which is closely related to engine load. The engine is therefore supplied with a more nearly ideal fuel/oil mixture under all operating conditions.

To adjust the oil pump, refer to **Figure 99**, then proceed as follows.

1. Remove the pump cover.
2. Remove all free-play from the throttle cable, using the cable adjuster at the throttle grip.
3. Open the throttle fully. With the twist grip fully open, check that oil pump control pulley

(A) can be turned about 0.08 in. (2mm) further, as measured along its rim.

4. If adjustment is necessary, loosen locknut (B), then adjust by turning cable adjuster (C) as required. Don't forget to tighten the locknut.

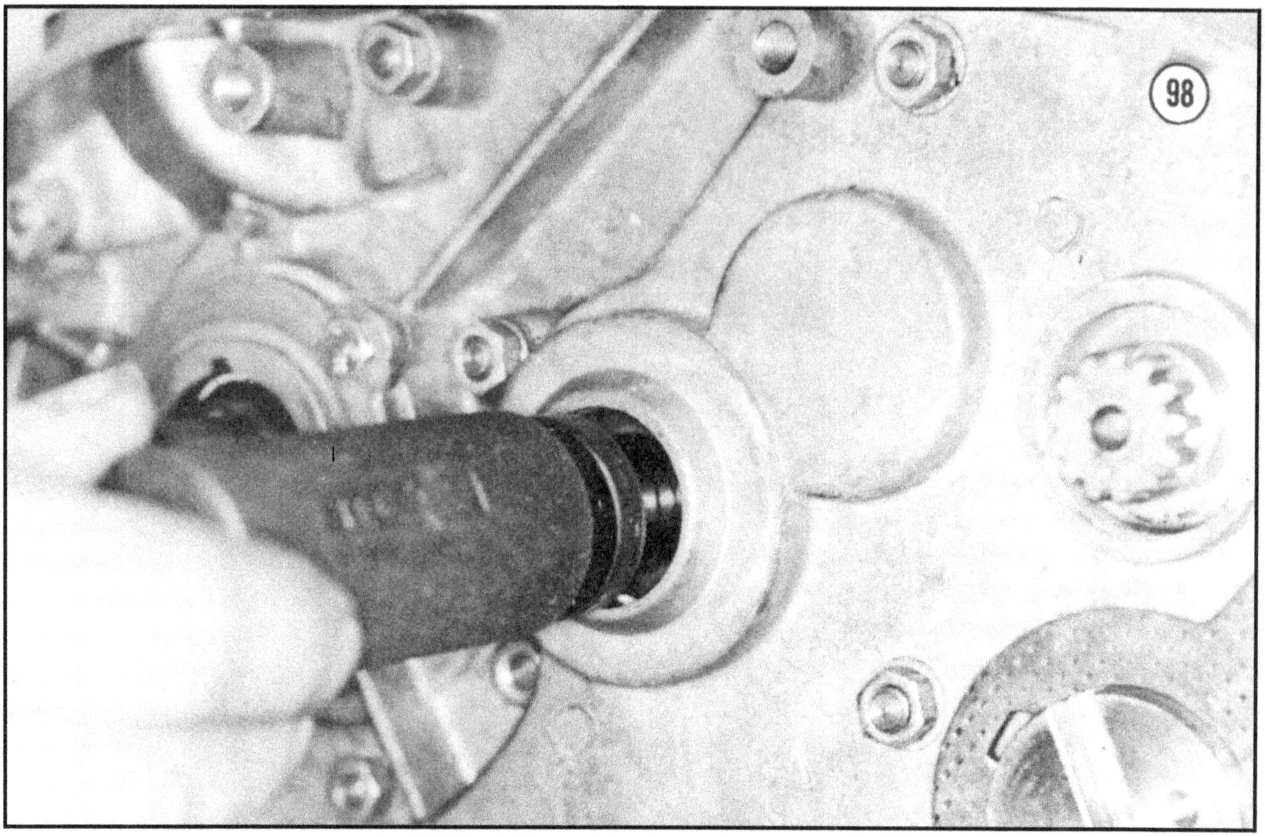
98

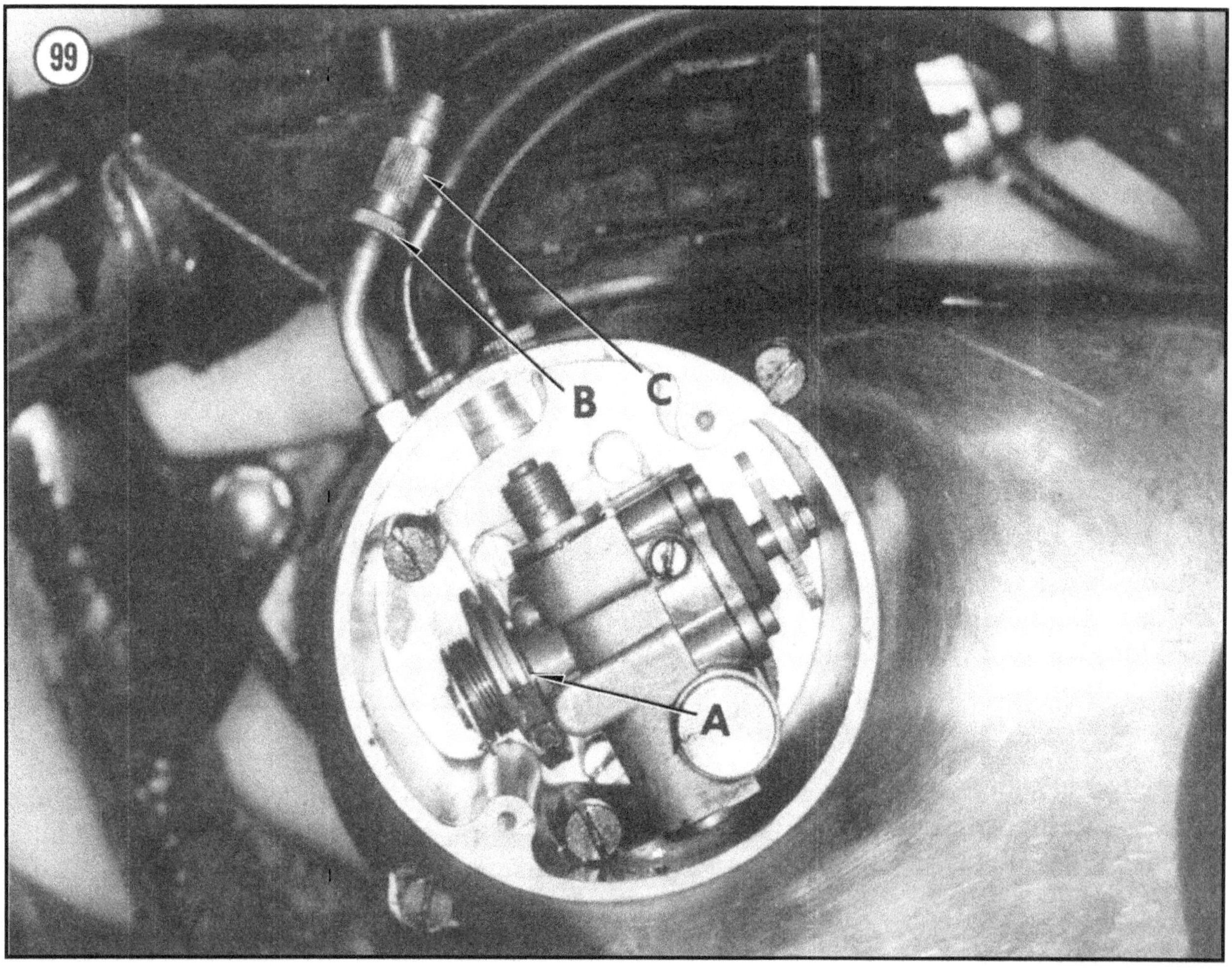
99
B
C
A

CHAPTER THREE

ELECTRICAL SYSTEM

This chapter covers operating principles and troubleshooting procedures for the ignition, charging, and lighting systems. Montesa machines are equipped with either a conventional flywheel magneto ignition system or a capacitor discharge system, which uses no breaker points. All models use flywheel magnetos as the source of electrical system power.

MAGNETO IGNITION SYSTEM

A magneto is a mechanically driven alternating current generator which develops the power required to fire the spark plug. On machines equipped with lights, additional coils within the magneto develop the power required for lighting.

Magneto Operation

Figure 1 illustrates a typical magneto ignition system. As the flywheel rotates, magnets in the flywheel move past the ignition source coil and thereby induce a current within the coil. The breaker points are so adjusted that they are opened by a cam attached to the engine crankshaft just as the piston reaches firing position. When the points open, energy developed in the ignition source coil is delivered to the ignition coil, which is a form of transformer, where it is stepped up to the very high voltage required to fire the spark plug.

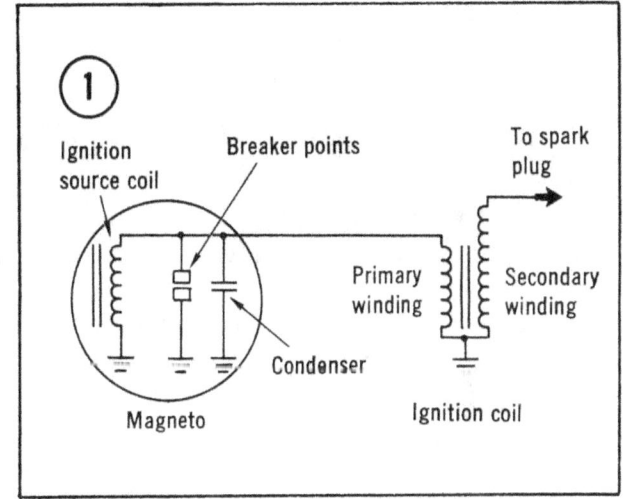

Breaker Points

Figure 2 illustrates typical breaker points. Normal use of the motorcycle causes the points to burn and pit gradually. If the points are not too pitted, they can be dressed with a few strokes of a clean point file. Do not use emery cloth or sandpaper, as particles can remain on the points and cause arcing and burning. If a few strokes of the file does not smooth the points completely, replace them.

Oil or dirt may get on the points, resulting in premature failure. Common causes for this condition are defective crankshaft seals, improper lubrication of the breaker cam, or lack of care when the crankcase cover is removed.

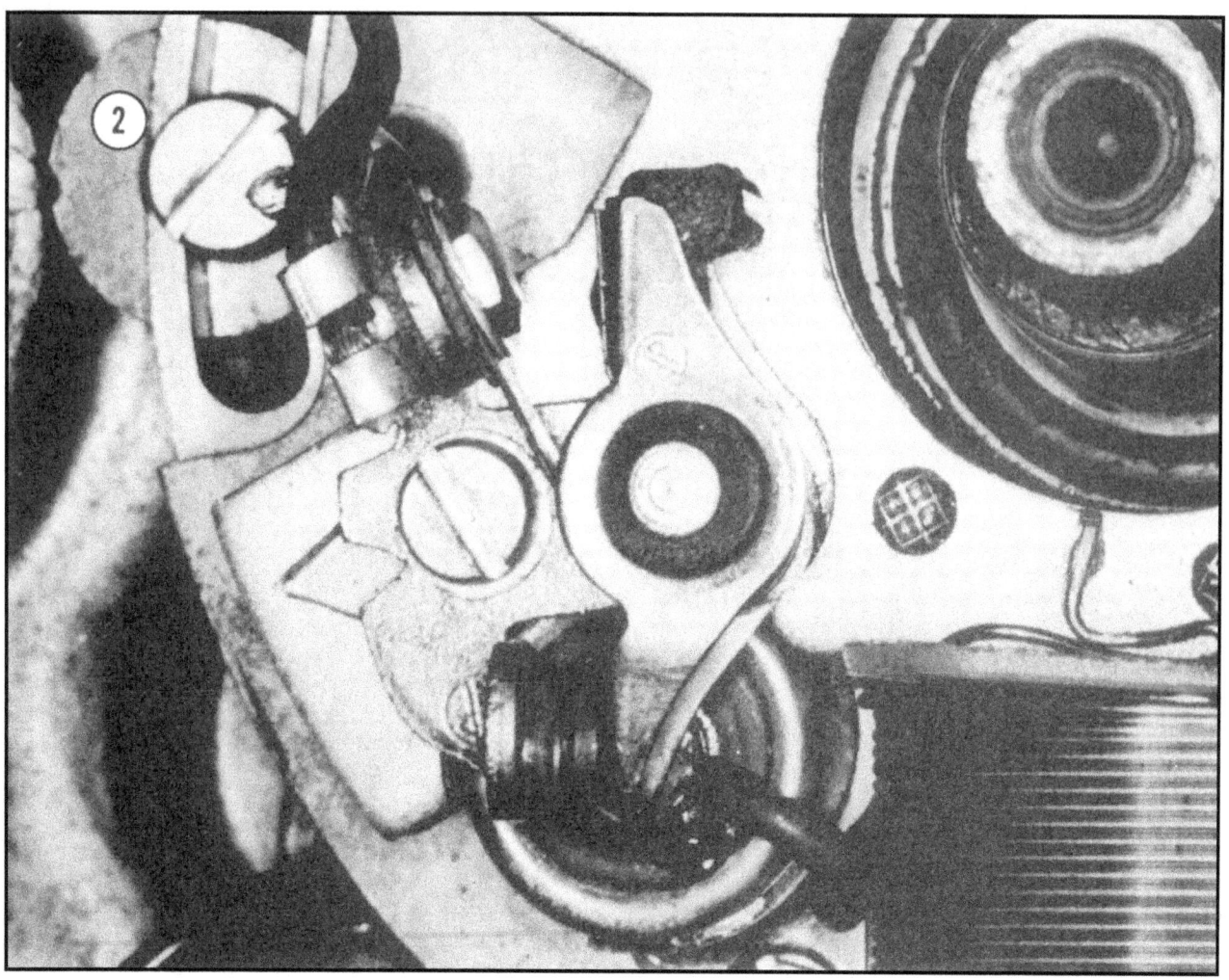

If the point spring is weak, the points will bounce and cause misfiring at high speeds.

Clean and regap the points from time to time. To clean the points, dress them lightly with a point file, then remove all residue with lacquer thinner. Close the points on a piece of clean white paper such as a business card. Continue to pull the card through the closed points until no particles or discoloration remains on the card. Finally, rotate the engine and observe the points as they open and close. If they do not meet squarely, replace them.

Breaker Point Installation

To install new breaker points, proceed as follows.

1. Remove the right crankcase cover.
2. Hold the flywheel in position, then remove the flywheel retaining nut (**Figure 3**). Note that this nut has a left-hand thread, and must be turned clockwise for removal.
3. Pry out the lockwasher with a small screwdriver.
4. Install the flywheel puller (**Figure 4**) by screwing it into the flywheel to its full depth, then turn the puller screw clockwise to remove the flywheel.
5. Remove 2 wires from the breaker points, then remove the attachment screw (**Figure 5**).
6. Reverse the removal procedure to install the new points. Be sure that both wire terminals are clean and tight, and that there is no oil between the fixed contact and the magneto base plate.
7. Be sure to adjust breaker point gap and ignition timing.

Adjusting Point Gap

For proper ignition system operation, point gap must be adjusted periodically. It is also necessary to adjust new points after they are installed. Adjust the points with the flywheel installed; if the flywheel was removed, install it

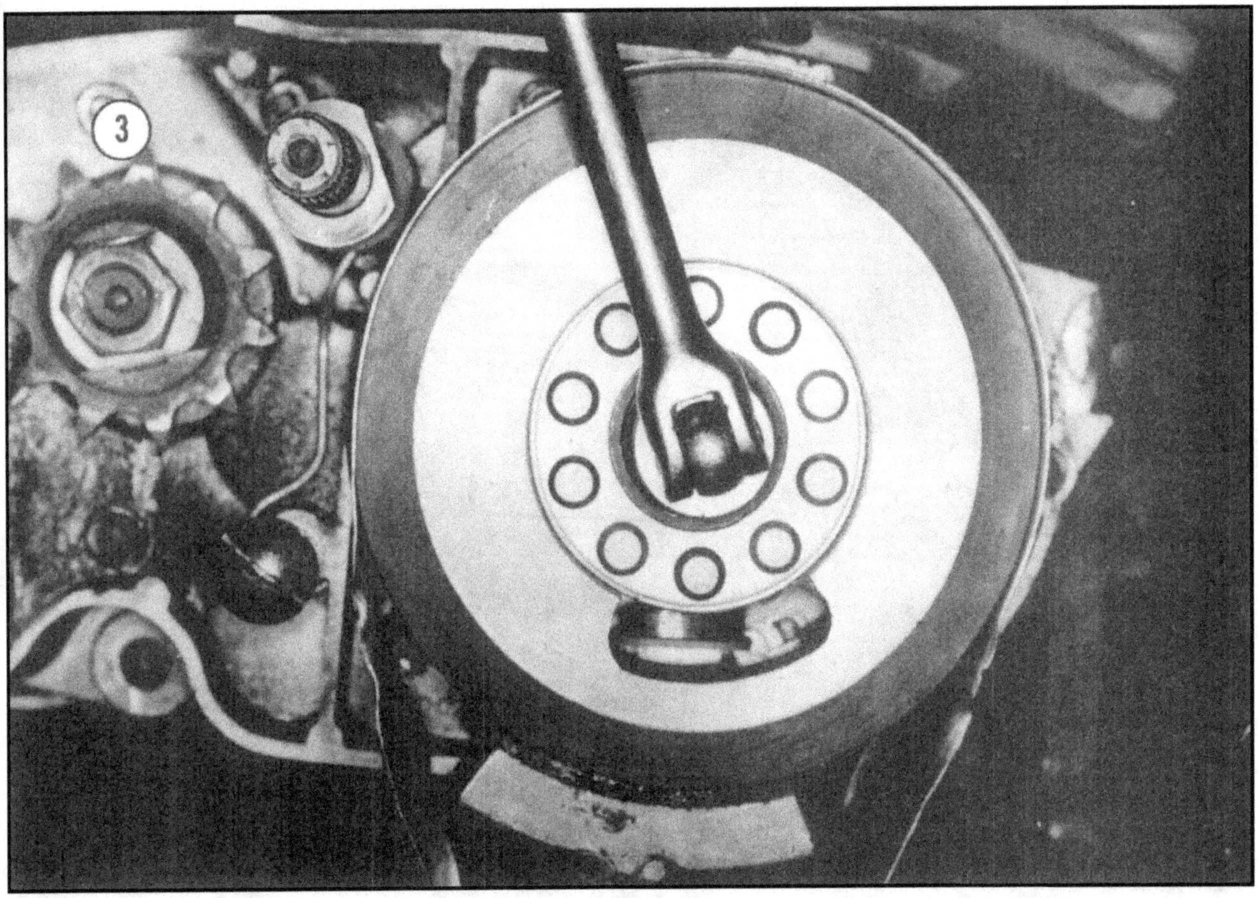

53

temporarily, but do not tighten the flywheel nut.

1. Rotate the flywheel slowly until the points are visible through the slot, and open to their maximum gap.

2. Check that point gap is 0.015 in. (0.38mm) with a feeler gauge inserted through the flywheel slot into the gap between the points. If the gap is not correct, loosen the attachment screw slightly, then move fixed point (**Figure 6**) as required with a screwdriver inserted between the pry points shown in **Figure 7**.

3. Tighten the clamp screw and recheck the adjustment.

4. Check ignition timing, and adjust if necessary.

Ignition Timing

Any change in point gap, including that resulting from normal breaker point and rubbing block wear, causes a change in ignition timing. If the spark occurs too early, severe engine damage may result. Overheating and loss of power will result from too late a spark. To adjust timing, proceed as follows.

1. Using a suitable adapter, mount a dial gauge in place of the spark plug (**Figure 8**) so that piston position may be determined.

2. Turn the flywheel slowly until the piston is at top dead center, then set the dial gauge to zero.

3. Connect an ohmmeter, buzzer, or other device for determining continuity across breaker

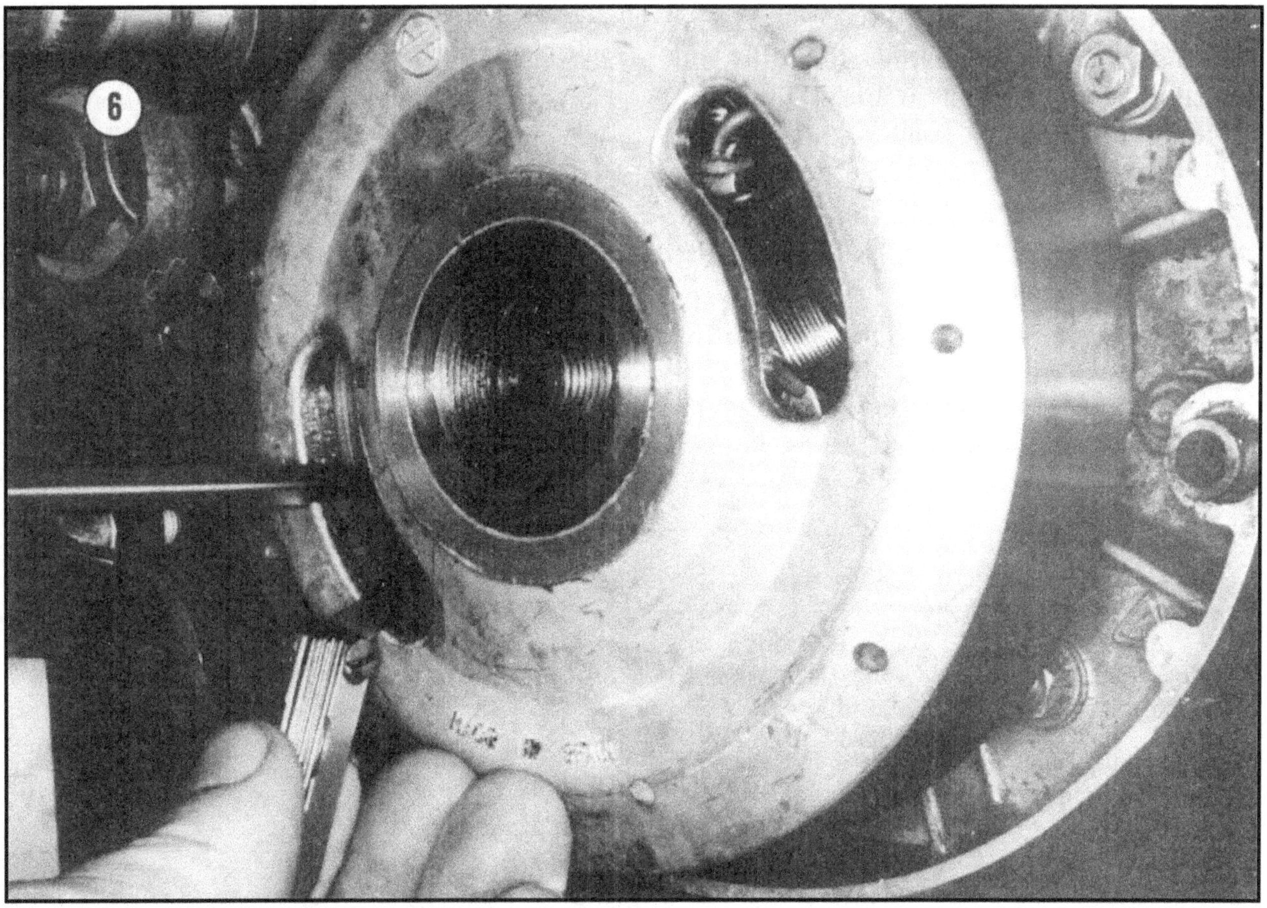
6

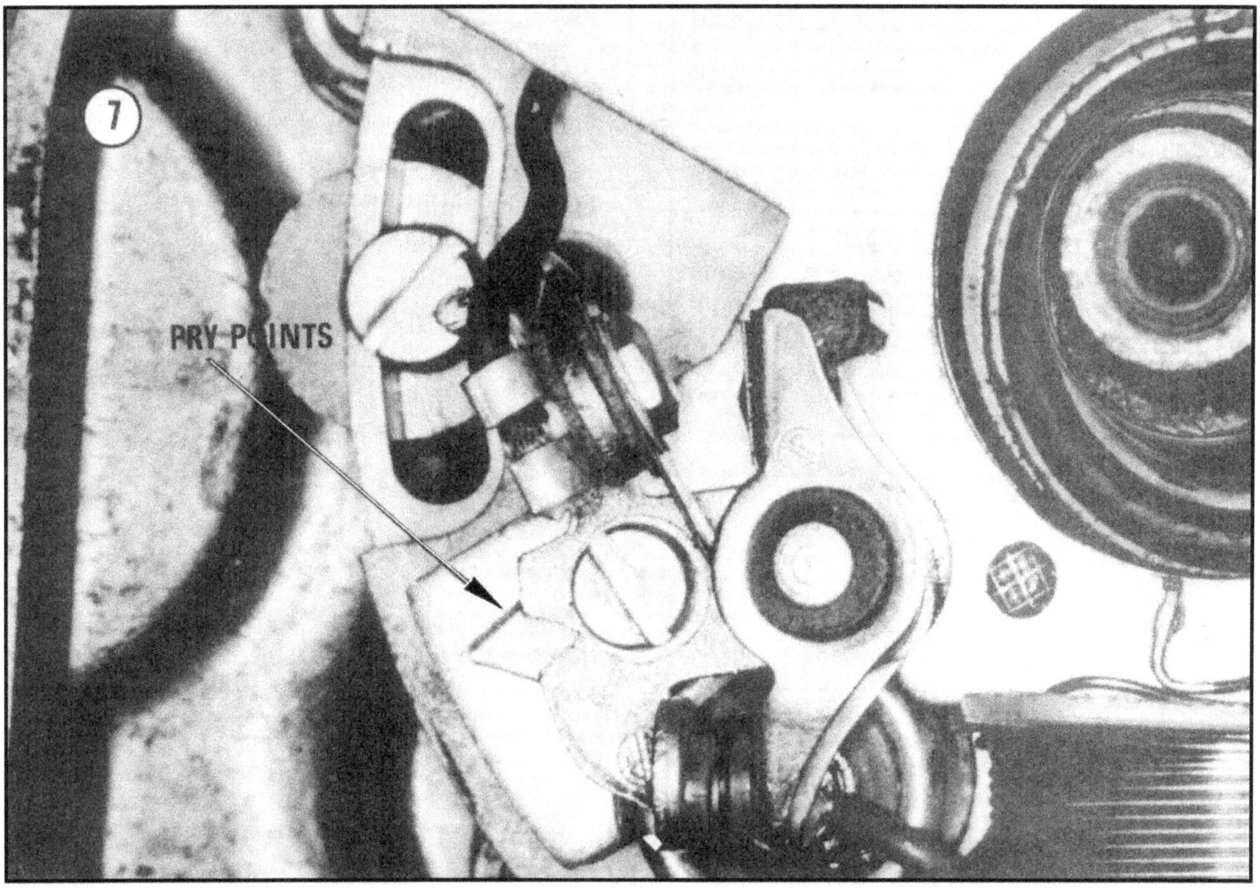
7
PRY POINTS

points. A convenient method for doing so is to disconnect the wire from terminal 1 at the ignition coil, then connect one test lead to the wire which was disconnected. Connect the other lead from the tester to any convenient ground.

4. Turn the flywheel opposite to normal engine rotation until the piston is lowered approximately 0.5 in. (13mm).

5. Very slowly rotate the flywheel in its normal direction until the continuity tester indicates that the points have just opened. Observe the dial gauge indication. **Table 1** lists piston distance below top dead center at which the points should open for each model.

Table 1   IGNITION TIMING BTDC

Model	Distance Inch	Millimeter
Texas	0.118	3.00
Impala, Impala Sport	0.118	3.00
Commando 175	0.118	3.00
Kenya	0.118	3.00
250 Trial	0.118	3.00
Impala Cross 175	0.138	3.50
Impala Cross 250	0.216	5.50
Enduro	0.138	3.50
Sport 250	0.157	4.00
Cota 247		
To Serial Number 21M2999	0.157	4.00
Cota 247		
From Serial Number 21M3000	0.098	2.50
La Cross	0.236	6.00
Scorpion 250	0.157	4.00
Cappra 250	0.151	4.00
Cappra 250 GP	0.152	4.00
Cappra 250-Five	0.157	4.00
Cappra 250 MX	0.118	3.00
Cappra 360 GP/DS	0.157	4.00
Cappra 125 MX		
To Serial Number 18M0052	0.157	4.00
Cota 123	0.118	3.00
Cota 123 Trail	0.118	3.00
Cota 172	0.118	3.00
Cota 247 Trail	0.098	2.50

If the breaker points do not open at the specified distance, it will be necessary to adjust the timing. There are two methods for doing so. The first may be used if the points opened within approximately 0.02 in. (0.5mm) of the specified distance. Under such conditions, ignition timing may be varied slightly by making a minor adjustment to the point gap, as described earlier. To do so, set the piston the specified distance below top dead center, then adjust the stationary breaker point until the continuity tester indicates that the points just open. Be sure to tighten the lock screw and recheck the adjustment. Experience has shown that ignition system operation will be satisfactory if breaker point gap is within the range of 0.012-0.016 in. (0.3-0.4mm).

If, after servicing the breaker points, ignition timing was too far off to adjust by changing point gap, it will be necessary to move the magneto base.

1. Readjust point gap to 0.015 in. (0.38mm) if the points were disturbed.

2. Remove the flywheel as described earlier.

3. Refer to **Figure 9**. Loosen the 3 magneto mounting screws enough so that the magneto base plate may be turned.

4. If the points opened at a distance greater than the distance specified, rotate the magneto base clockwise to retard the ignition timing. Conversely, if the piston was too close to top dead center when the points opened, rotate the magneto counterclockwise to advance the timing. Tighten the 3 mounting screws securely.

5. Replace the flywheel temporarily, then recheck the adjustment. Minor adjustment may then be accomplished by changing point gap as described earlier.

6. Install the flywheel. Be sure to use a new lockwasher. Note that this is a special "left-hand" lockwasher; a standard one will not work. Tighten the flywheel nut securely.

Ignition Coil

The ignition coil is a form of transformer which develops the high voltage required to jump the spark plug gap. The only maintenance required is that of keeping the electrical connection clean and tight, and occasionally checking to see that the coil is mounted securely.

If the condition of the coil is doubtful, there are several checks which should be made.

1. Using an ohmmeter, measure resistance between both primary terminals, as shown in **Figure 10**. Resistance should be approximately one ohm.

2. Measure the resistance between either primary terminal and the secondary high voltage terminal (**Figure 11**). Resistance should be in the range of 5,000-11,000 ohms.

3. Scrape the paint from the coil housing down to bare metal. Set the ohmmeter to its highest range, then measure the insulation resistance between this bare spot and any terminal (**Figure 12**). Insulation resistance must be at least 3 megohms (3 million ohms).

4. If these checks don't reveal any defects, but the coil condition is still doubtful, substitute a known good one.

Be sure that you connect the primary wires correctly when you replace the coil. The ground wire connects to the number 15 terminal on the coil.

Condenser

The condenser is a sealed unit that requires no maintenance. Be sure that both connections are clean and tight.

Two tests can be made on the condenser. Measure condenser capacity with a condenser tester. Capacity should be 0.18-0.25 microfarad. The other test is insulation resistance, which should not be less than 5 megohms, measured between the condenser pigtail and case.

In the event that no test equipment is available, a quick test of the condenser may be made by connecting the condenser case to the negative terminal of a 12-volt battery, and the positive lead to the positive battery terminal. Allow the condenser to charge for a few seconds, then quickly disconnect the battery and touch the condenser pigtail to the condenser case. If you observe a spark as the pigtail touches the case, you may assume that the condenser is okay.

Arcing between the breaker points is a common symptom of condenser failure.

Magneto Troubleshooting

The magneto is a simple, rugged device which should give little trouble. If malfunction is suspected, perform the following checks, with all wiring disconnected.

1. Block the ignition points open with a business card or similar piece of paper.

10

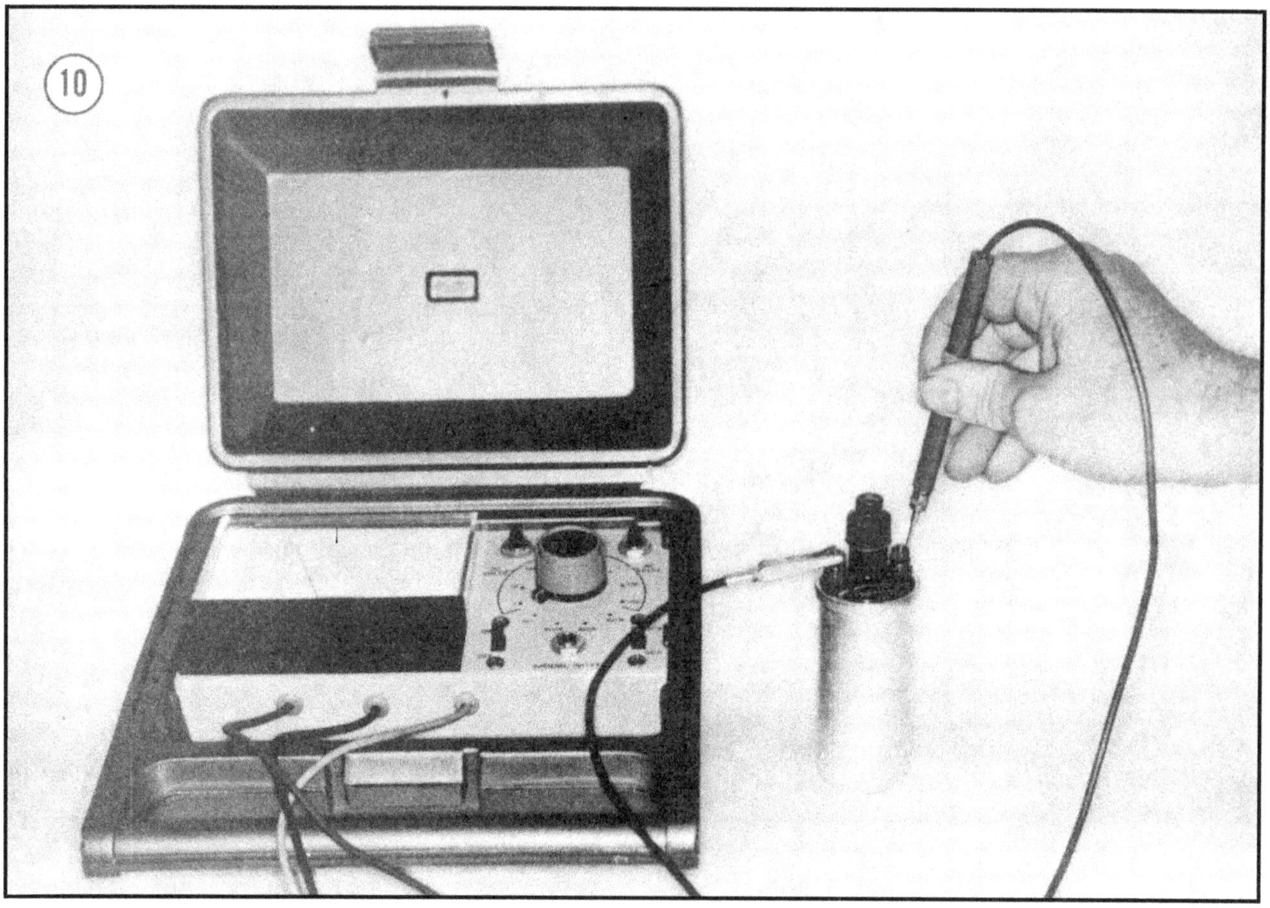

11

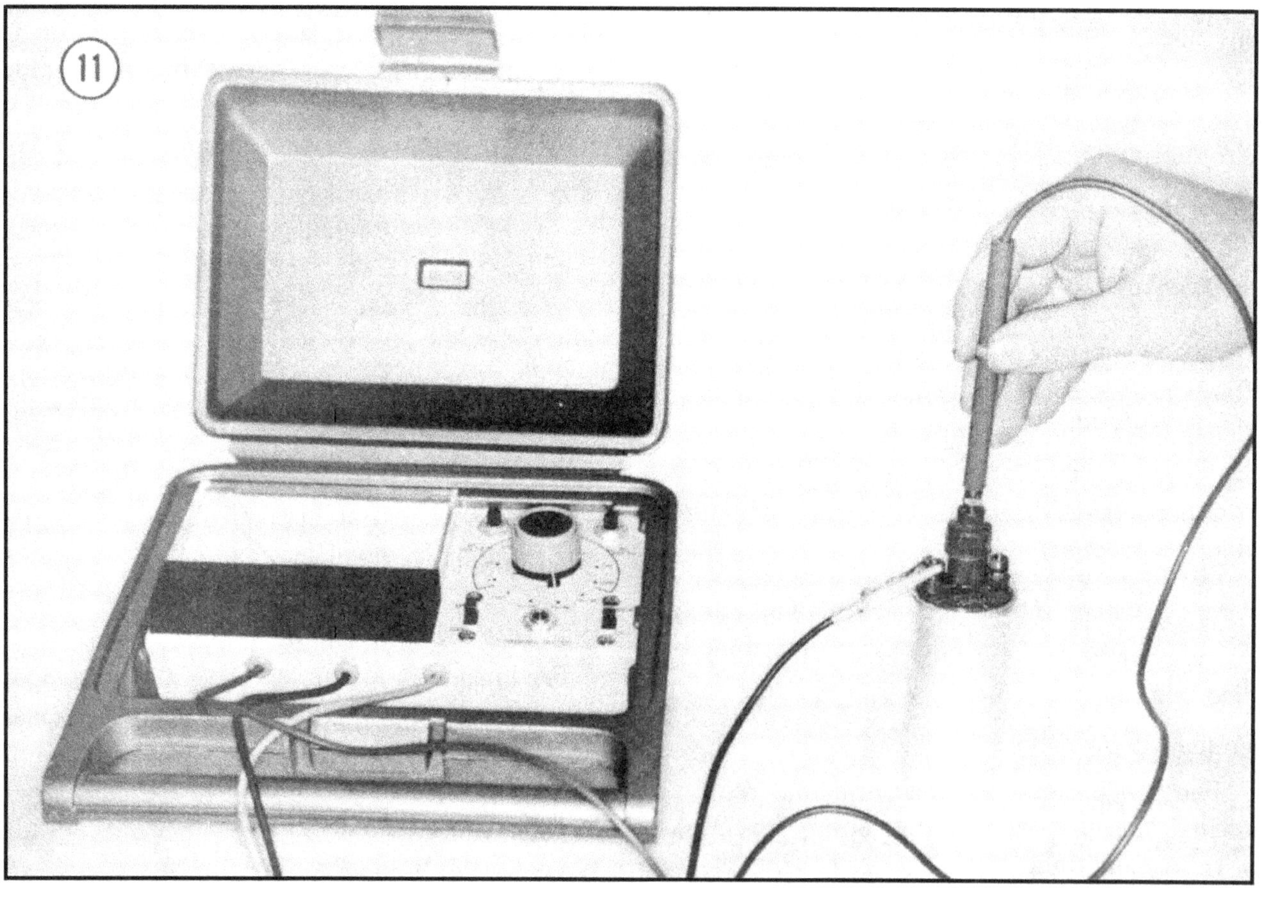

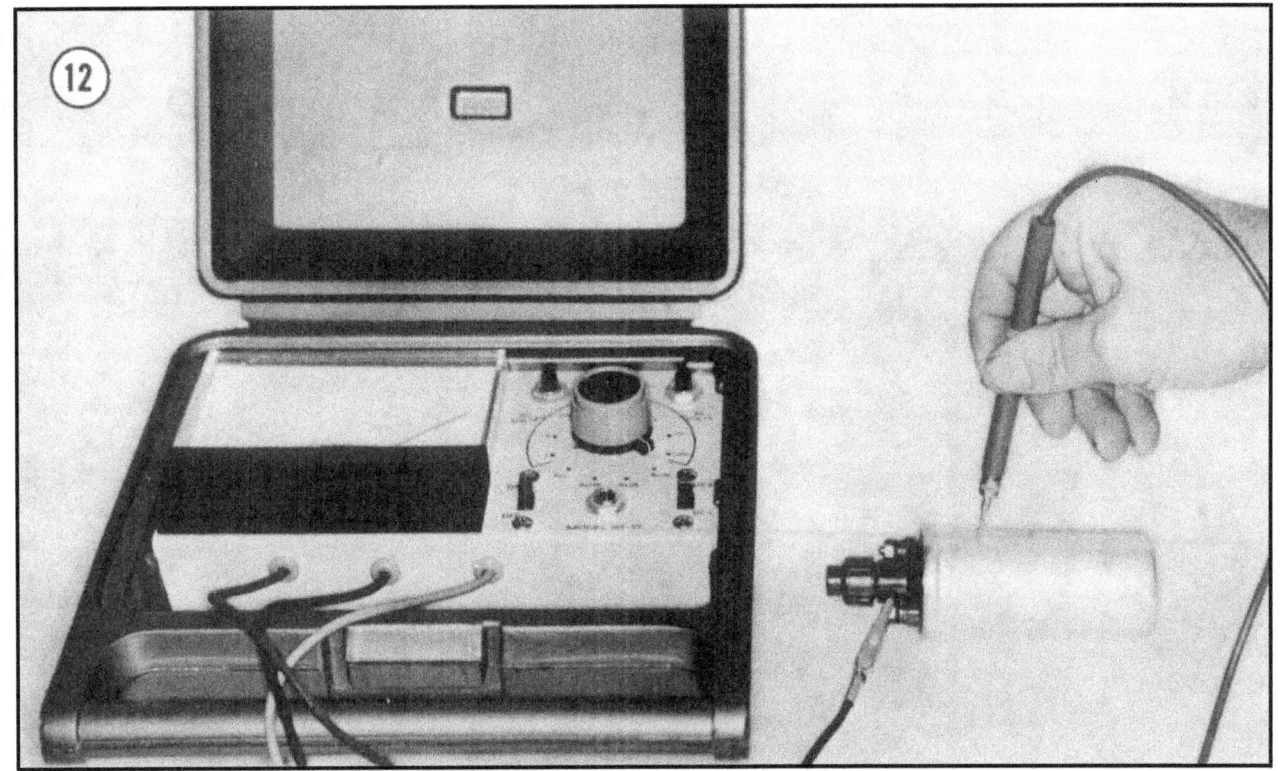

2. With an ohmmeter set to its highest range, check that the movable breaker point is not shorted to ground. Both wires must be disconnected from the points for this test. If there is any indication at all on the ohmmeter, replace the points.

3. Check the condenser. Replace it if there is any doubt about its condition.

4. Examine each coil for evidence of chafing. This condition is not likely to occur on late model magnetos, but may be found on earlier ones.

5. With the points blocked open, measure resistance between each lead from the magneto and ground (**Figure 13**). Typical readings are listed in **Table 2**.

Sport models without lights may be equipped with the type of ignition source shown in **Figure 14**. Resistance of this coil should be approximately 0.5 ohm.

Table 2   RESISTANCE TO GROUND

Wire	Resistance to Ground (Ohm)
Black	0.6
Pink	0.6
Yellow	0.3
Green	0.3

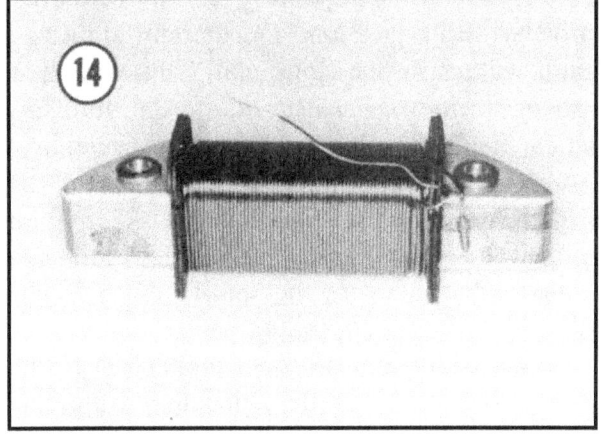

ELECTRONIC IGNITION SYSTEM

Some models are equipped with electronic ignition. This system uses no breaker points, cams, or other moving parts. Because of the extremely fast rise time of the generated high voltage, spark plug fouling is minimized.

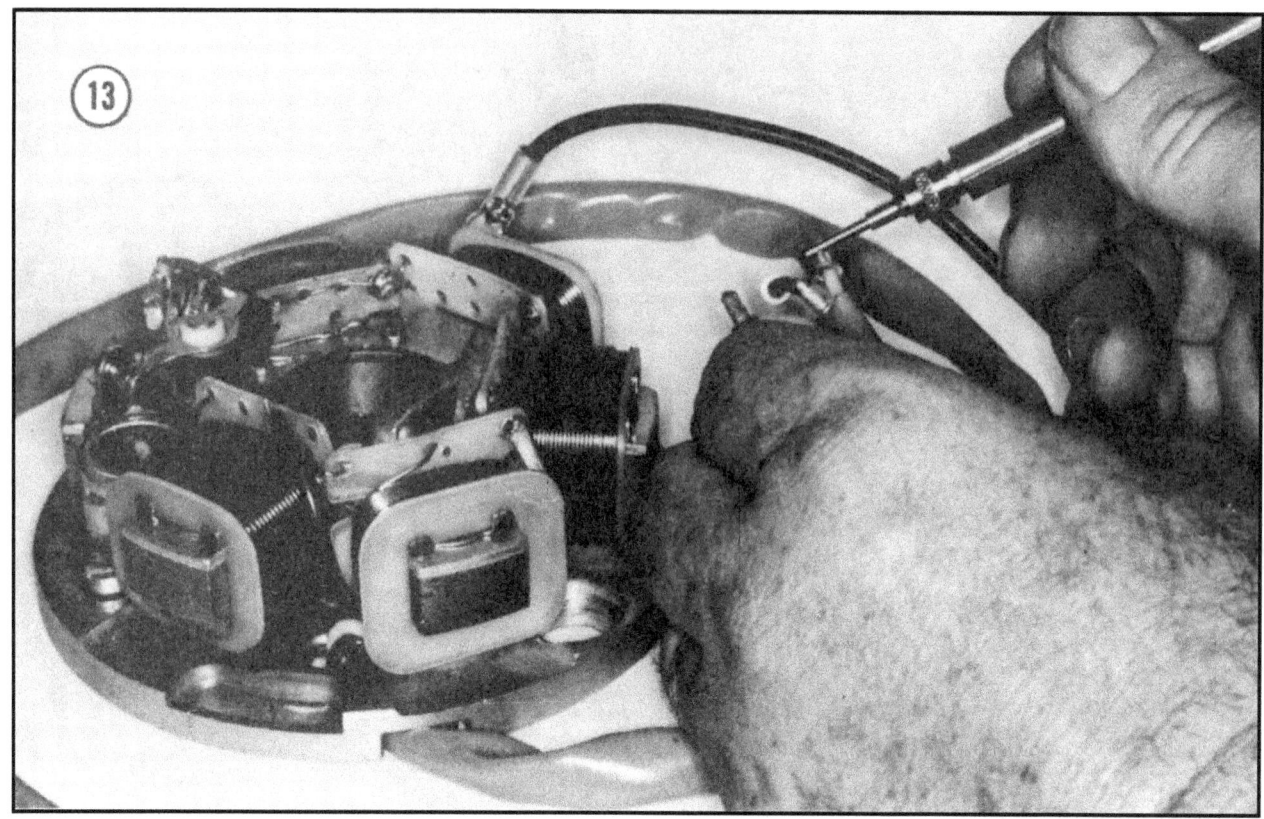

System Operation

Figure 15 is a schematic diagram of the electronic ignition system. Alternating current is developed in the source coil (1) as a magnet rotates past the coil. This current is rectified by the diode (2), and then changes the capacitor (3). The thyristor (4) is normally in a nonconducting state, and prevents discharge of the capacitor. A small magnet attached to the magneto flywheel moves past the signal coil (7) as the piston approaches firing position, and thereby induces a small voltage in the signal coil. This voltage is applied to the trigger electrode to the thyristor, which then immediately conducts, providing a discharge path for the capacitor through the primary winding of the ignition coil (8). Ignition voltage is stepped up in the ignition coil to a value sufficient to fire the spark plug (5). The resistor (6) acts as a limiter.

Figure 16 illustrates system connections. Note that a kill button must be connected to the blue terminal only.

Electronic Ignition Maintenance

No maintenance is required on the electronic ignition system other than occasional checks to be sure that all connections are clean and secure. Be sure that the mounting bracket on the electronic converter unit makes good electrical contact with the motorcycle frame. Failure to maintain a good connection at this point may result in ignition system malfunction.

Ignition Timing

Because there are no breaker points or other moving parts, ignition timing adjustment differs considerably from that of conventional magneto ignition systems.

1. Install a dial gauge or ignition timing gauge in the spark plug hole. This installation is the same as for the conventional magneto ignition system.
2. Rotate the engine until the dial gauge indicates top dead center, then set the dial gauge to zero.
3. Rotate the engine opposite to its normal running direction until the dial gauge indicates that the piston is in timing position. **Table 3** lists piston distances below top dead center for each model with electronic ignition.

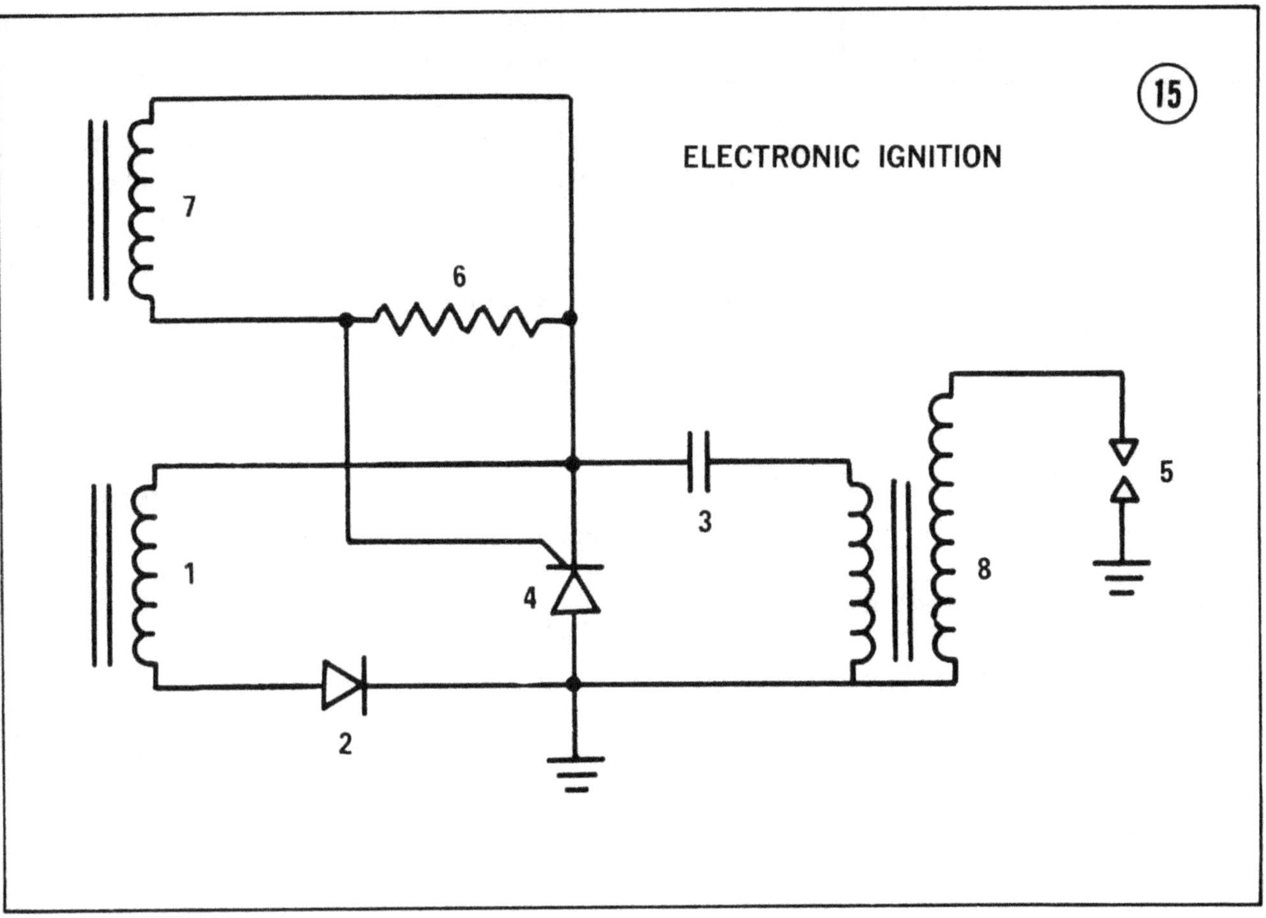
15
ELECTRONIC IGNITION
7
6
1
2
3
4
5
8

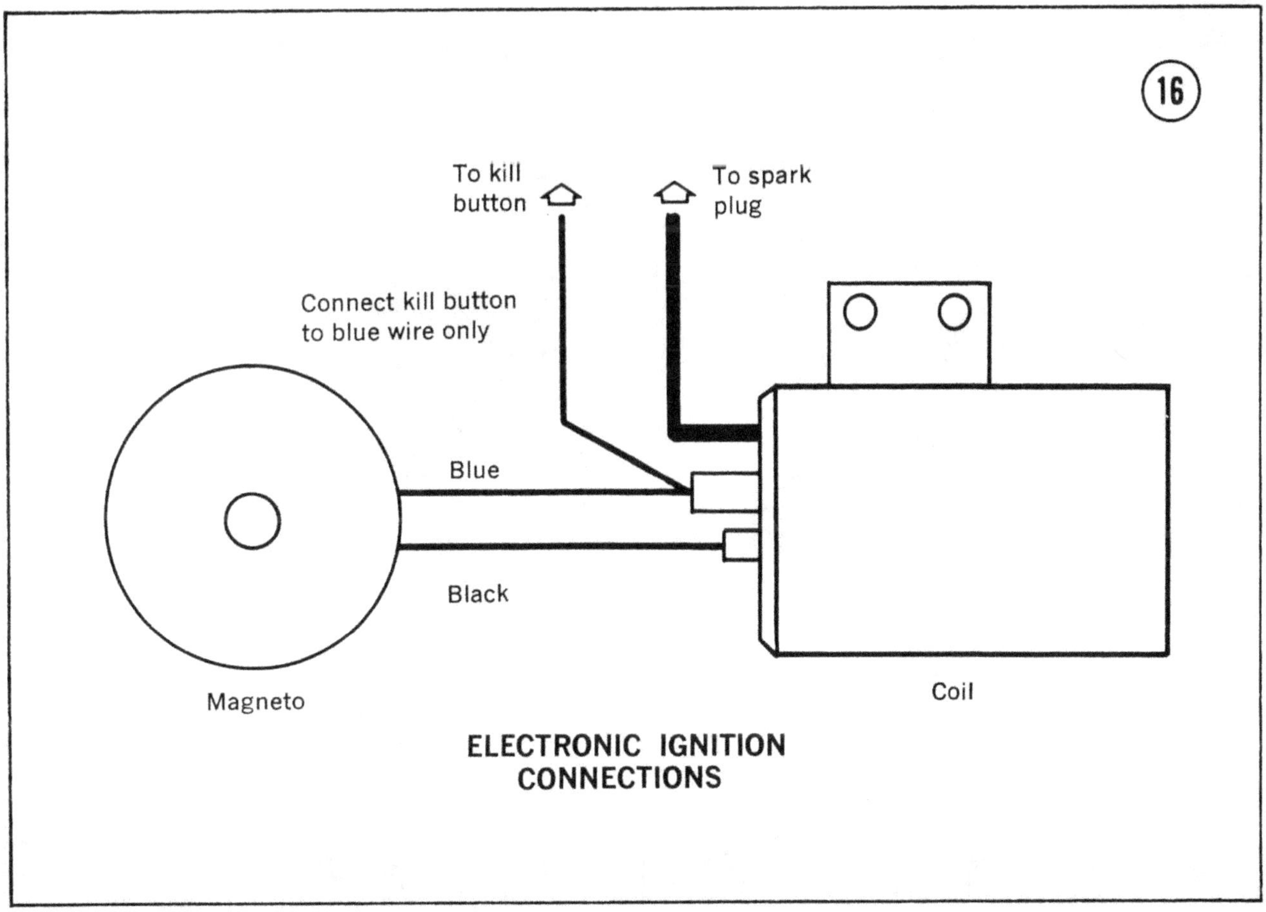
16
To kill button
To spark plug
Connect kill button to blue wire only
Blue
Black
Magneto
Coil
ELECTRONIC IGNITION CONNECTIONS

**Table 3 IGNITION TIMING —
ELECTRONIC IGNITON SYSTEMS**

Model	Distance	
	Inch	(Millimeter)
Cappra 125 MX	0.118	(3.0)
Cappra 250 MX	0.118	(3.0)
Cappra 250 VR	0.098	(2.5)
King Scorpion	0.118	(3.0)
Cappra 125 VA	0.059	(1.5)
Enduro 250	0.118	(3.0)
Rapita 250	0.118	(3.0)
Cappra 250 V-75	0.098	(2.5)

4. Insert a timing gauge rod through the hole in the flywheel and into the stator plate hole, as shown in **Figure 17**. No adjustment is required if the 2 holes line up.

5. If the 2 holes do not align, rotate the flywheel slightly to align the holes. Note the number of degrees and direction of flywheel rotation required for alignment.

6. Remove the flywheel. Note that for flywheels on the left side of the engine, retaining nuts have left-hand threads.

7. Loosen 3 stator plate screws slightly, then rotate the stator plate the same number of degrees noted in Step 5, *but in the opposite direction*.

8. Temporarily install the flywheel.

9. Repeat Steps 3 through 8 to check for proper adjustment.

10. Install a new lockwasher and tighten the retaining nut securely. Note that for left side flywheels, a special left-hand lockwasher is required.

Electronic Ignition Troubleshooting

Since the electronic ignition system units are sealed, troubleshooting is best accomplished by substitution. Tests that may be made are listed below.

1. Clean and tighten all connections. Be sure that the connection between the coil mounting

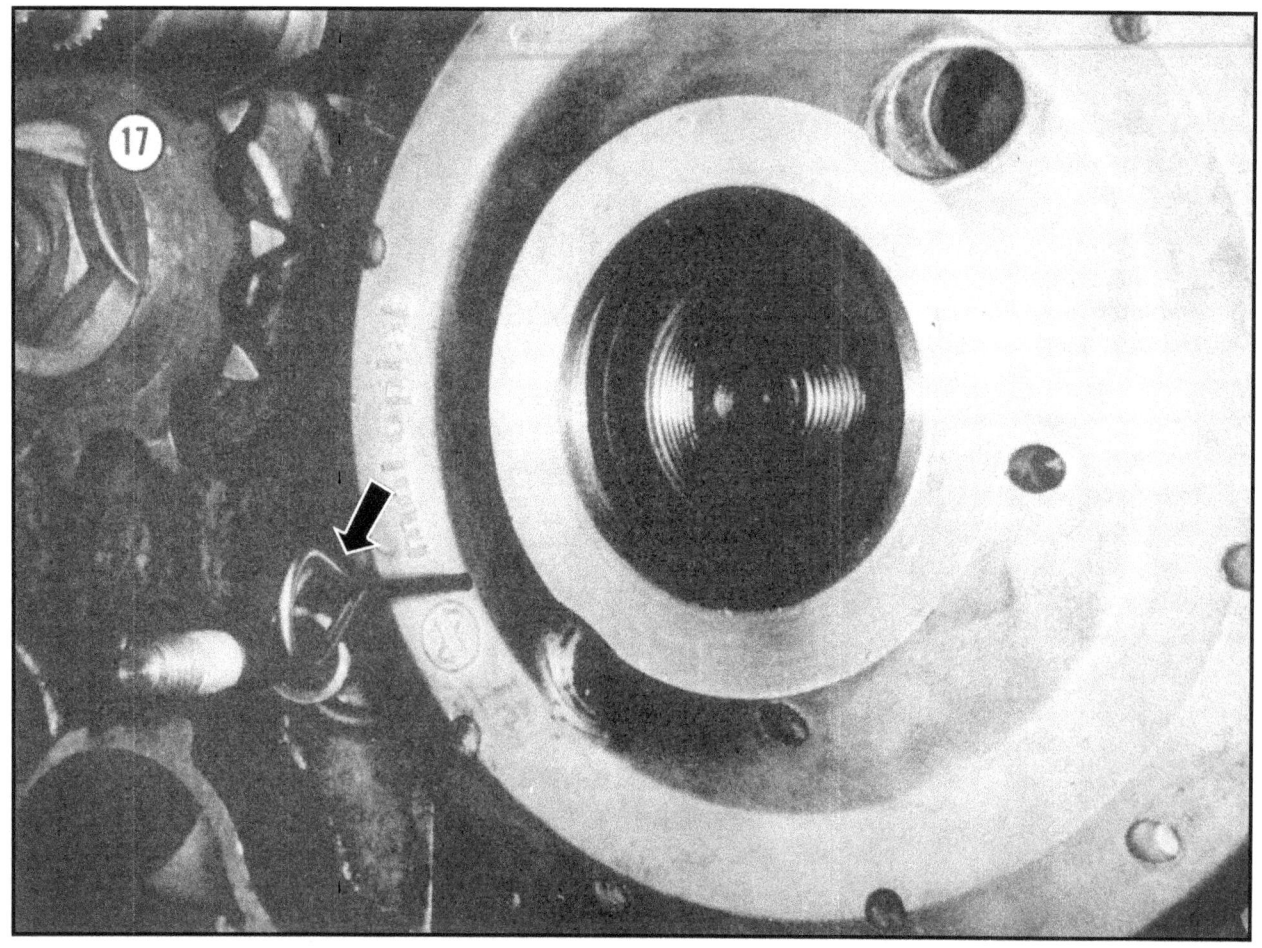

bracket and the motorcycle frame is clean, free of corrosion, and tight.

2. Disconnect the spark plug cable and hold it approximately ¼ in. (6mm) from the cylinder head.

3. Crank the engine briskly. If a strong, blue-white spark jumps between the cable and cylinder head, the ignition system is okay.

Measurements made with an ohmmeter are not conclusive. Resistance readings will vary, depending on ohmmeter type, range used, and battery voltage. Some typical values are presented in the following tests. Note that for some ohmmeters, lead color does not indicate polarity of test current.

1. Connect the negative lead from the ohmmeter to ground. Connect the positive lead in turn to the blue and black wires. Resistance should indicate 200 to 800 ohms. If an electronic ohmmeter is used, resistance may read as high as 25,000 ohms.

2. Reverse the ohmmeter lead, and repeat each measurement. Resistance should be essentially infinite.

3. Measure resistance between the black and blue leads. Resistance should be 10 ohms in either direction.

4. Connect either ohmmeter lead to the coil mounting bracket. Connect the other lead to the spark plug lead. Resistance should be about 10,000 ohms.

5. Connect one ohmmeter lead to the mounting bracket. Set the ohmmeter to its highest range. Carefully observe the meter, then connect the other test lead to the blue terminal. The ohmmeter needle should flick downscale momentarily, then settle at infinity.

6. Repeat Step 5, but testing the black terminal.

Electronic Ignition Cautions

The electronic ignition is simple and should give no trouble. Damage may occur, however, if certain precautions are not observed.

1. Never stop the machine by disconnecting the spark plug lead.

2. Connect a kill button, if required, to the blue wire only.

3. Do not interchange the blue and black wires.

4. Keep all connections clean and tight. Be sure that the mounting brackets to frame connection is clean and tight.

RECTIFIER

Machines with batteries are also equipped with a rectifier. The rectifier serves 2 purposes. First, it converts alternating current generated by the magneto into direct current for charging the battery. It also prevents the battery from discharging through the charging coil in the magneto when the engine is not running, or is running too slowly to charge the battery.

To test the rectifier, refer to **Figure 18**. Connect the test circuit shown, using the motorcycle battery and a small 6-volt lamp. If the lamp lights with the rectifier leads connected one way, but not when the leads are reversed, the rectifier is okay. If the lamp lights when the leads are connected either way, the rectifier is shorted. If the lamp does not light at all, the rectifier is open. Replace the magneto if the rectifier is shorted or open.

An alternate test method is to use an ohmmeter.

1. Disconnect all wires from the magneto.

2. Connect one ohmmeter lead to the red (low charge) wire coming from the magneto. Connect the other ohmmeter lead to ground.

3. Note the ohmmeter indication.

4. Reverse the test connections, then again note the ohmmeter indication.

5. If resistance indications were the same, either high or low, in Steps 3 and 4, the rectifier is faulty. If one reading was high and the other low, the rectifier is OK.

6. Repeat Steps 2 through 5 for the white (high charge) wire.

SPARK PLUG

The spark plug recommended by the factory is usually the most suitable for your machine. If your riding conditions are mild, it may be advisable to go to a spark plug one step hotter than normal. Unusually severe riding conditions may require slightly colder plugs.

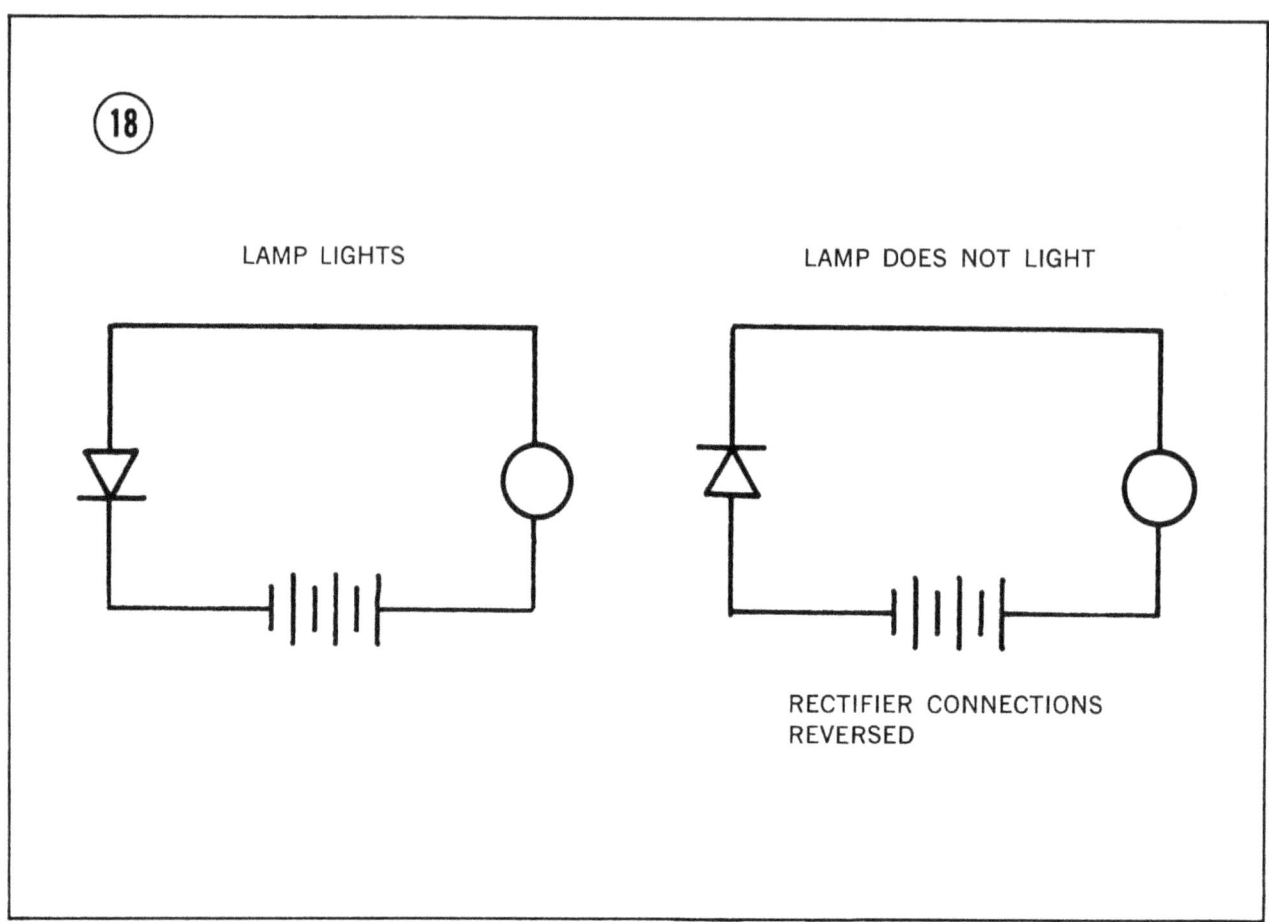

The proper heat range for the spark plug is determined by the requirement that the plug operate hot enough to burn off unwanted deposits, but not so hot that they burn themselves or cause preignition. A spark plug of the correct heat range will show a light tan color on the portion of the insulator within the cylinder after the plug has been in service.

If the insulator appears to be burned or white, the plug is too hot. Possibly the insulator and the center electrode will even show evidence of melting. Such a plug should be replaced with a colder one.

Unburned residue in the form of fluffy black carbon or grimy oil deposits indicate a spark plug that is too cold. The insulator color may range from dark brown to black. Try using a hotter plug if these conditions are found.

Remove and clean the spark plug approximately every 600 miles (1,000 kilometers). After cleaning, inspect it for worn or eroded electrodes. Replace it if there is any doubt about its condition. If the plug is found to be serviceable, file the center electrode square, then adjust the gap by bending the outer electrode only. Measure the gap with a round wire spark plug gauge only; a flat gauge will yield an incorrect reading. Spark plug gap for all models is 0.020-0.024 in. (0.5-0.6mm).

Should you encounter difficulty removing the spark plug, apply penetrating oil to the base of plug and allow time for the oil to work in. Be sure to clean the seating area on the cylinder head and use a new gasket when you replace the spark plug. Install the plug finger-tight, then tighten it an additional ½ turn. Remember that faulty spark plugs are the greatest cause for starting failures in 2-stroke engines.

BATTERY

Check the battery occasionally for sulphation or deposits in the bottom of the cells. Replace the battery if such conditions exist, or if the battery will not accept or hold a charge.

Maintain the battery electrolyte level between the minimum and maximum marks on the battery case. Use only distilled water to fill the cells.

If the battery requires water more frequently than once a month, check the charging system. It's possible the battery is being overcharged.

Battery life should normally be 2 to 3 years. This will be shortened by any of the following conditions:
1. Overcharging.
2. Leaving the battery in a discharged state.
3. Freezing—a fully charged battery will freeze at a much lower temperature than one that is discharged. If the machine is exposed to cold weather, be sure to keep battery fully charged.
4. Allowing the electrolyte level to drop below the tops of the plates.
5. Adding anything to the electrolyte except distilled water.

If the motorcycle is not to be used for an extended period, charge the battery fully, remove it from the machine, and store it in a cool, dry place. Recharge the battery every 2 months while it is in storage, and again before it is put back into service.

Be very careful when you install the battery to connect it properly. If the battery is installed backward, the rectifier and magneto will be damaged.

Determine the state of charge of the battery with a hydrometer. To use this instrument, place the suction tube into the filler opening and draw in just enough electrolyte to lift the float. Hold the instrument in a vertical position and take the reading at eye level.

The specific gravity of the electrolyte varies with temperature, so it's necessary to apply a temperature correction to the reading you obtain. For each 10° that the battery temperature exceeds 80°F, add 0.004 to the indicated specific gravity. Subtract 0.004 from the indicated value for each 10° that the battery temperature is below 80°F.

Specific gravity of a fully charged battery is 1.260. If specific gravity is below 1.220, recharge the battery.

Montesa machines with batteries have 2 charging wires coming from the magneto. If the bike is operated under conditions of sustained high speeds with little use of any electrical accessories, connect the red wire to the battery. If the battery is chronically undercharged, disconnect the red wire and connect the white wire to provide a higher charging rate.

LIGHTS

Machines which are intended to be ridden on public streets are equipped with lights. Check them periodically to be sure that they are working properly.

Headlight

The headlight unit consists primarily of a lamp body, a dual-filament bulb, a lens and reflector unit, a rim, and a socket. To adjust the headlight, loosen the mounting bolts and move the assembly as required.

Brake Light Switch

The switch is actuated by the brake pedal. Adjust the switch so that the stoplight goes on just before braking action occurs.

CHAPTER FOUR

CARBURETION

For proper operation, a gasoline engine must be supplied with fuel and air, mixed in the proper proportions by weight. A mixture in which there is an excess of fuel is said to be rich. A lean mixture is one which contains insufficient fuel. It is the function of a carburetor to supply the proper mixture to the engine under all operating conditions.

Montesa motorcycles are equipped with one of 4 different carburetors: the Bing (**Figure 1**), the Amal monobloc (**Figure 2A**), the Amal concentric (**Figure 2B**), or the Amal Mark II (**Figure 3**).

CARBURETOR OPERATION

Figure 4 is an exploded view of a typical carburetor. The essential functional parts are a float and float valve mechanism for maintaining a constant fuel level in the float bowl, a pilot system for supplying fuel at low speeds, a main fuel system which supplies the engine at medium and high speeds, and a tickler system, which supplies the very rich mixture needed to start a cold engine. The operation of each system is discussed in the following paragraphs.

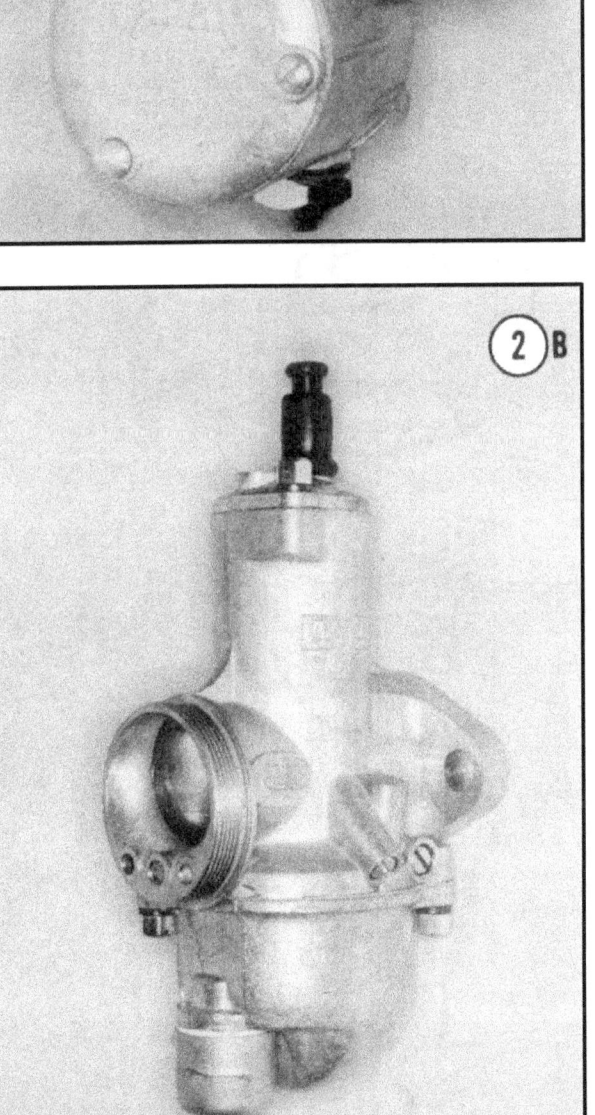

Float Mechanism

Figure 5 illustrates a typical float mechanism. Proper operation of the carburetor is dependent on maintaining a constant fuel level in the carburetor bowl. As fuel is drawn from the float bowl, the float level drops. When the float drops, the float valve moves away from its seat and allows fuel to flow past the valve and seat into the bowl. As this occurs, the float rises, pressing the valve against its seat and shutting off the flow of fuel.

It can be seen from this discussion that a small piece of dirt trapped between the valve and seat will prevent the valve from closing and allow fuel to rise beyond the normal level. One result is flooding. **Figure 6** illustrates this condition.

Pilot System

Under idle or low speed conditions, at less than ⅛ throttle, the engine doesn't require much fuel or air, and the throttle valve is almost closed. A separate pilot system is required for

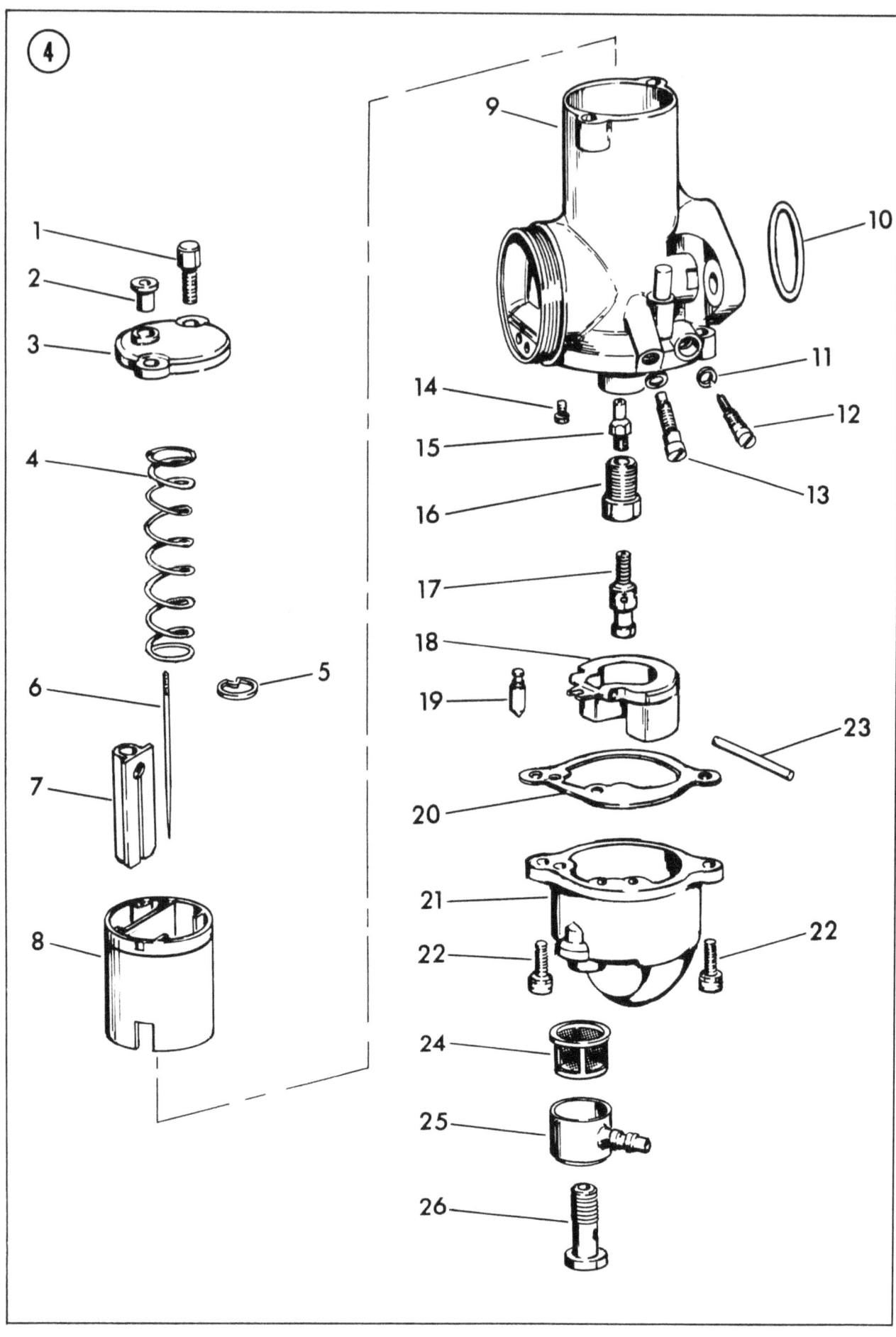

AMAL CARBURETOR

1. Screw
2. Ferrule
3. Mixing chamber cap
4. Spring
5. Jet needle clip
6. Jet needle
7. Choke valve
8. Throttle valve
9. Mixing chamber body
10. O-ring
11. O-ring
12. Pilot air screw
13. Throttle stop screw
14. Pilot jet
15. Needle jet
16. Jet holder
17. Main jet
18. Float
19. Float needle
20. Gasket
21. Float bowl
22. Screw
23. Float pivot
24. Filter screen
25. Banjo
26. Banjo bolt

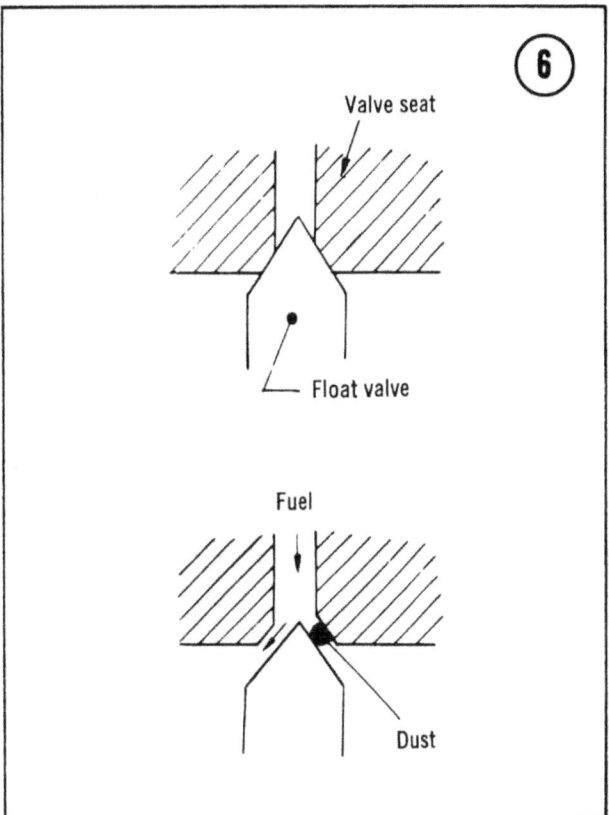

operation under such conditions. **Figure 7** illustrates its operation.

Air is drawn through the pilot air inlet and controlled by the pilot air screw. It is mixed with fuel drawn through the pilot jet. The air/fuel mixture then travels from the pilot outlet into the main air passage, where it is further mixed with air prior to being drawn into the engine. The pilot air screw controls the idle mixture.

If proper idle and low speed mixture cannot be obtained within the normal adjustment range of the idle mixture screw, refer to **Table 1** for possible causes.

Table 1 MIXTURE ADJUSTMENT CORRECTIONS

Too rich
Clogged pilot air intake
Clogged air passage
Clogged air bleed opening
Pilot jet loose

Too lean
Obstructed pilot jet
Obstructed jet outlet
Worn throttle valve
Carburetor mounting loose

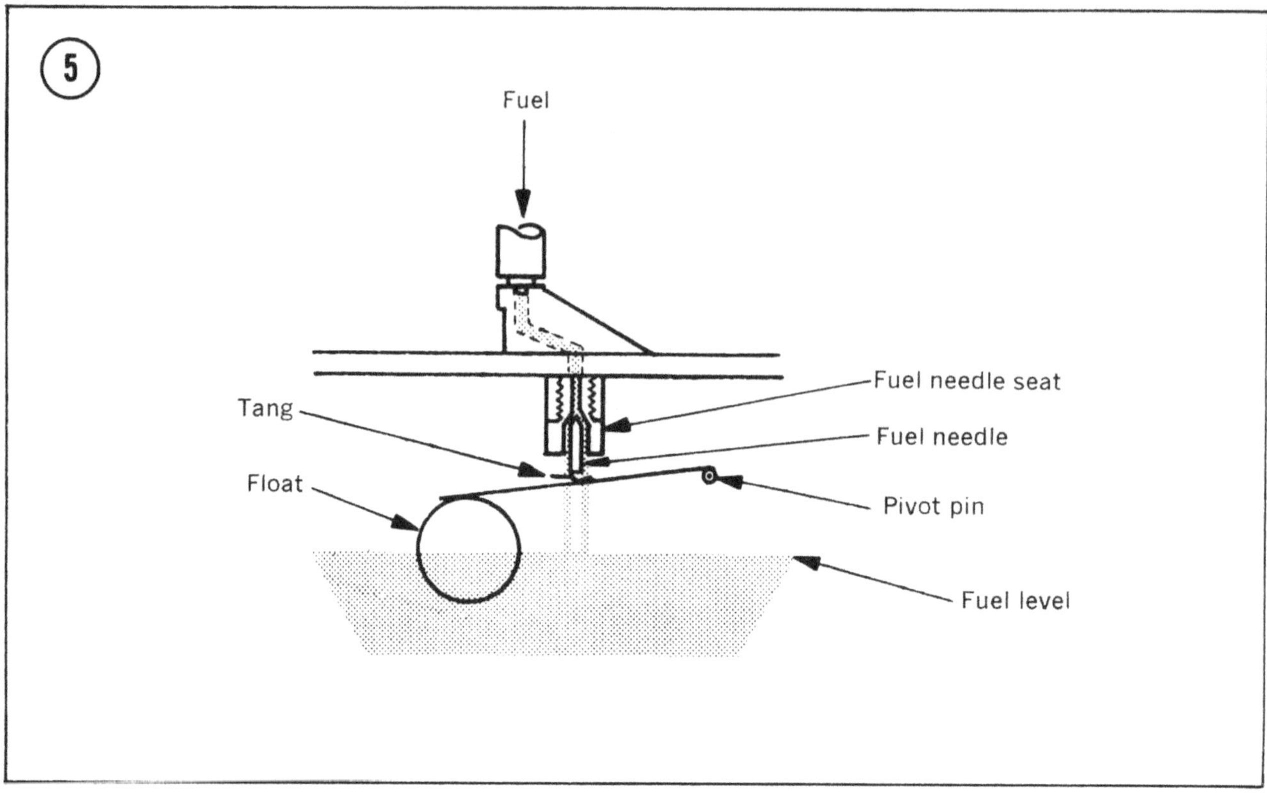

(5)

Fuel

- Fuel needle seat
- Tang
- Fuel needle
- Float
- Pivot pin
- Fuel level

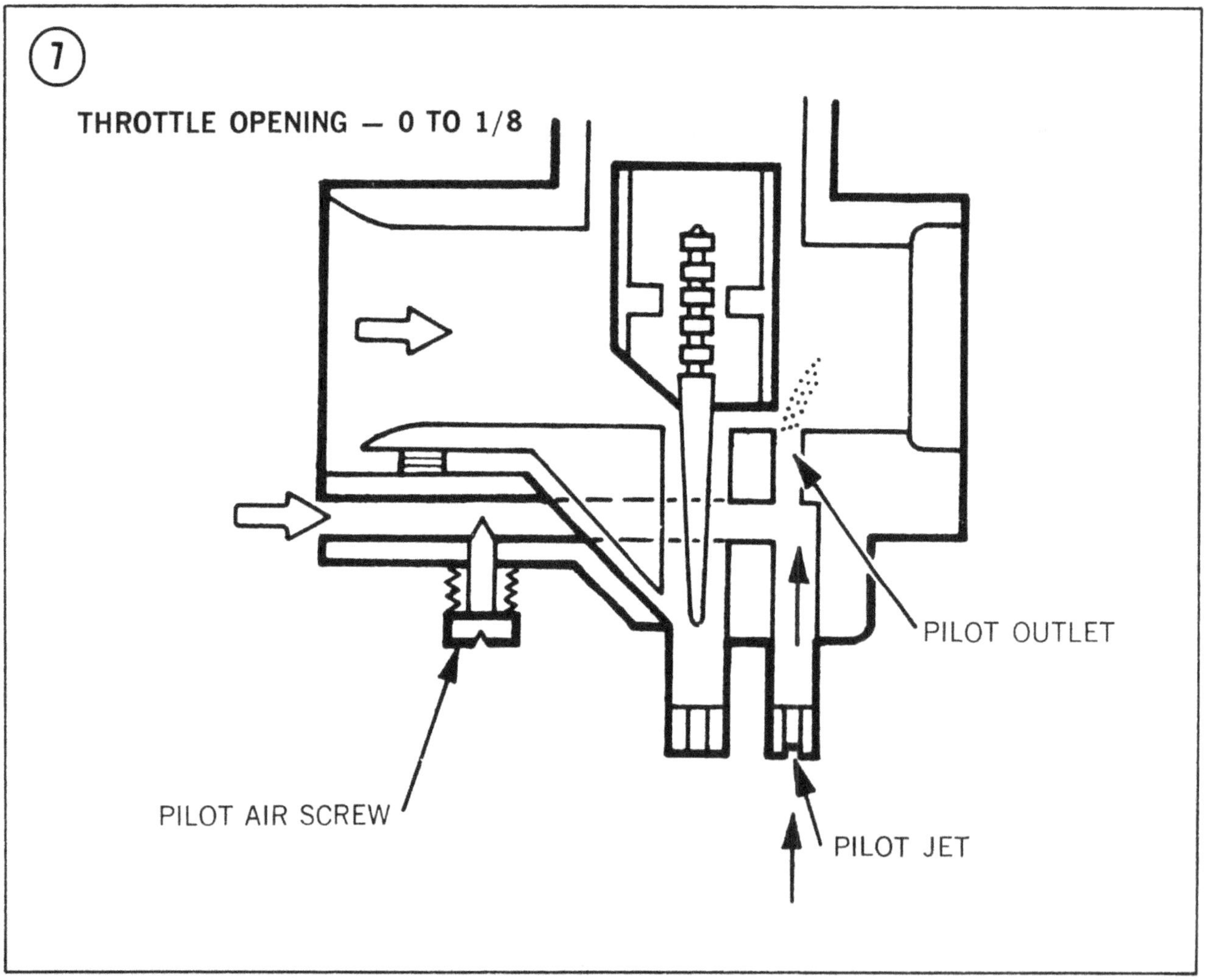

(7)

THROTTLE OPENING – 0 TO 1/8

PILOT OUTLET

PILOT AIR SCREW

PILOT JET

Main Fuel System

As the throttle is opened still more, to about ¼ open, the pilot circuit begins to supply less of the mixture and the main fuel system, illustrated in **Figure 8**, begins to function. The main jet, the needle jet, the jet needle, and the air jet make up the main fuel circuit. As the throttle valve opens more than about ⅛ of its travel, air is drawn through the main port, and passes under the throttle valve in the main bore. The velocity of the air stream reduces pressure around the jet needle. Fuel then passes through the main jet, past the needle jet and jet needle, and into the air stream where it is atomized and sent to the cylinder. As the throttle valve opens, more air flows through the carburetor, and the jet needle, which is attached to the throttle slide, rises to permit more fuel to flow.

A portion of the air bled past the air jet passes through the needle jet bleed air inlet into the needle jet, where it is mixed with the main air stream and atomized.

Airflow at small throttle openings is controlled primairy by the cutaway on the throttle slide.

As the throttle is opened wider, to about ¾, the circuit draws air from 2 sources, as shown in **Figure 9**. The first is air passing through the venturi; the second is through the air jet. Air passing through the venturi draws fuel through the needle jet. The jet needle is tapered, and therefore allows more fuel to pass. Air passing through the air jet passes to the needle jet to aid atomization of the fuel there.

Figure 10 illustrates the circuit at high speeds. The jet needle is withdrawn almost completely from the needle jet. Fuel flow is then controlled by the main jet. Air passing through the air jet continues to aid atomization of the fuel as described in the foregoing paragraphs.

Any dirt which collects in the main jet or in the needle jet obstructs fuel flow and causes a lean mixture. Any clogged air passage, such as the air bleed opening or air jet, may result in an overrich mixture. Other causes of a rich mixture

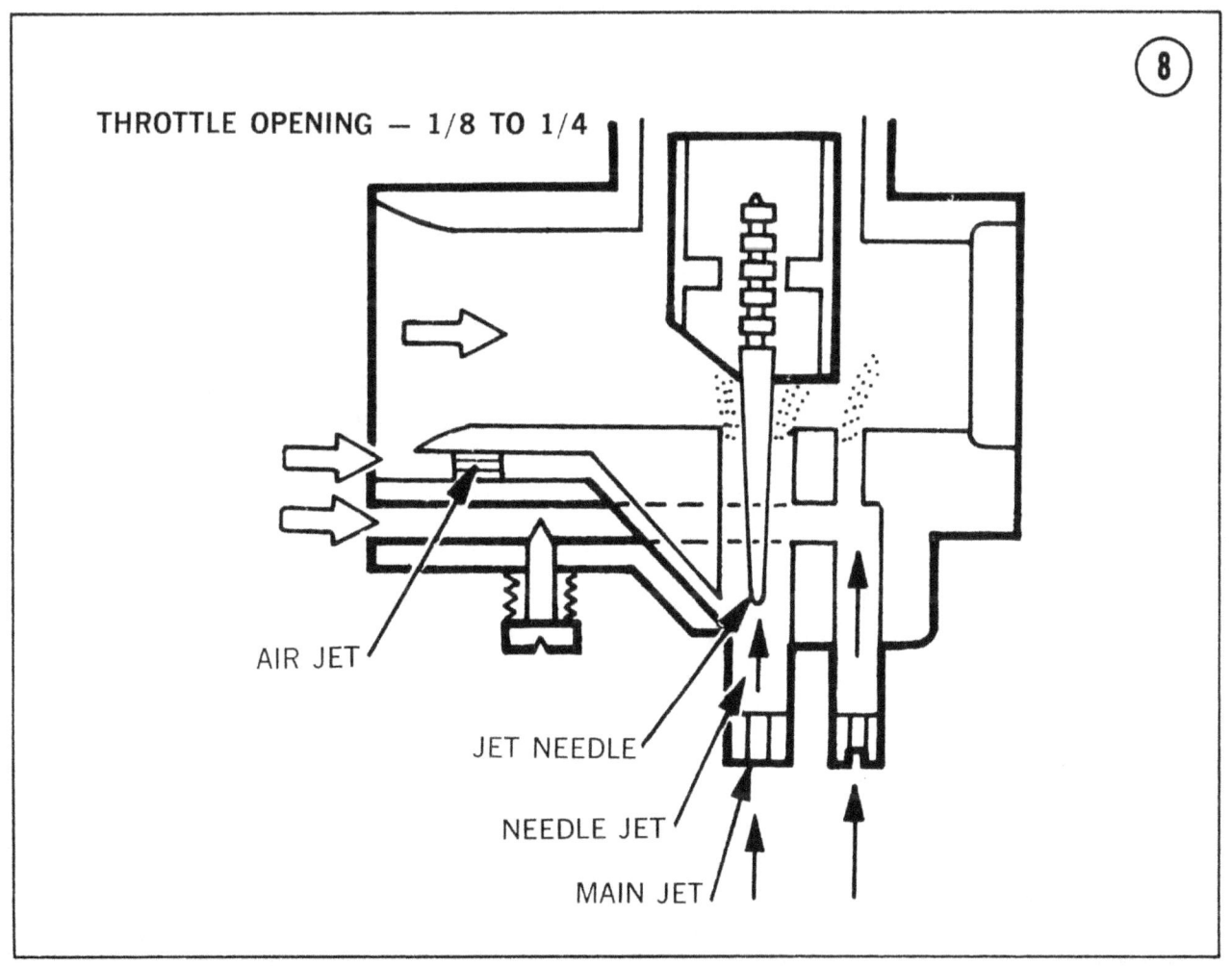

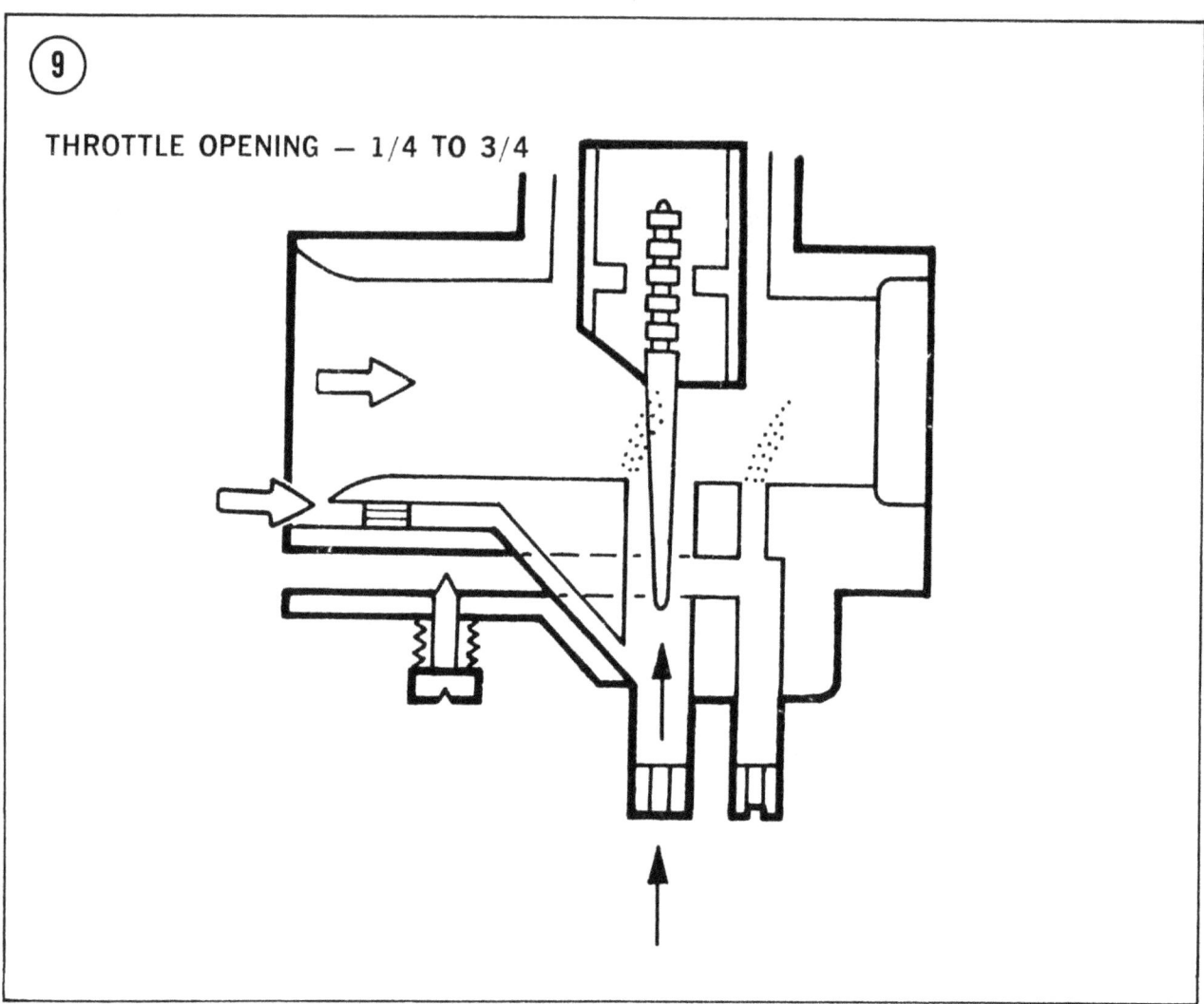

are a worn jet needle, a worn needle jet, loose needle jet, or loose main jet. If the jet needle is worn, it should be replaced; however, it may be possible to effect a temporary repair by placing the jet needle clip in a higher groove.

Tickler System

A cold engine requires a far richer mixture than normal. The tickler system provides this. When the rider presses the tickler button, the float is forced downward, causing the float needle valve to open, and allowing extra fuel to flow into the float chamber.

CARBURETOR OVERHAUL FREQUENCY

There is no set rule regarding frequency of carburetor overhaul. A carburetor used primarily for street riding may go 5,000 miles without attention. If the bike is used in dirt, the carburetor may need an overhaul in less than 1,000 miles. Poor engine performance, hesitation, and little or no response to idle mixture adjustment are all symptoms of possible carburetor malfunction. As a general rule, overhaul the carburetor each time you perform a routine decarbonization of the engine.

AMAL MONOBLOC CARBURETOR

Disassembly

1. Remove the mixing chamber top (**Figure 11**), if the top was not removed previously.
2. Withdraw the throttle valve (**Figure 12**).
3. Remove the float chamber cover (**Figure 13**).
4. Remove the spacer from the float pivot shaft (**Figure 14**), then the float (**Figure 15**).
5. Remove the float needle (**Figure 16**).

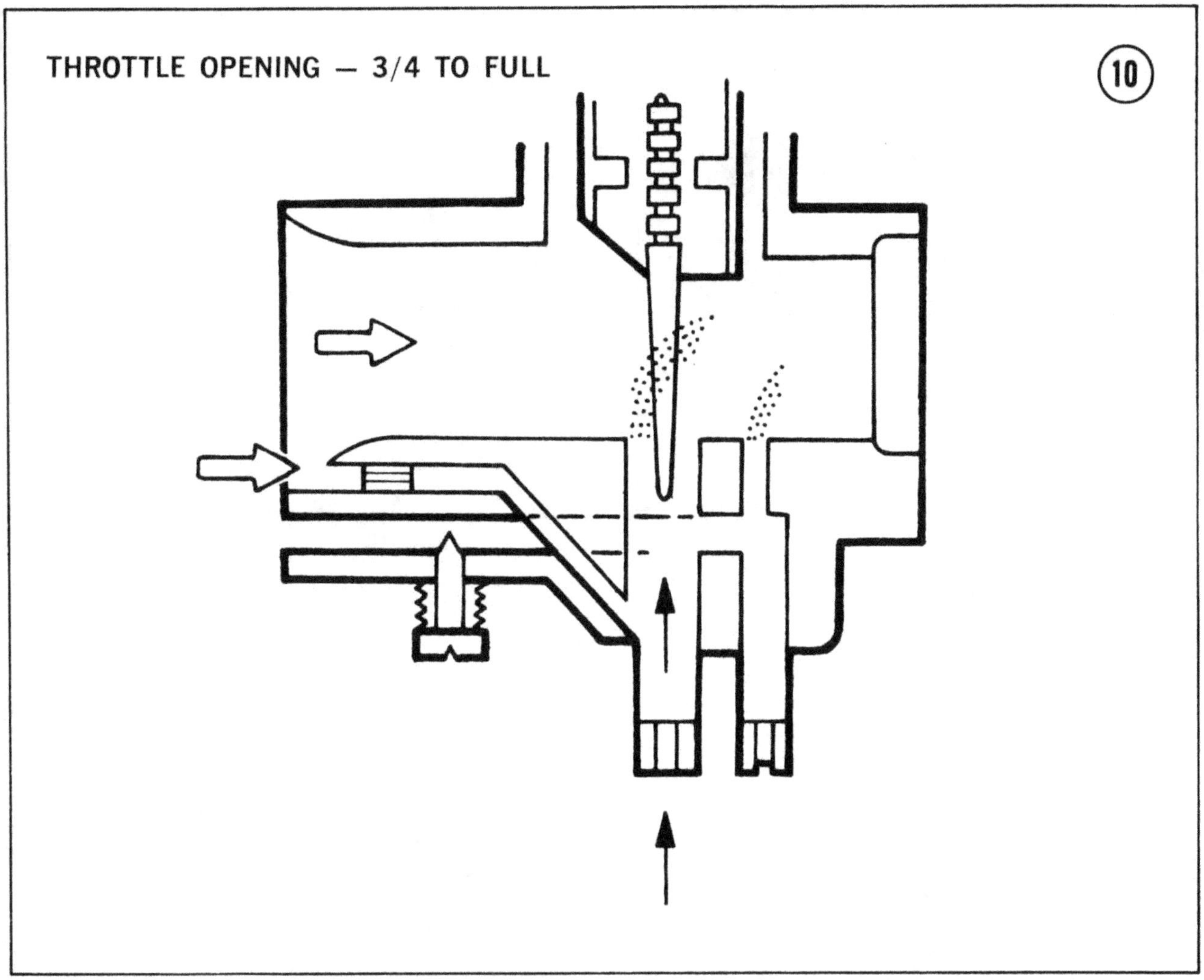

THROTTLE OPENING — 3/4 TO FULL

⑩

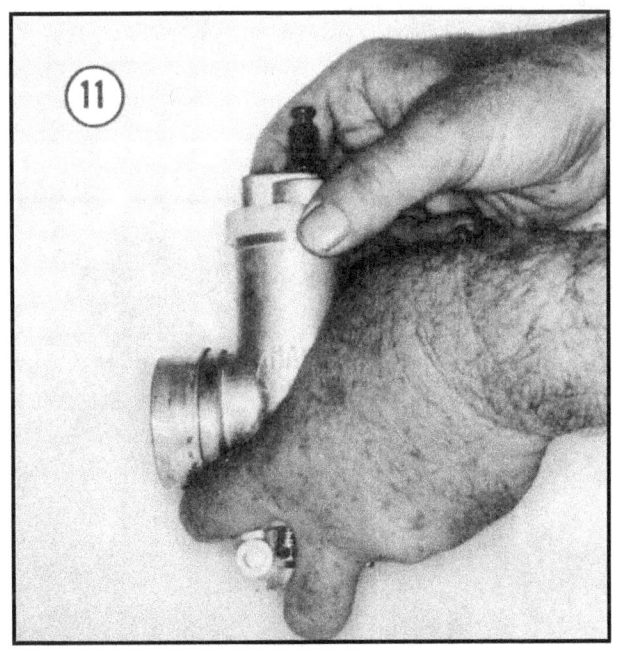

⑪

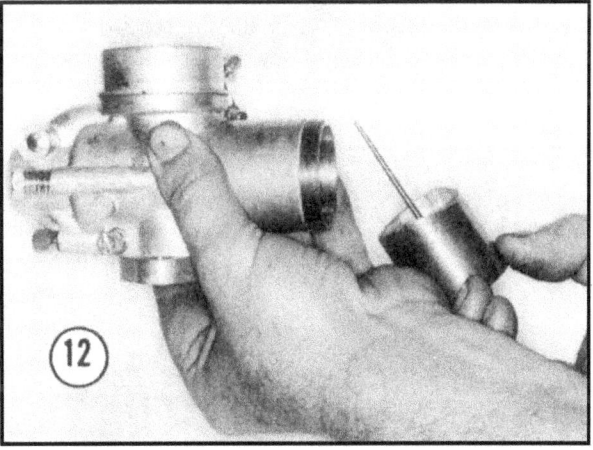

⑫

6. Remove the main jet cover (**Figure 17**), then the main jet (**Figure 18**).

7. Remove the jet holder (**Figure 19**), then unscrew needle jet from jet holder (**Figure 20**).

8. Remove the pilot jet cover (**Figure 21**), then the pilot jet (**Figure 22**).

9. Remove the banjo bolt, then the fuel inlet banjo fitting (**Figure 23**).

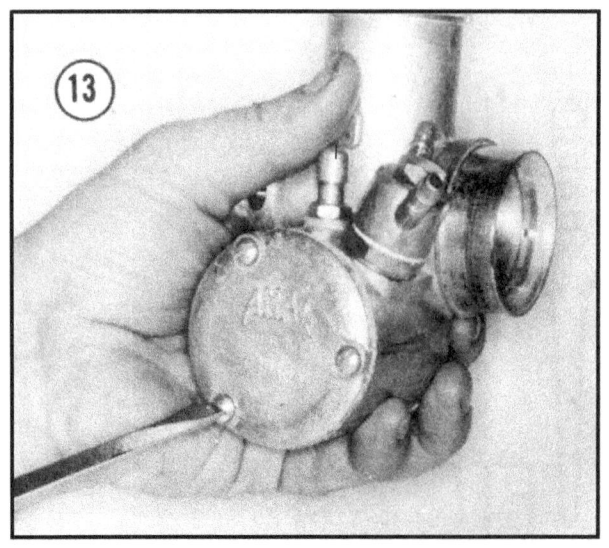
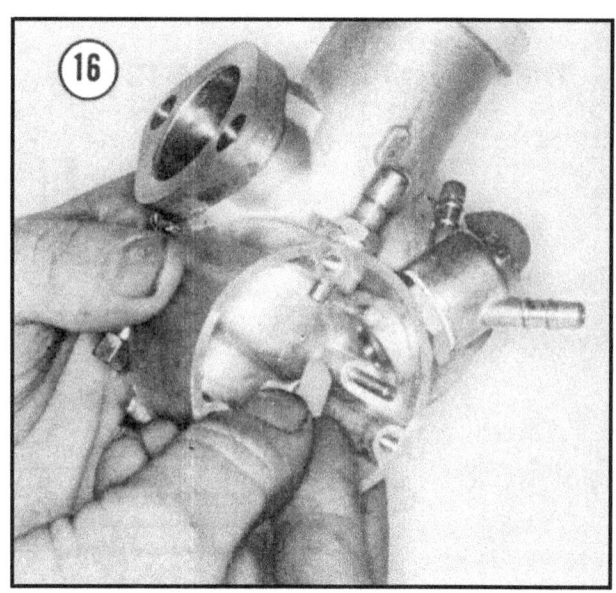
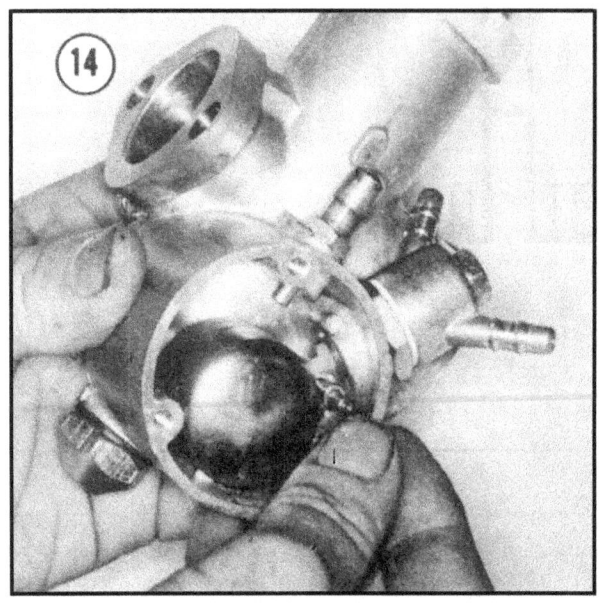
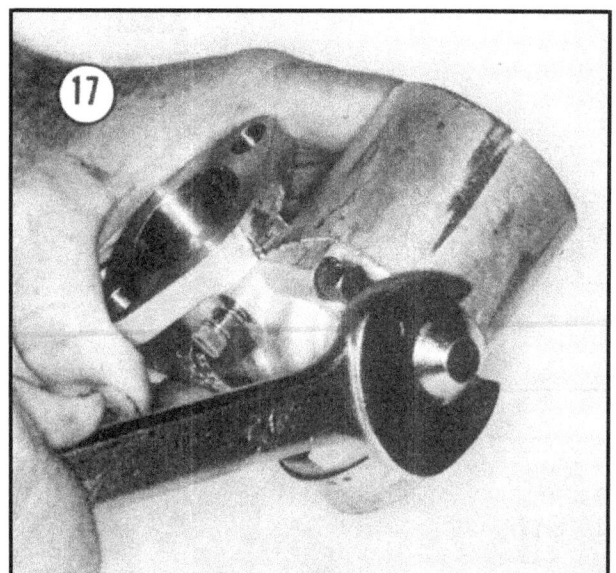
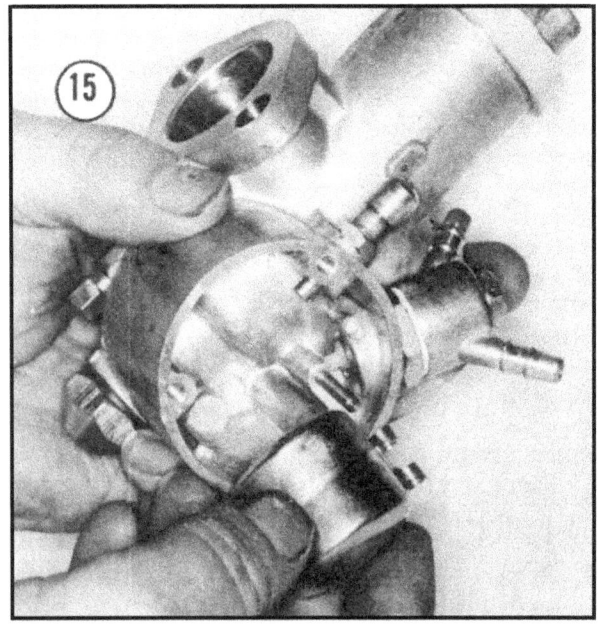
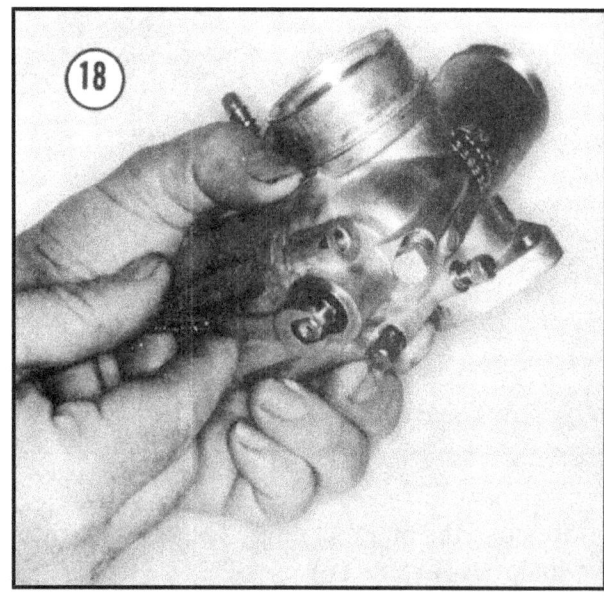

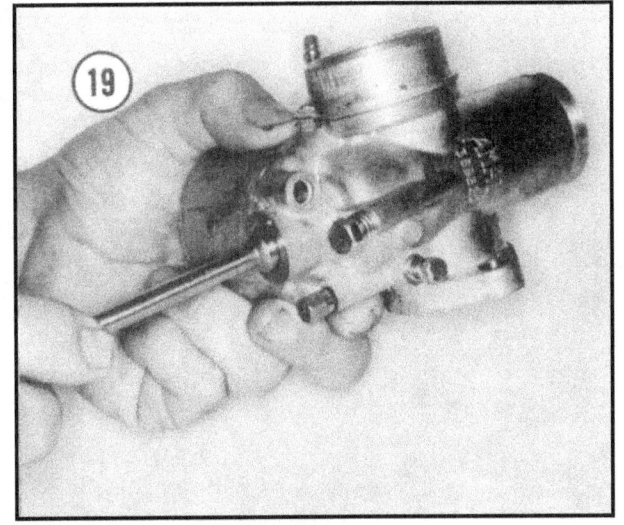

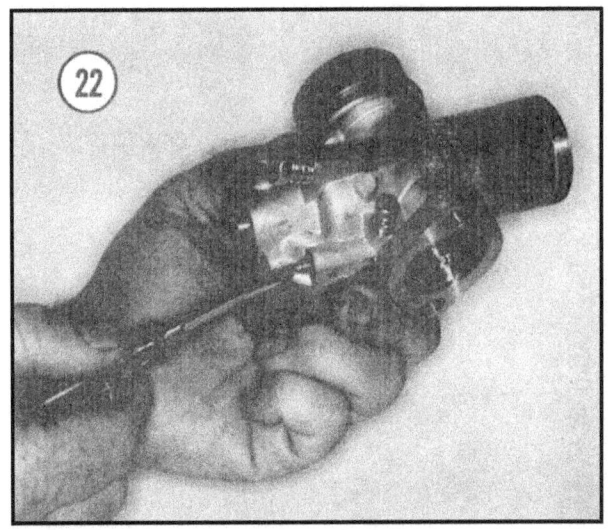

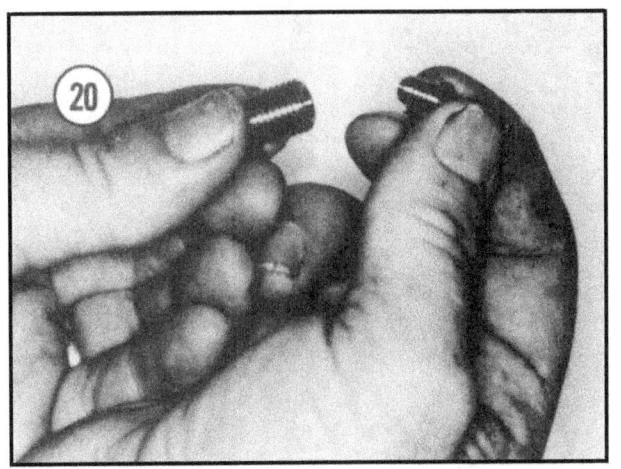

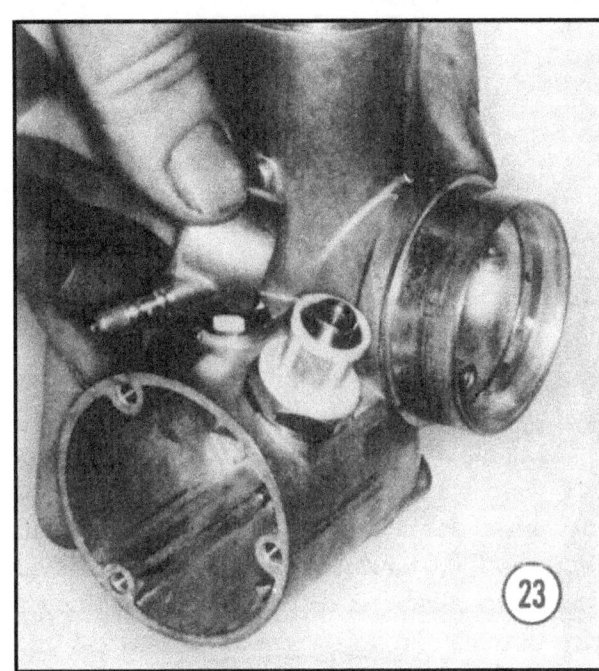

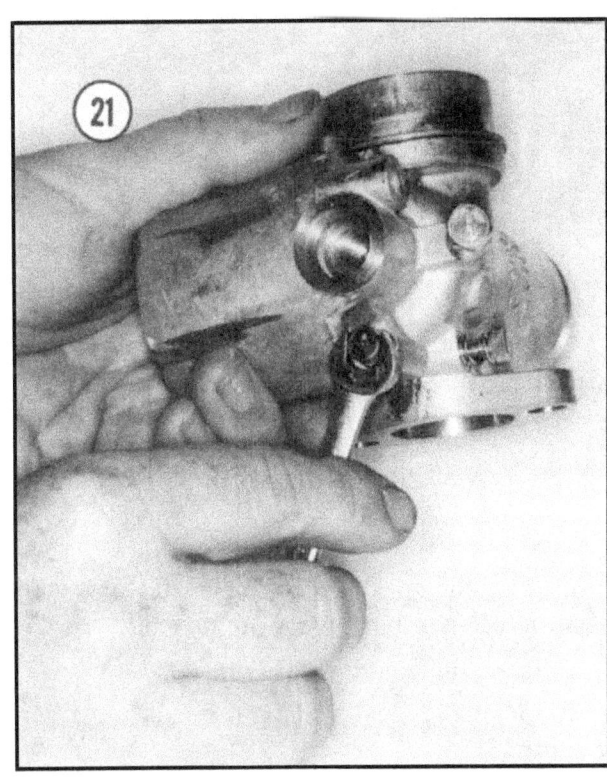

10. Remove the fuel strainer (**Figure 24**), then the float needle seat.

11. Remove the pilot air screw, tickler button, and throttle stop screw.

Inspection

Shake the float to check for gasoline inside. If fuel leaks into the float, the float chamber fuel level will rise, resulting in an overrich mixture. Replace the float if it is deformed or leaking.

Replace the float valve if its seating end is scratched or worn. Press the float valve gently with your finger and make sure it seats properly. If it doesn't seat properly, fuel will overflow, causing an overrich mixture and flooding the float chamber whenever the fuel petcock is open.

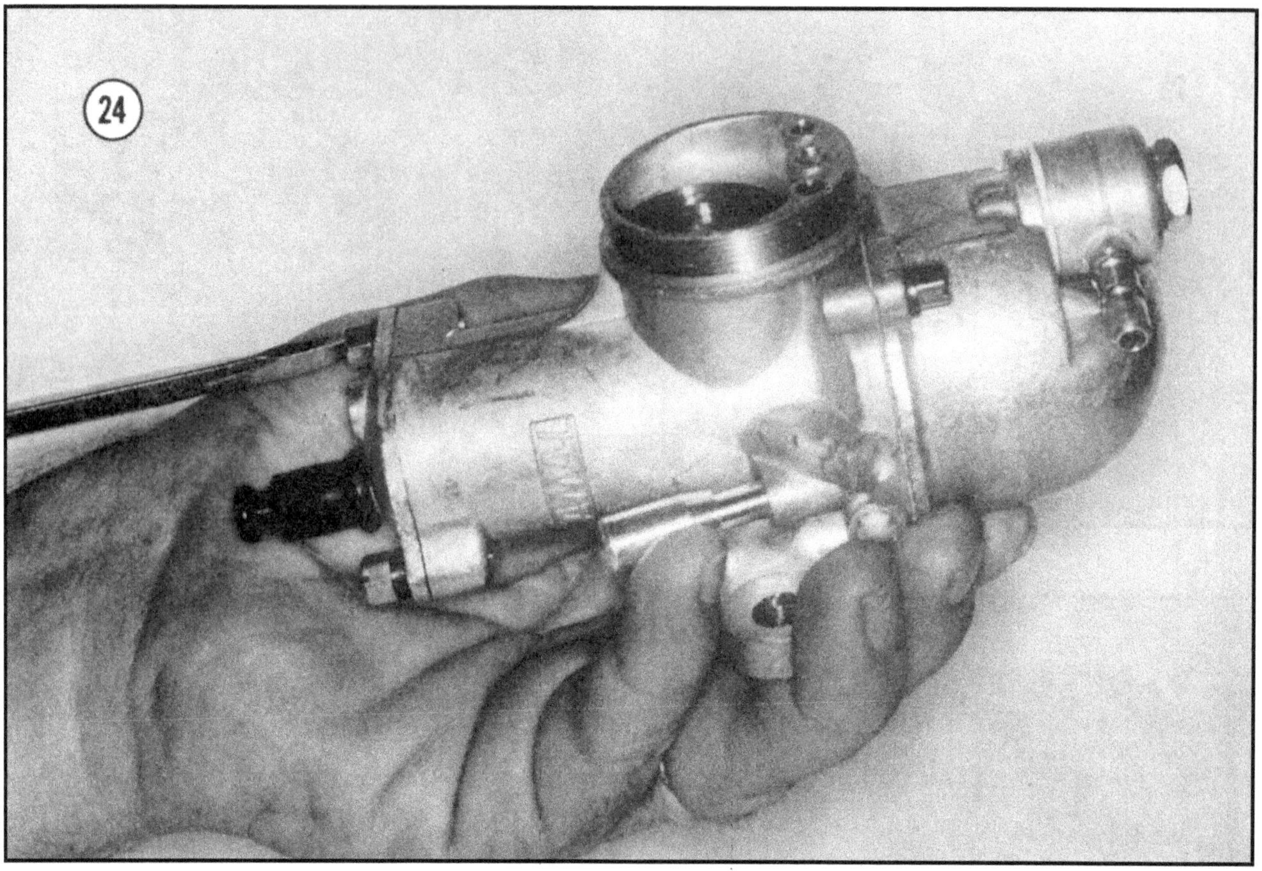

Clean all parts in carburetor cleaning solvent. Dry them with compressed air. Clean the jets and other delicate parts with compressed air after the float bowl has been removed. Never attempt to clean jets or passages by running a wire through. To do so will cause damage and destroy their calibration. Do not use compressed air to clean an assembled carburetor, since the float and float valve can be damaged.

Reassembly

Reverse the disassembly procedure to reassemble the carburetor. Always use new gaskets upon reassembly.

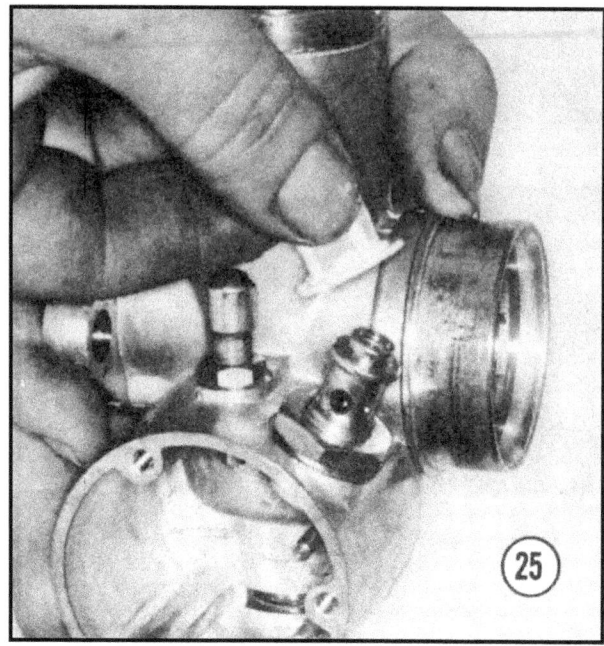

AMAL CONCENTRIC CARBURETOR

Disassembly

1. Remove the mixing chamber cap (**Figure 25**), if this step has not been performed previously.
2. Withdraw the throttle valve (**Figure 26**). Don't lose the spring or spring plate. Note the position of each part as it is removed.
3. Remove the float bowl (**Figure 27**).
4. Remove the float and float needle together (**Figure 28**).

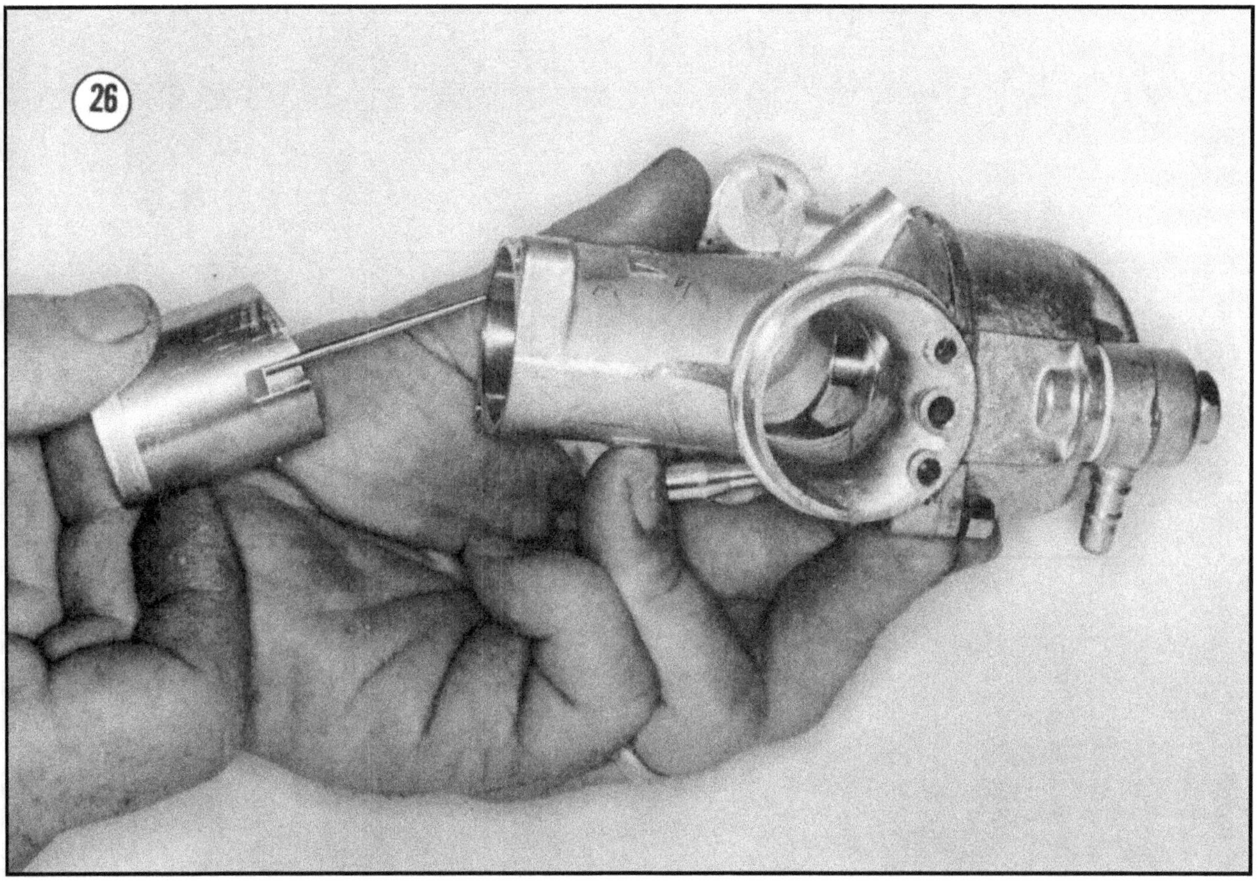

77

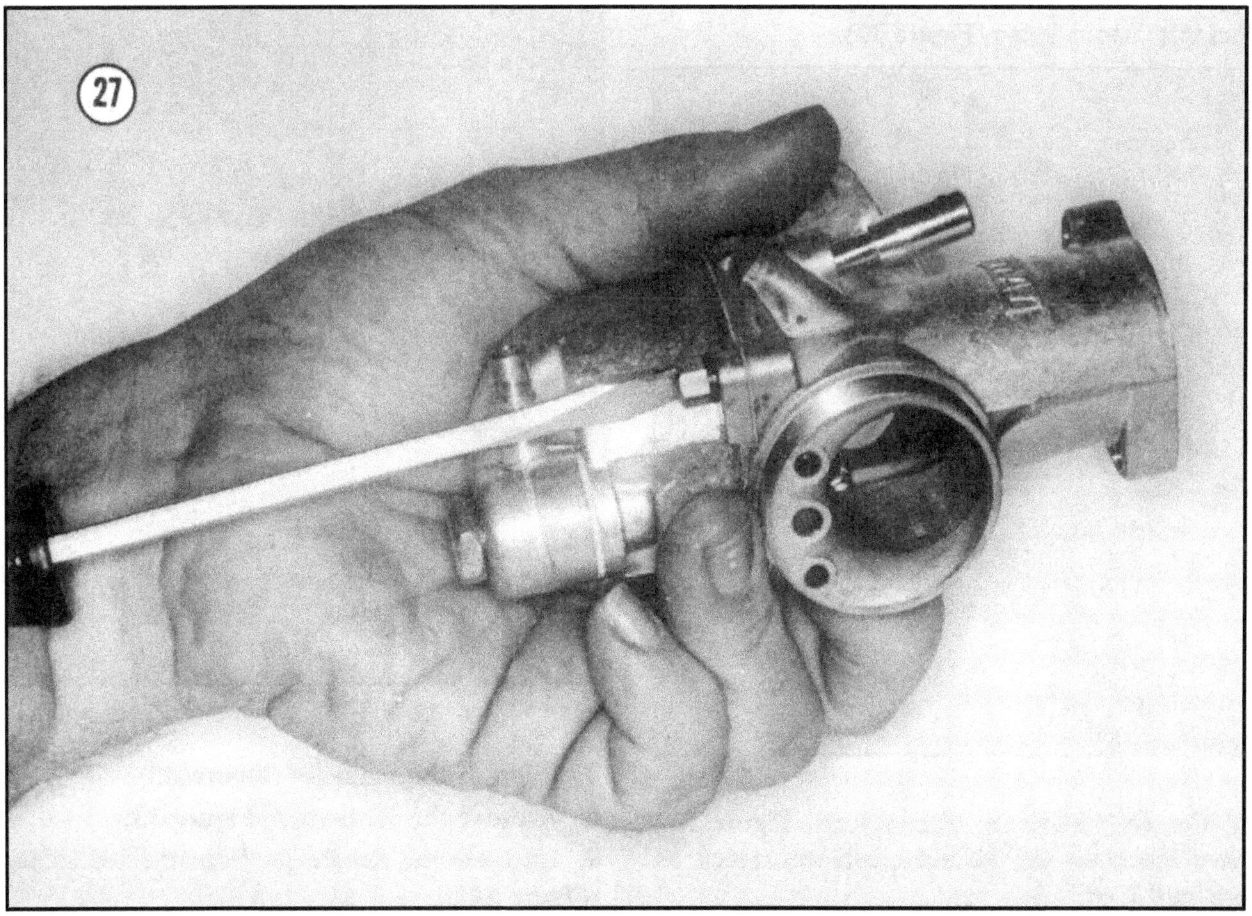

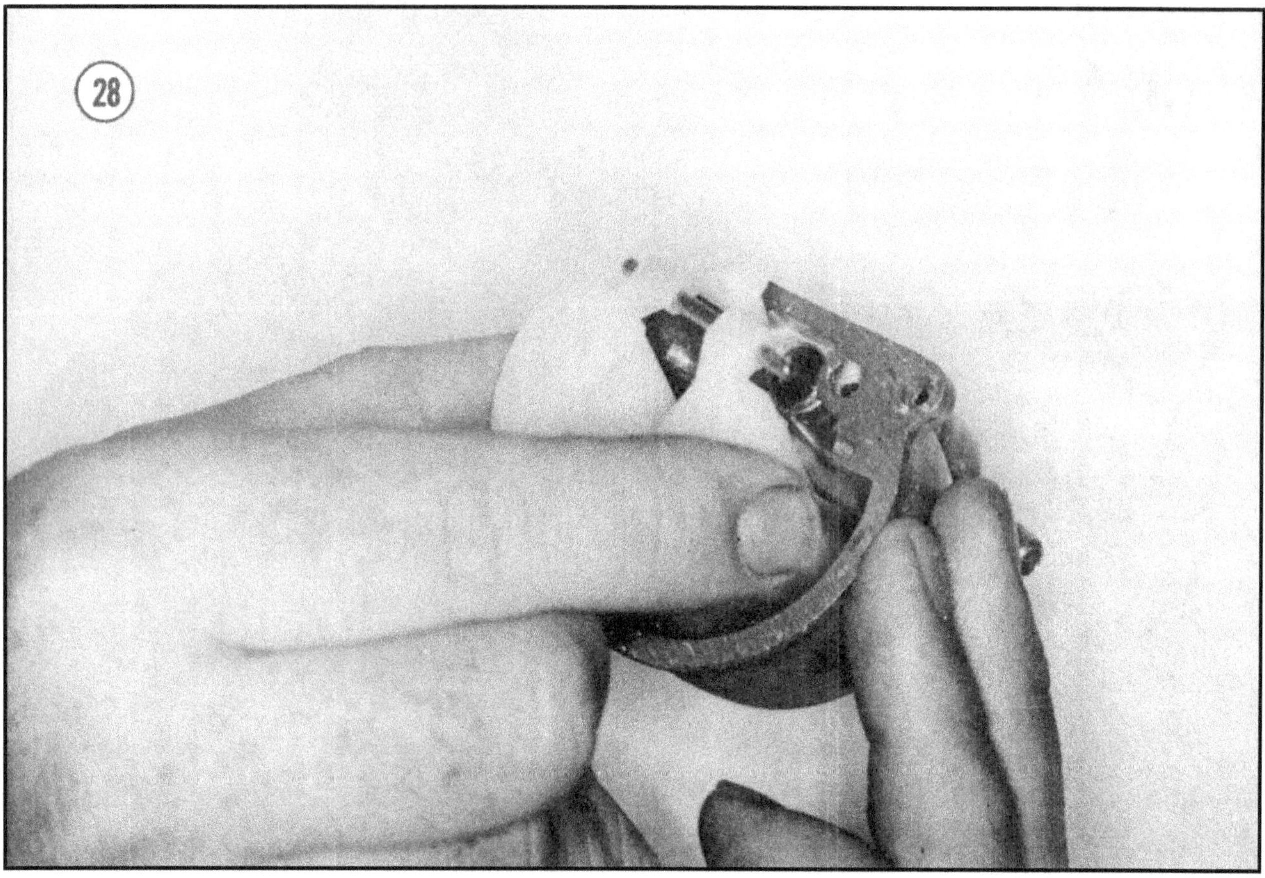

5. Remove the banjo bolt (**Figure 29**), then the fuel inlet banjo fitting (**Figure 30**).

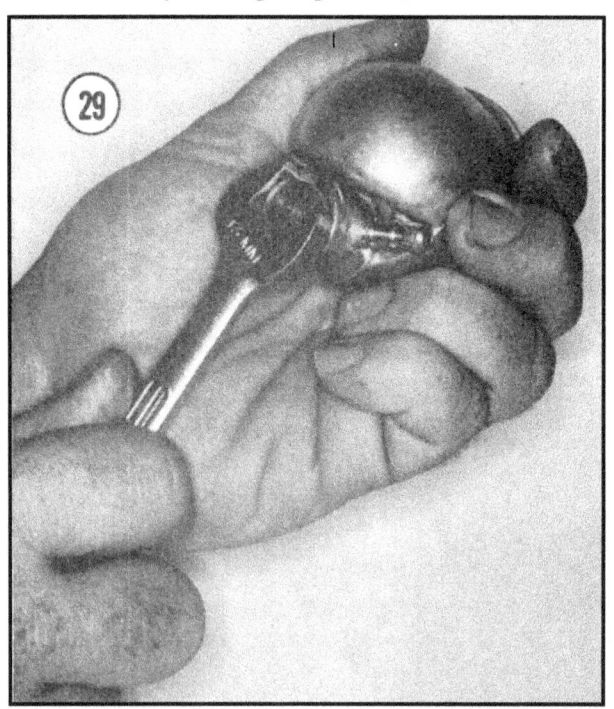

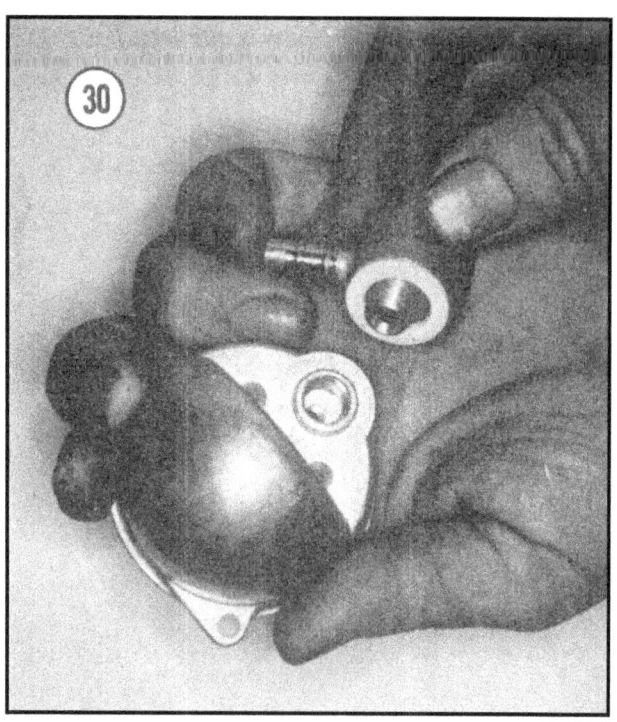

6. Carefully slide the filter screen (**Figure 31**) from the main jet. Do not crush the screen as you pull it off.

7. Remove the main jet (**Figure 32**).
8. Remove the jet holder (**Figure 33**).
9. Unscrew the needle jet from the jet holder (**Figure 34**).

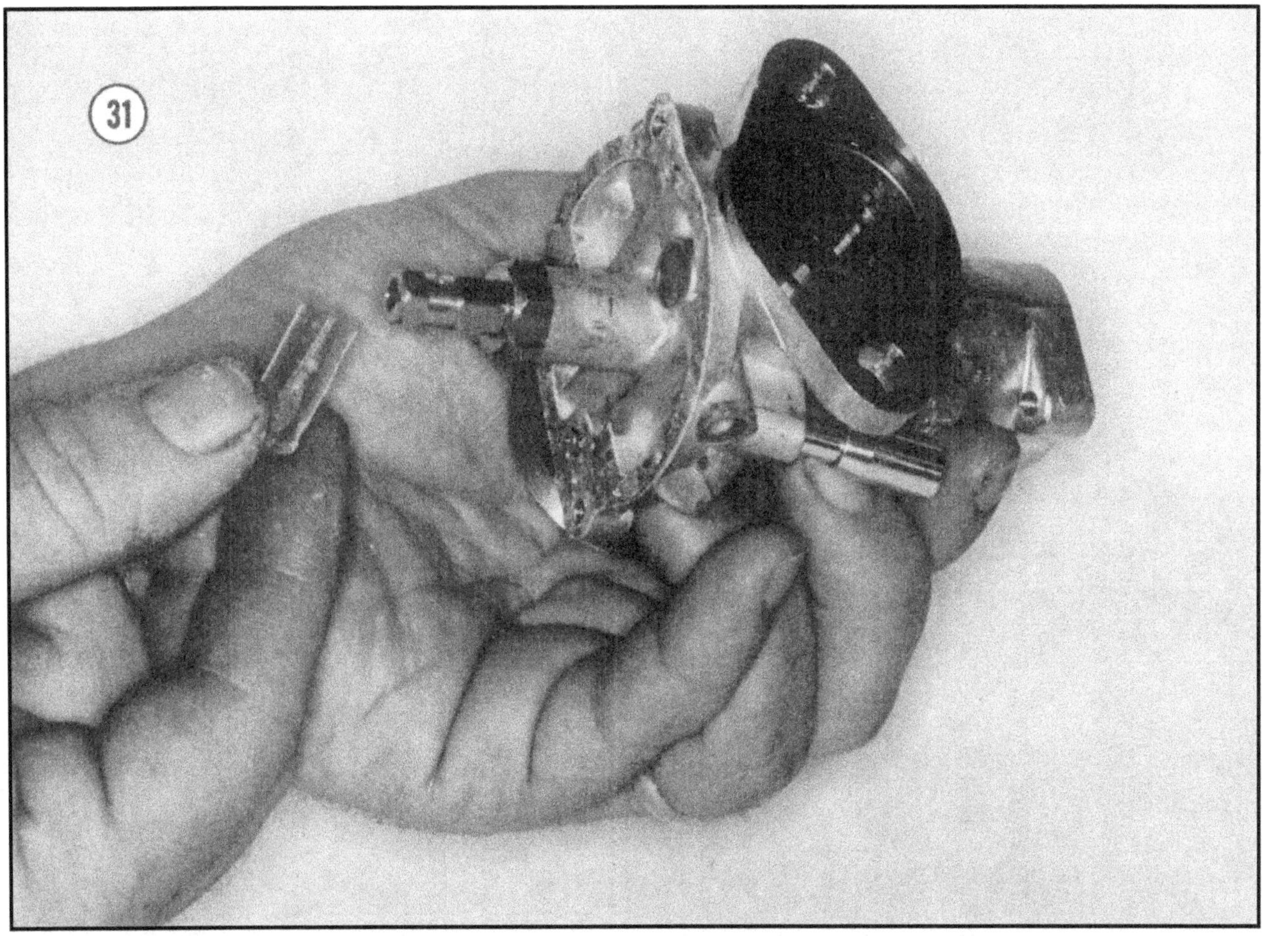

(31)

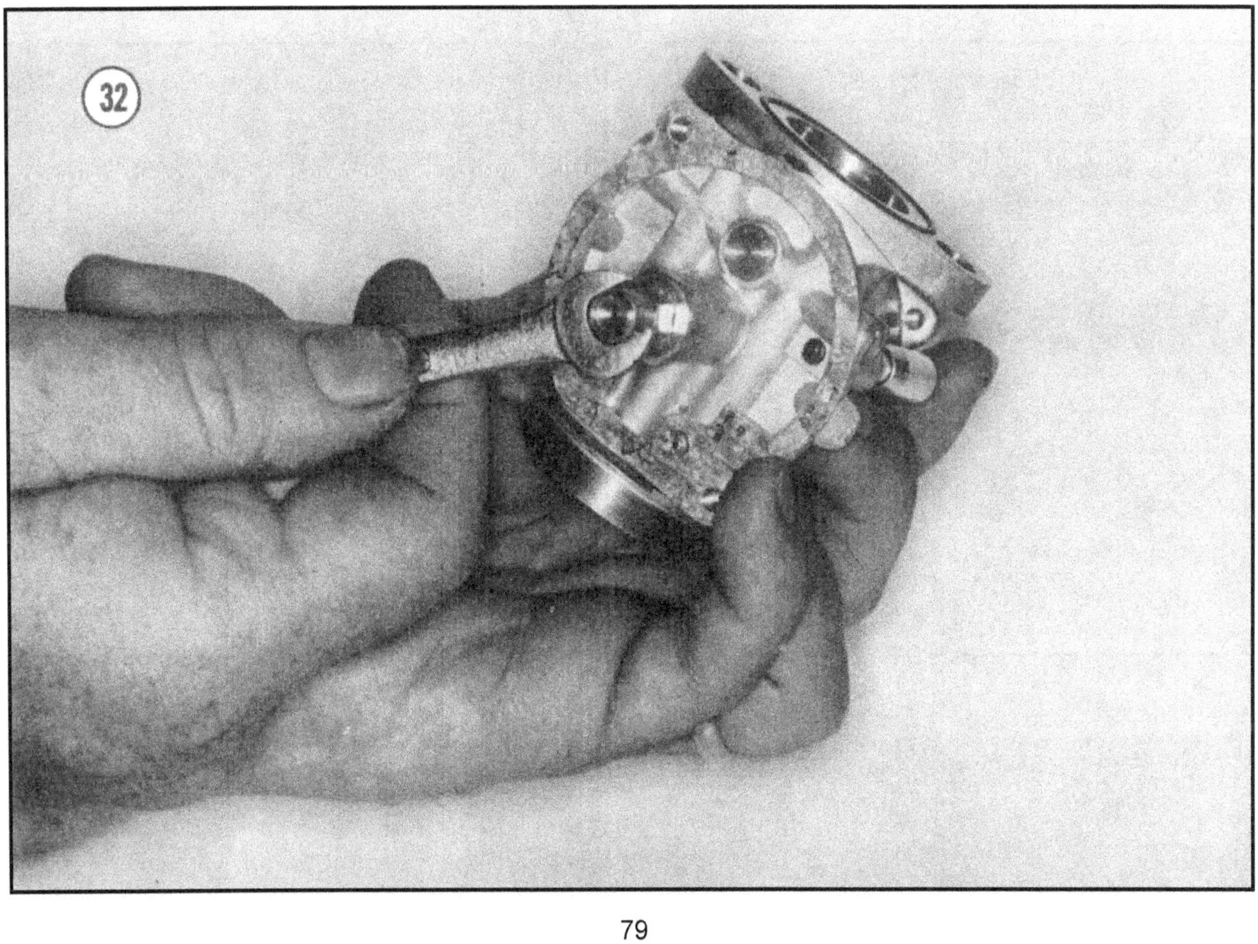

(32)

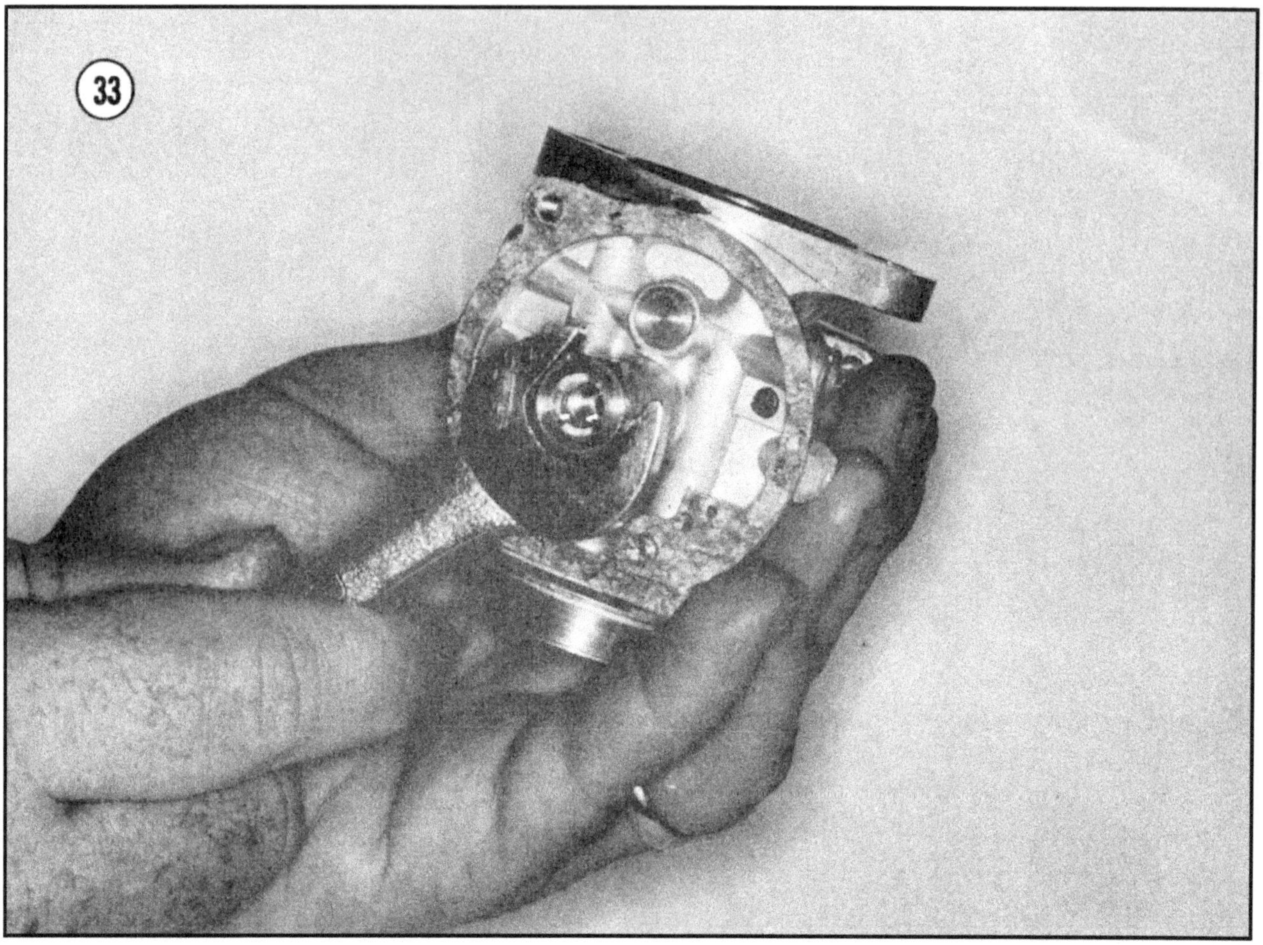

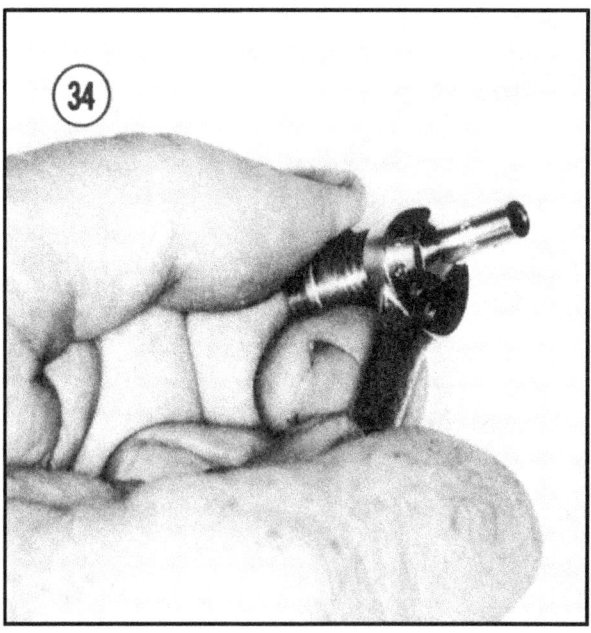
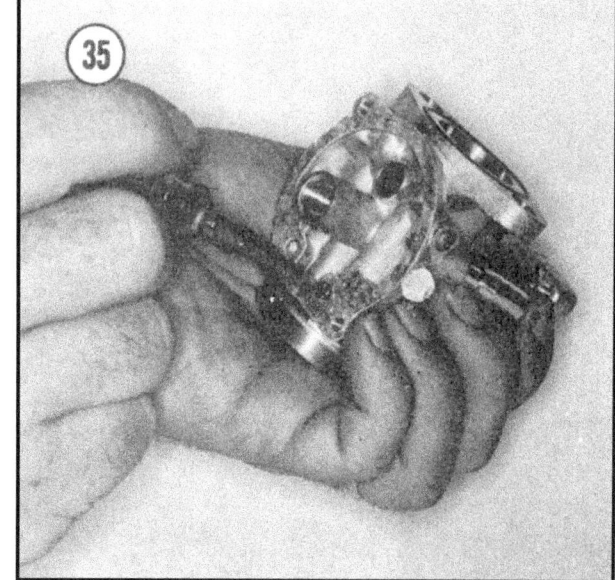

10. Remove the pilot jet (**Figure 35**).
11. Remove the mounting flange O-ring.
12. Remove the pilot air screw and the throttle stop screw.

Inspection

Shake the float to check for gasoline inside. If fuel leaks into the float, the float chamber fuel level will rise, resulting in an overrich mixture.

Replace the float if it is deformed or leaking.

Replace the float valve if its seating end is scratched or worn. Press the float valve gently with your finger and make sure it seats properly. If it doesn't seat properly, fuel will overflow, causing an overrich mixture and flooding the float chamber whenever the fuel petcock is open.

Clean all parts in carburetor cleaning solvent. Dry them with compressed air. Clean the jets and other delicate parts with compressed air after the float bowl has been removed. Never attempt to clean jets or passages by running a wire through. To do so will cause damage and destroy their calibration. Do not use compressed air to clean an assembled carburetor, since the float and float valve can be damaged.

Reassembly

Reverse the disassembly procedure to reassemble the carburetor. Always use new gaskets upon reassembly.

BING CARBURETOR

Disassembly

1. Remove 2 retaining screws, then the mixing chamber top (**Figure 36**). Be careful; the cover is spring loaded.

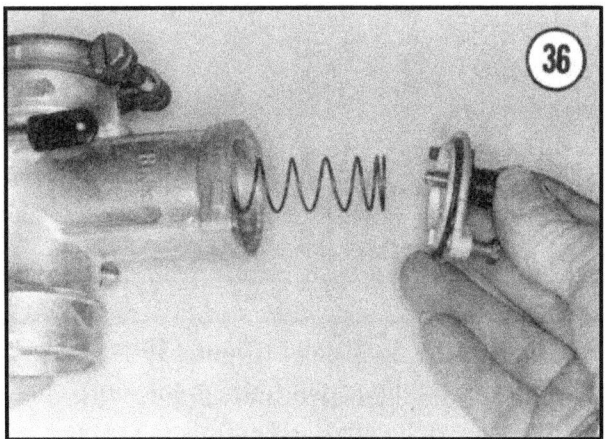

2. Remove the spring, then the throttle slide (**Figure 37**).

3. Push the float bowl retaining bail toward the carburetor inlet (**Figure 38**).

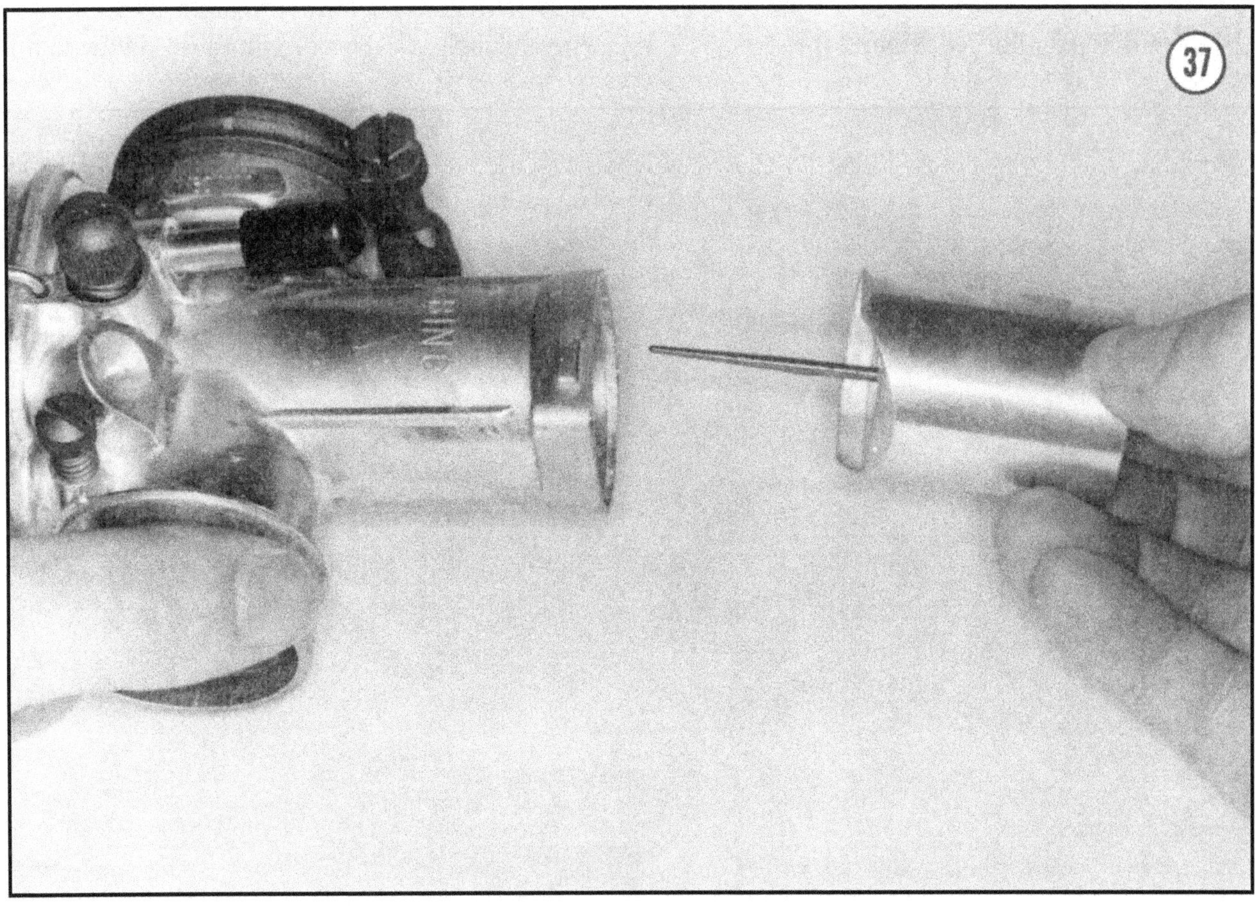

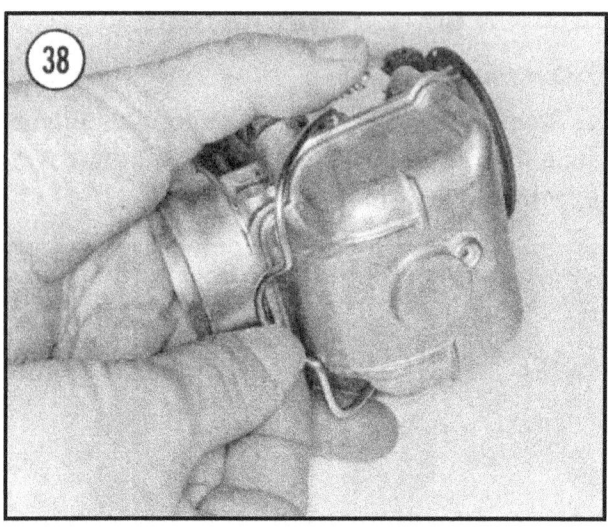

11. Remove the fuel inlet fitting (**Figure 46**).
12. Remove the idle mixture screw (**Figure 47**).
13. Remove the idle speed screw (**Figure 48**).
14. Remove the jet needle from the throttle slide (**Figure 49**).
15. Unscrew the main jet from the jet holder. See **Figure 50**.

Inspection

Shake the float to check for gasoline inside. If fuel leaks into the float, the float chamber fuel level will rise, resulting in an overrich mixture. Replace float if it is deformed or leaking.

Replace the float valve if its seating end is scratched or worn. Press the float valve gently with your finger and make sure it seats properly. If it doesn't seat properly, fuel will overflow, causing an overrich mixture and flooding the float chamber whenever the fuel petcock is open.

Clean all parts in carburetor cleaning solvent. Dry them with compressed air. Clean the jets and other delicate parts with compressed air after the float bowl has been removed. Never attempt to clean jets or passages by running a wire through. To do so will cause damage and

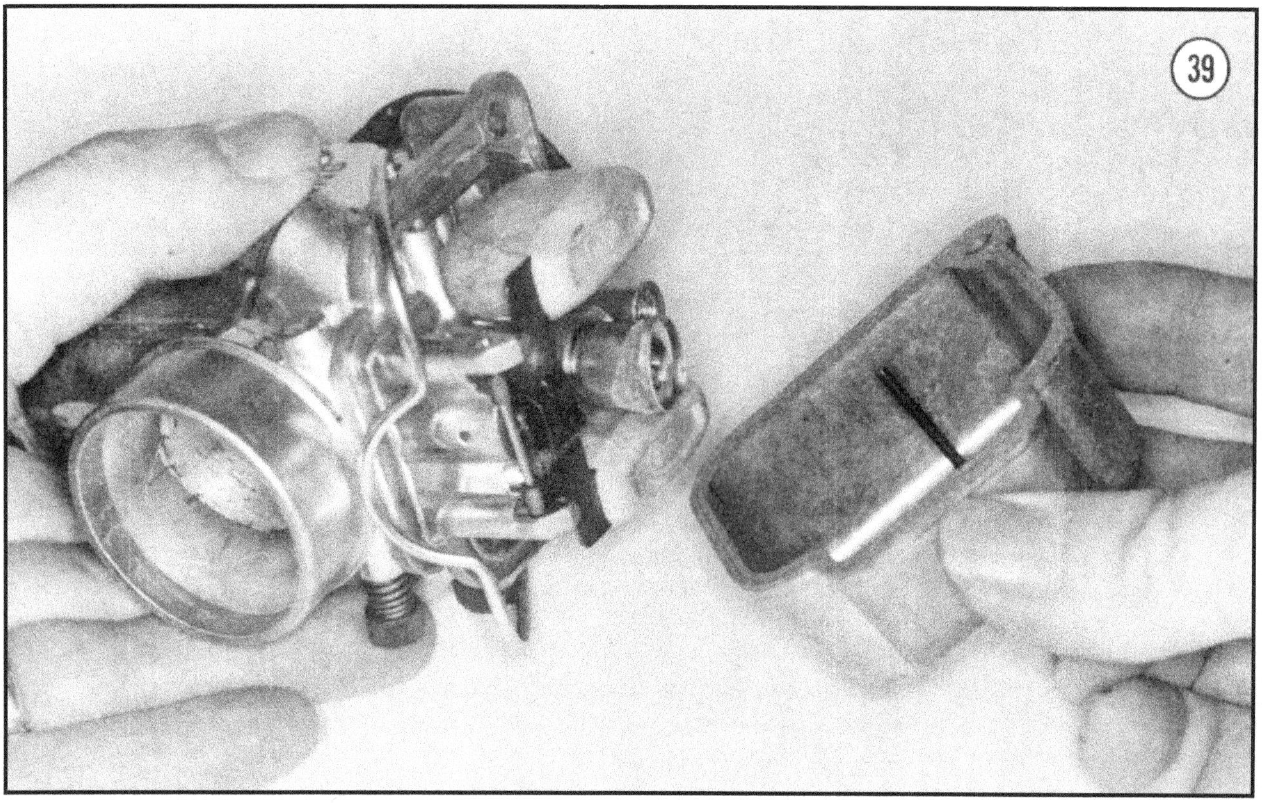

4. Remove the float bowl (**Figure 39**).
5. Pull out the float pivot pin (**Figure 40**), then gently remove the float assembly.
6. Pull out the float needle (**Figure 41**).
7. Carefully remove the strainer from the main jet (**Figure 42**).
8. Remove the jet holder (**Figure 43**).
9. Turn the carburetor upright. The needle jet will drop out (**Figure 44**). Push it out with a plastic rod if necessary.
10. Remove the pilot jet (**Figure 45**).

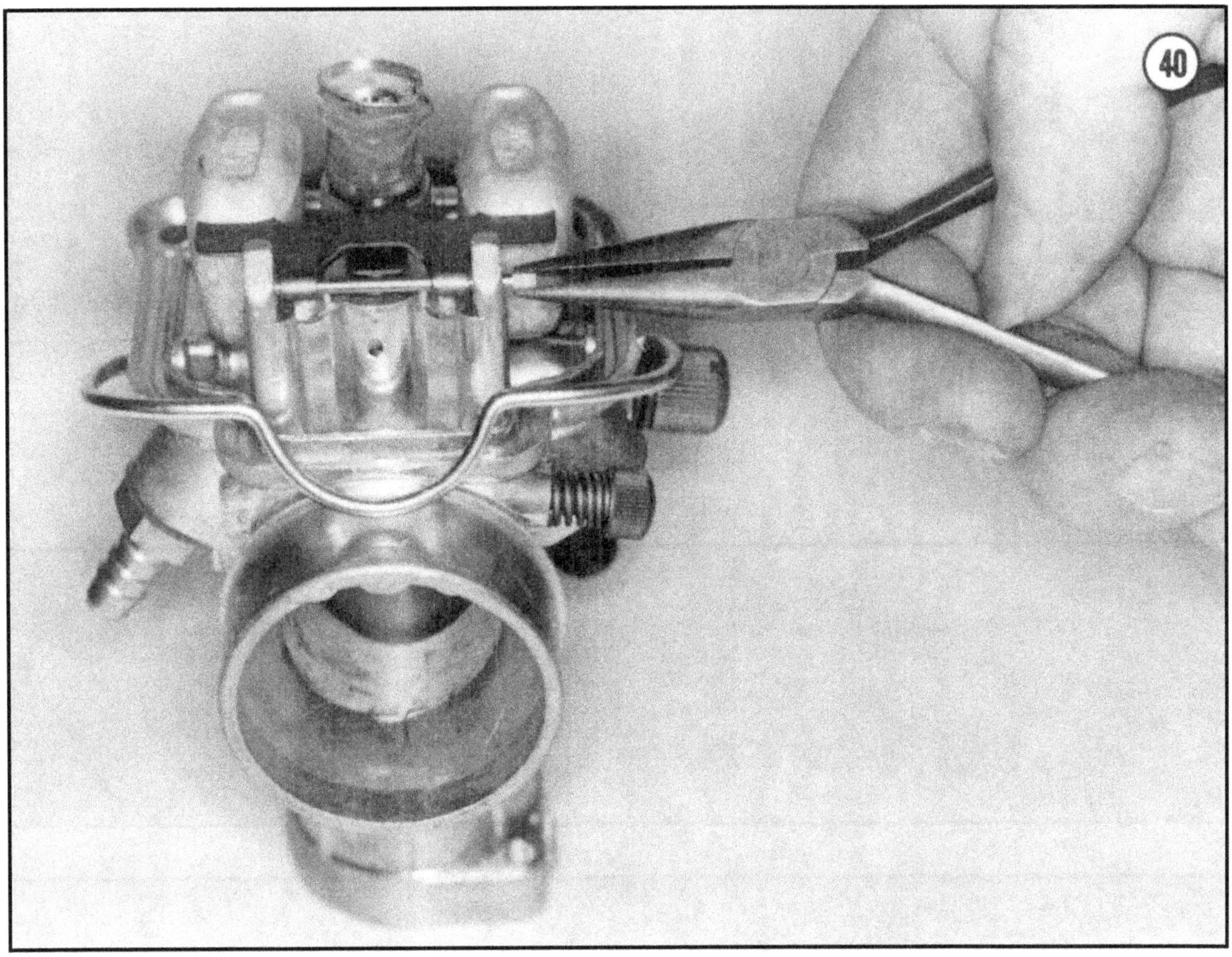

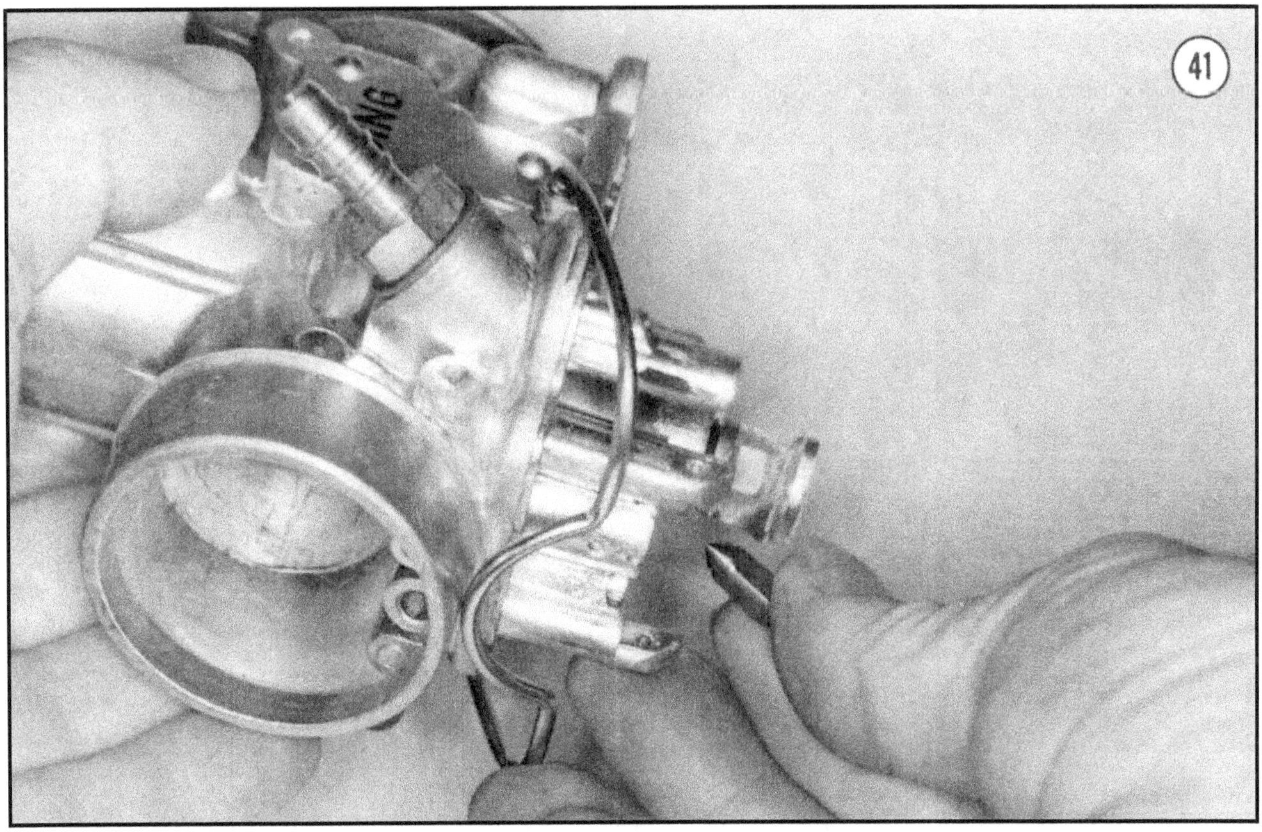

83

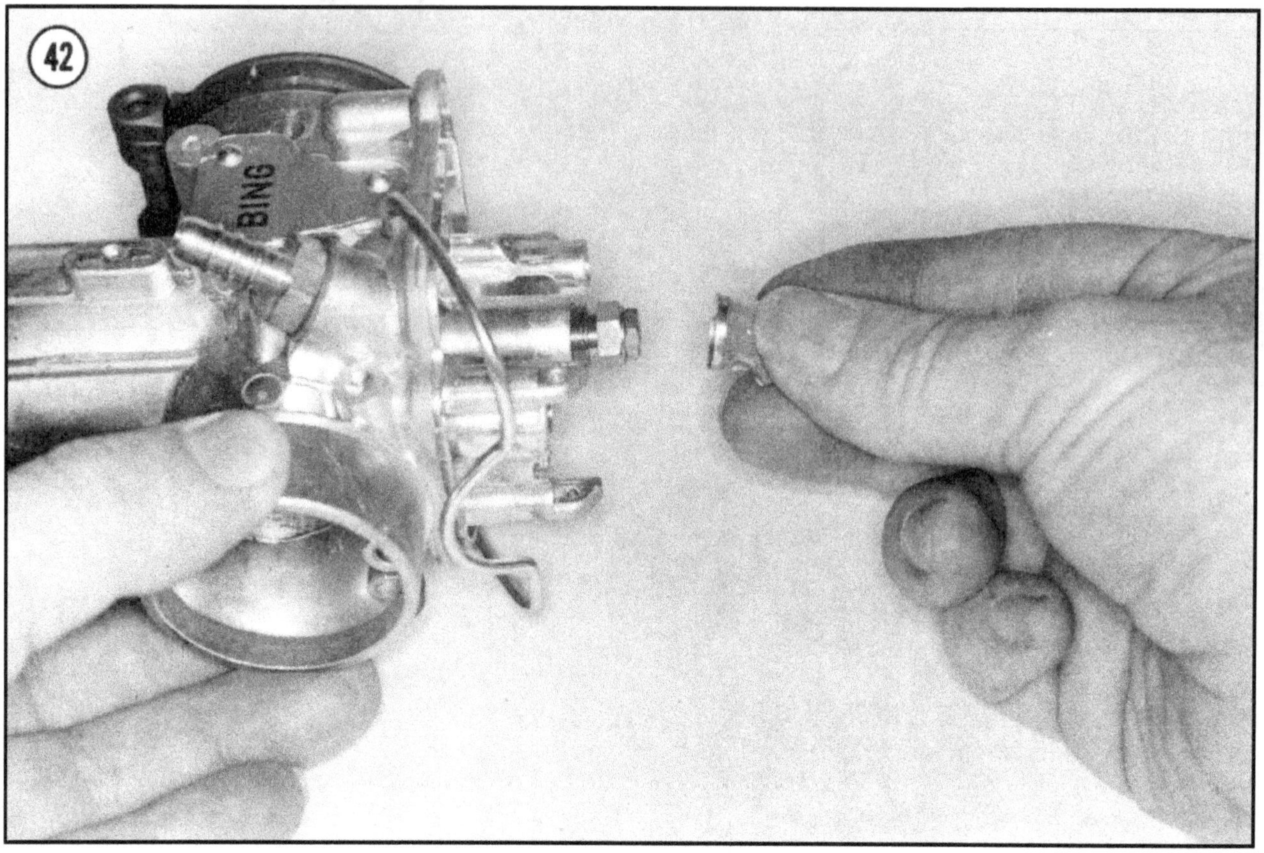

84

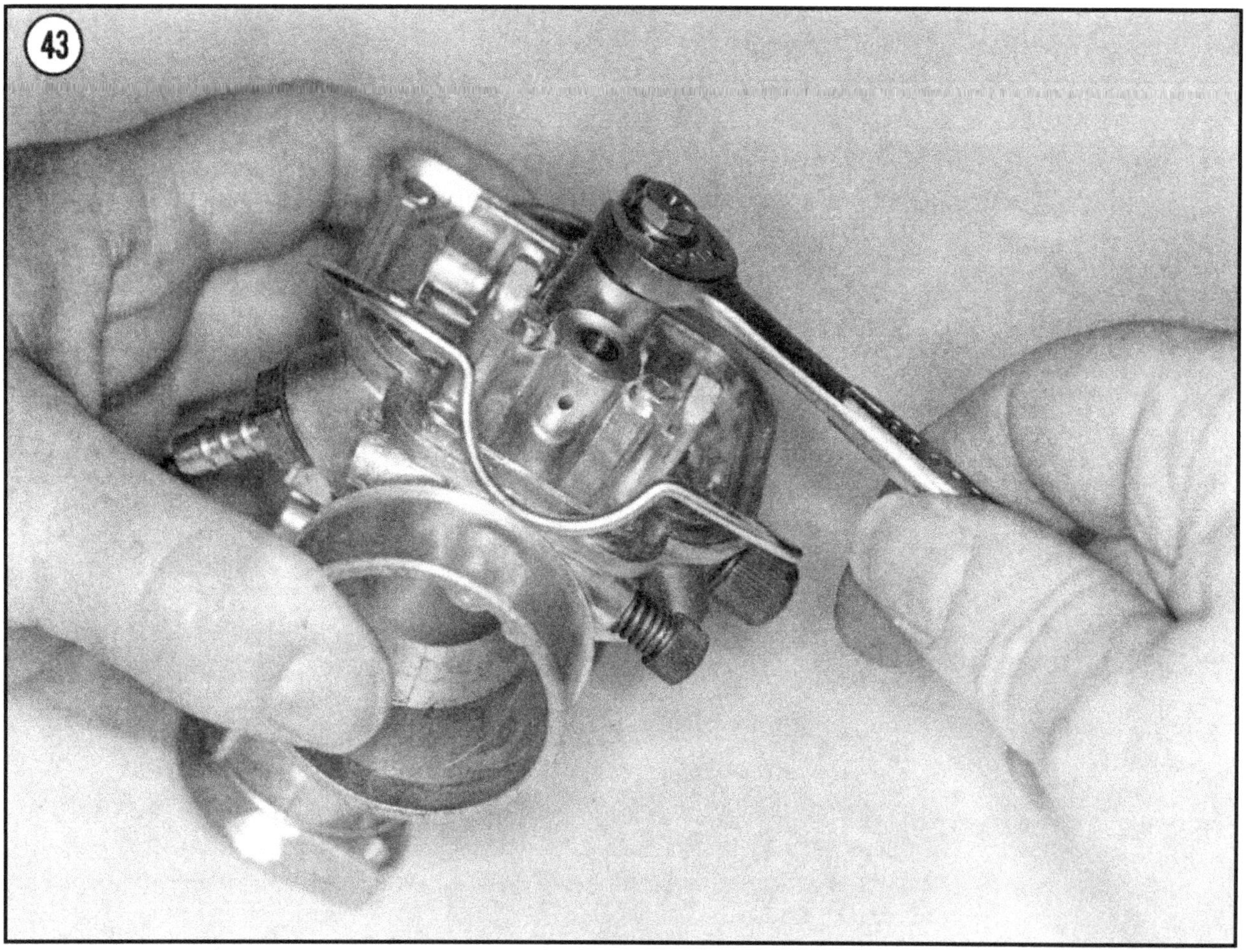

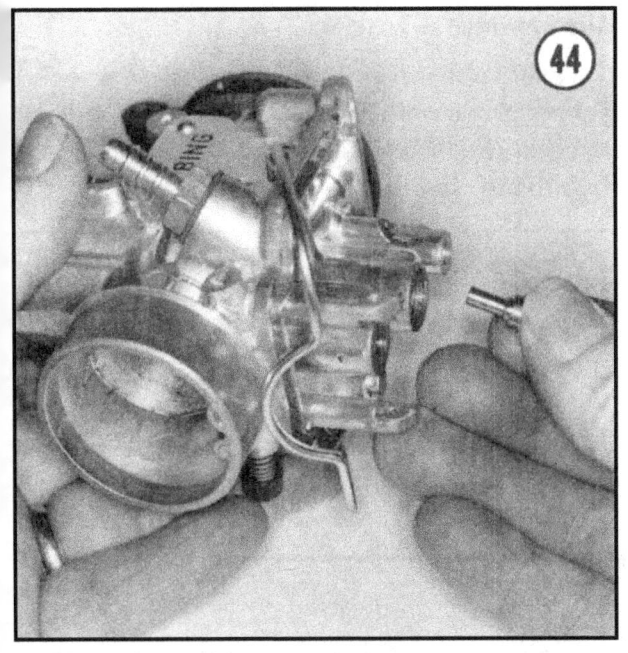

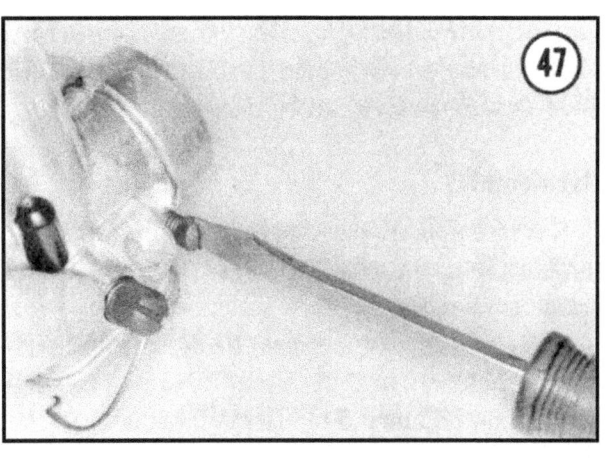

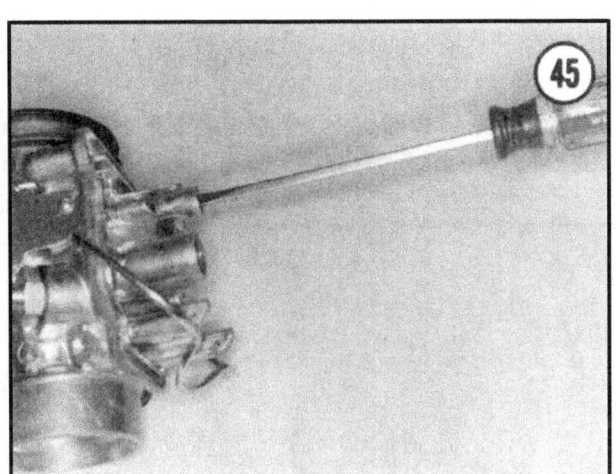

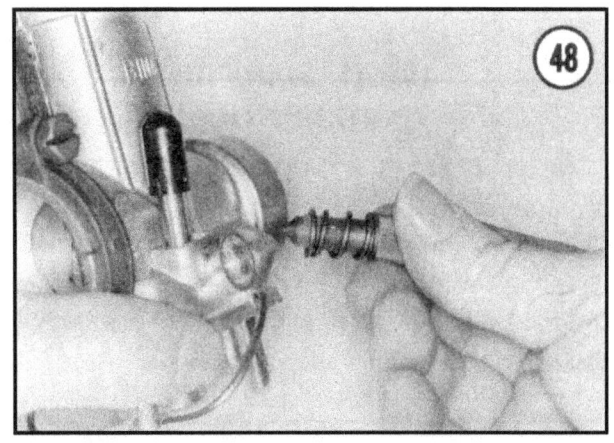

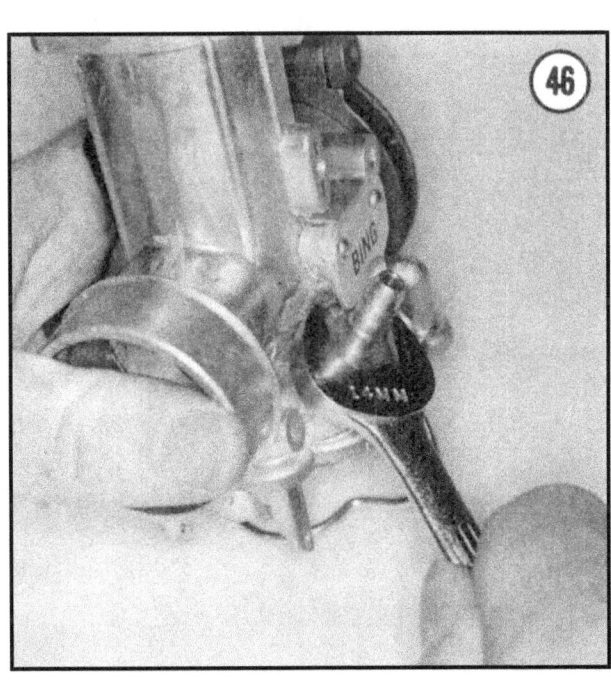

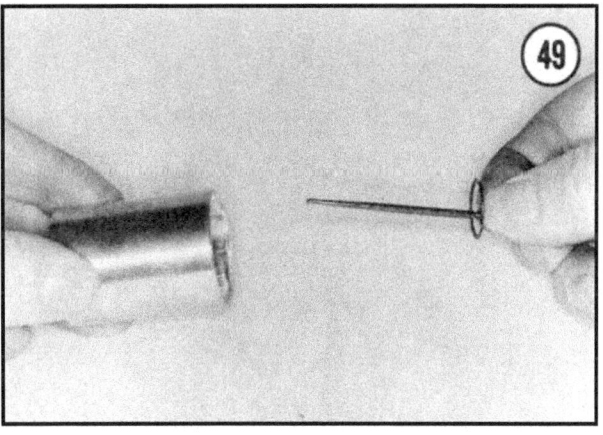

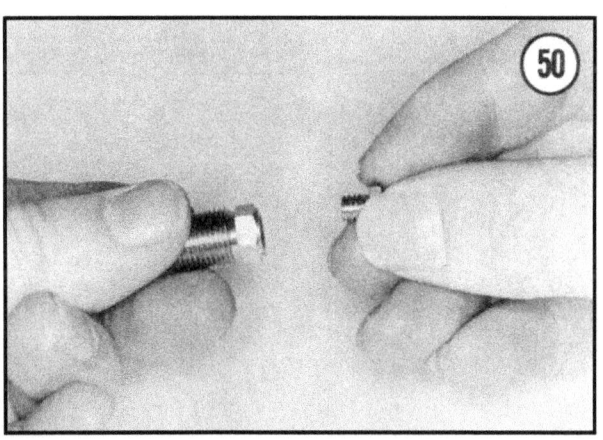

85

destroy their calibration. Do not use compressed air to clean an assembled carburetor, since the float and float valve can be damaged.

Reassembly

Reverse the disassembly procedure to reassemble the carburetor. Always use new gaskets upon reassembly.

After reassembly, be sure to adjust both floats so that they are parallel to the float bowl mounting surface (**Figure 51**). Bend the tang on the float lever if necessary.

AMAL MARK II CARBURETOR

A few of the newer Montesa motorcycles are equipped with the Amal Mark II carburetor. The new Amal shares many of the design and servicing procedures with the older style Amals and the Bing, but it differs in outside appearance and in detail.

Disassembly

1. Remove the mixing chamber top (**Figure 52**) if the top was not removed previously. Note the notch in the throttle slide and how it fits inside the mixing chamber.

2. Twist the handlebar twistgrip to give full throttle so the throttle valve return spring is fully compressed. Hold the valve and the cap while the knob on the end of the inner throttle cable is

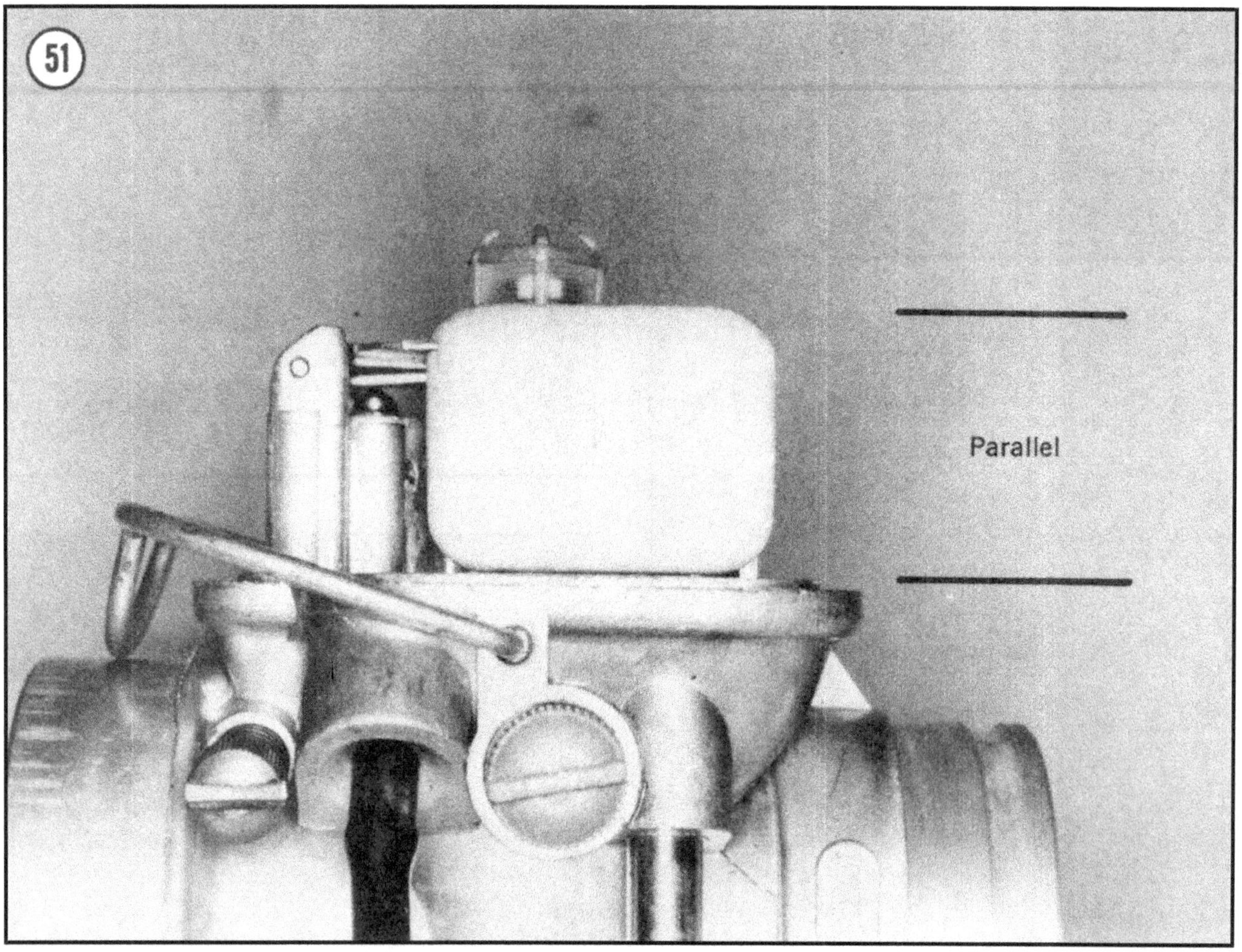

pushed down and to the side so the cable, mixing chamber top, throttle valve, return spring, keeper plate, jet needle, and clip (**Figure 53**) can be removed from the carburetor.

3. The main jet cover (**Figure 54**) can be removed for access to the main jet without disassembling the carburetor. Pull the filter screen from the main jet. The main jet can then be removed (**Figure 55**).

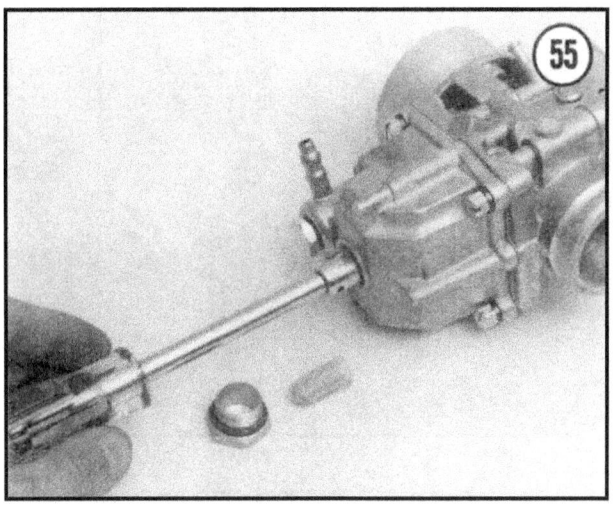

4. Remove the banjo bolt, then the fuel inlet fitting (**Figure 56**).

5. Remove the fuel strainer (**Figure 57**) and note how its flange serves as a gasket for the fuel inlet fitting.

6. Remove the 4 screws that retain the float bowl to the bottom of the carburetor (**Figure 58**).

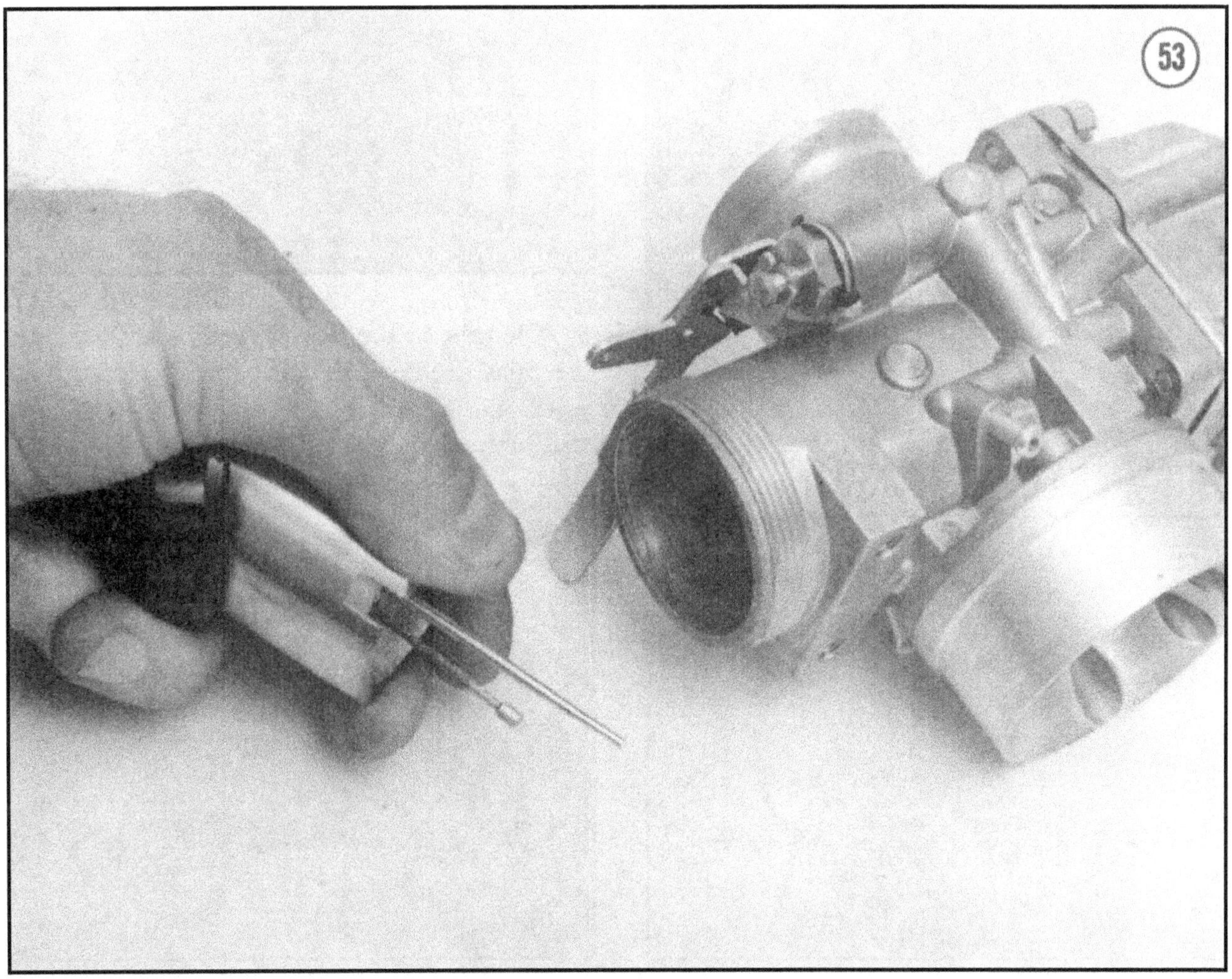

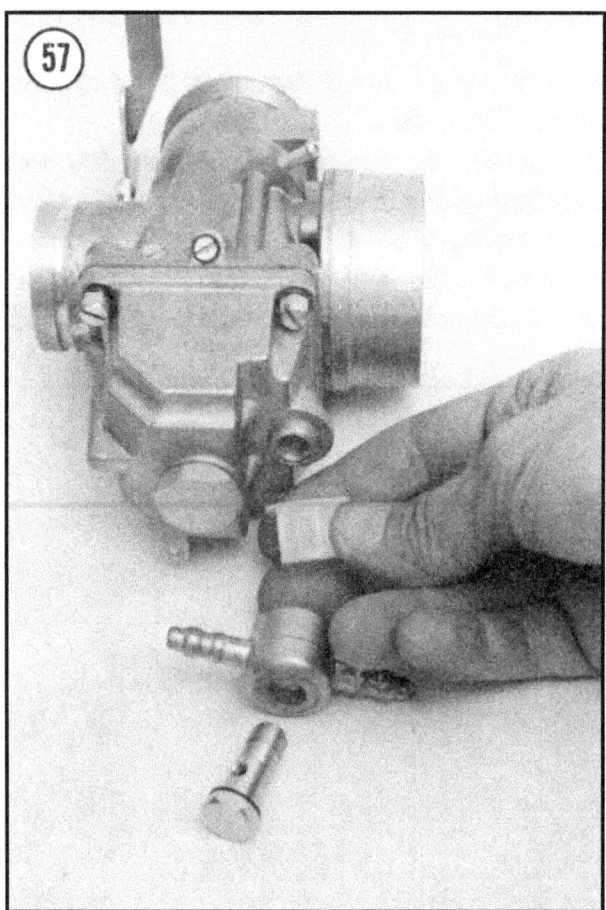

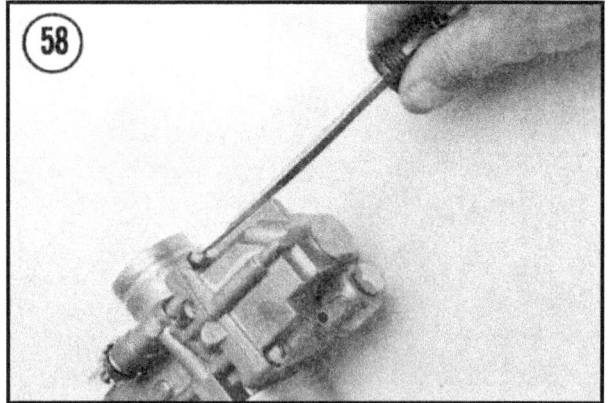

7. Hold the carburetor upright (**Figure 59**) while the float bowl is pulled from the bottom. The float assembly is now loose so be certain the pieces stay in place long enough so you can note their correct locations.

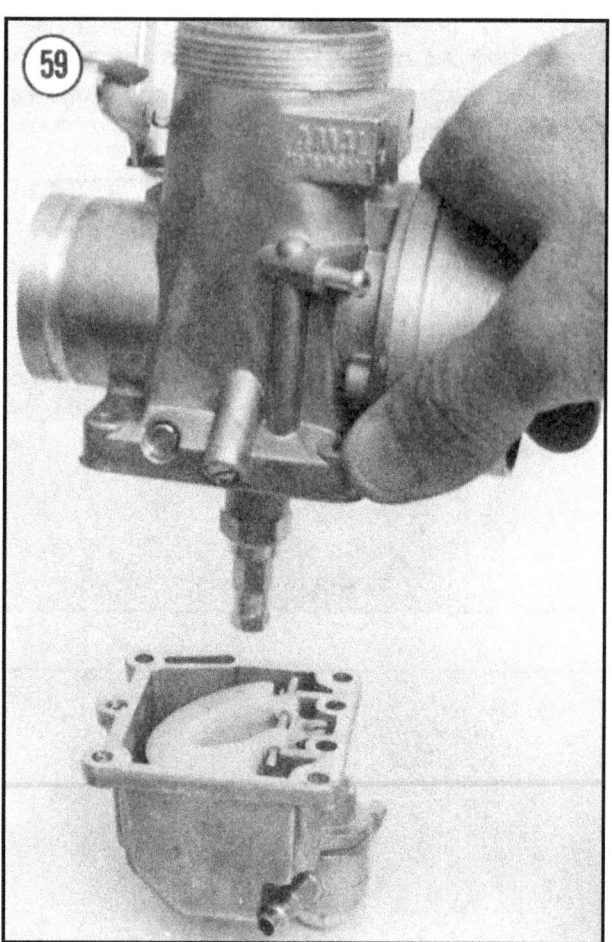

8. The tabs on the side of the plastic float hold the float needle. Lift the complete float, float pivot, and needle assembly from the float bowl and remove the needle (**Figure 60**).

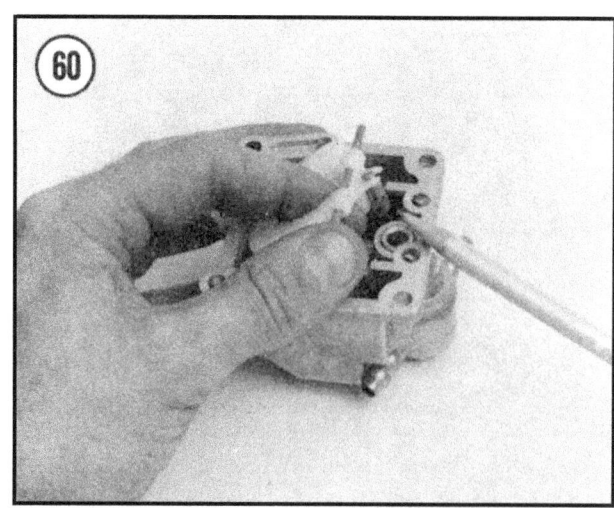

9. Remove the main jet and the main jet holder from the carburetor (**Figure 61**).

10. If you have not previously removed the main jet, hold the main jet holder with a wrench (**Figure 62**) while you remove the main jet.

11. Remove the pilot jet (**Figure 63**) and inspect its O-ring for signs of wear or cracking.

12. Remove the single brass nut that retains the complete choke assembly (**Figure 64**) and pull the choke from the carburetor.

13. The choke itself can be removed by moving the operating lever to the open position (**Figure 65**) so the choke can be pulled away from its retaining notches.

Inspection

Shake the float to check for gasoline inside. If fuel leaks into the float, the float chamber fuel level will rise, resulting in an overrich mixture. Replace float if it is deformed or leaking.

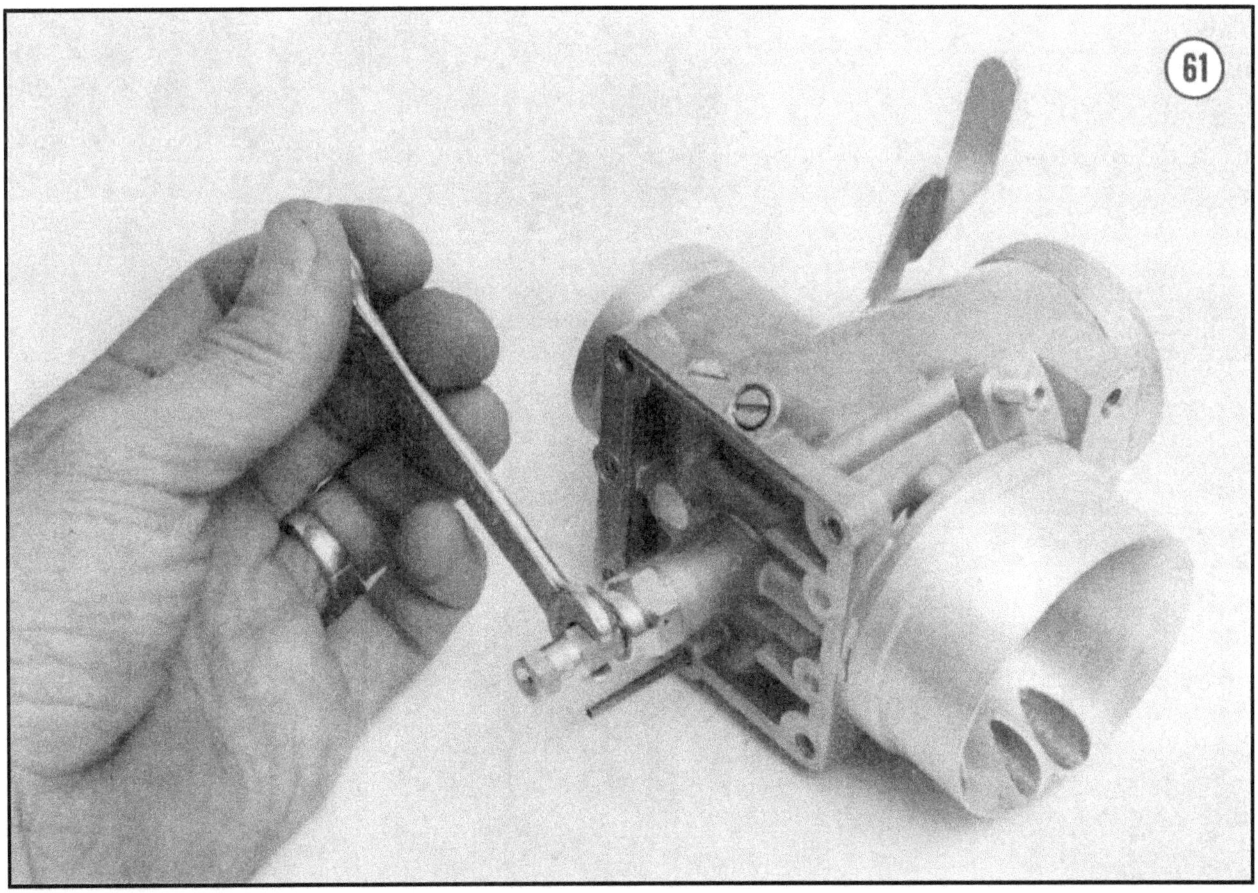

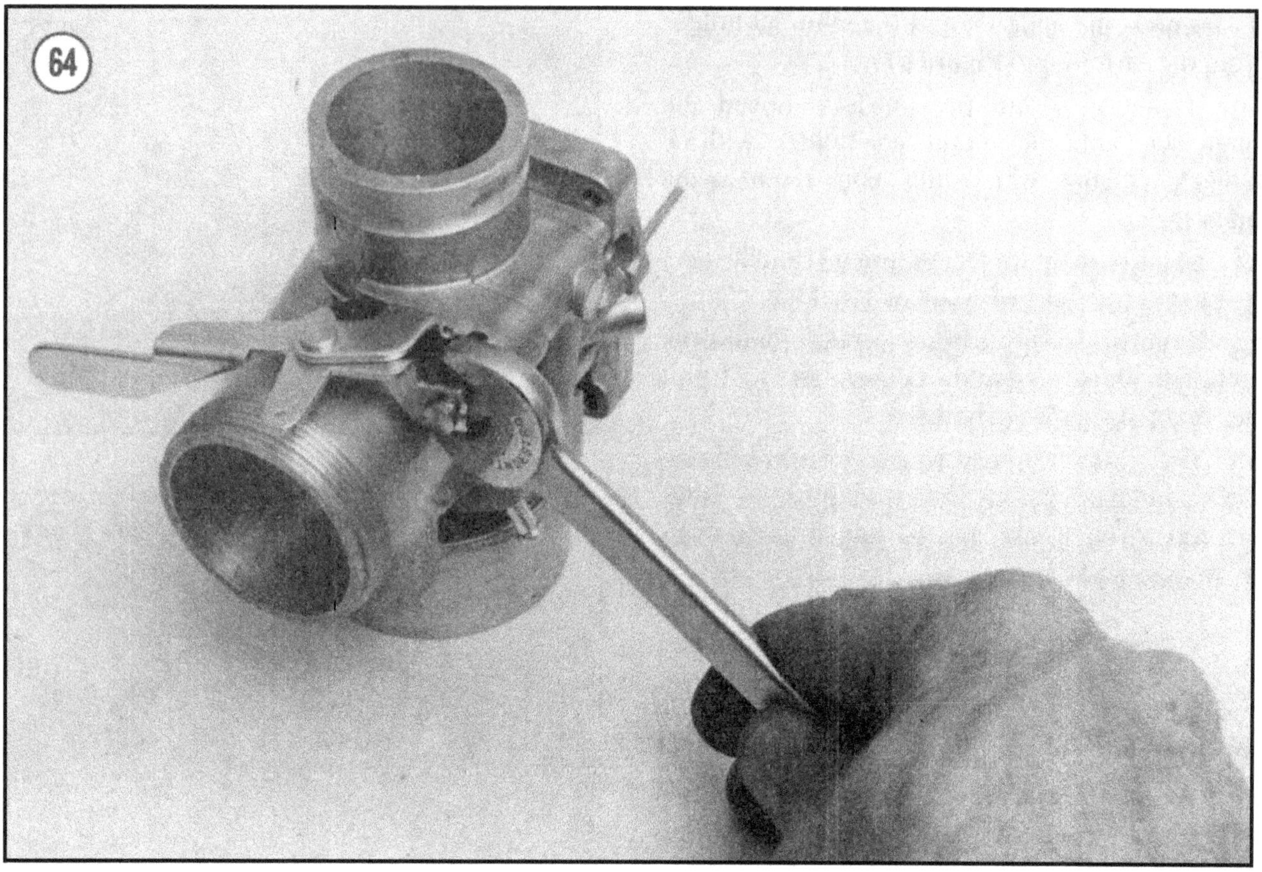

64

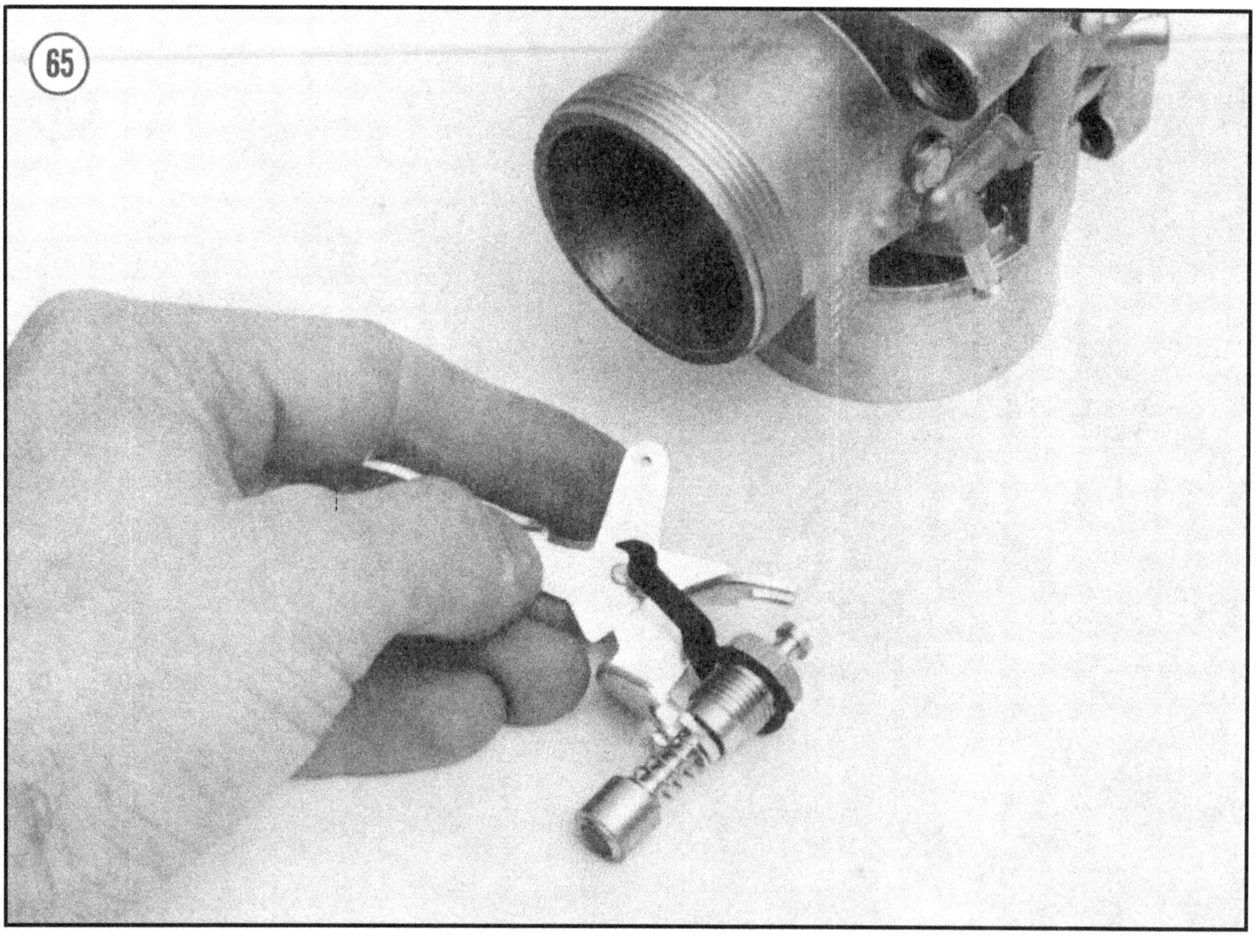

65

90

Replace the float valve if its seating end is scratched or worn. Press the float valve gently with your finger and make sure it seats properly. If it doesn't seat properly, fuel will overflow, causing an overrich mixture and flooding the float chamber whenever the fuel petcock is open.

Clean all parts in carburetor cleaning solvent. Dry them with compressed air. Clean the jets and other delicate parts with compressed air after the float bowl has been removed. Never attempt to clean jets or passages by running a wire through. To do so will cause damage and destroy their calibration. Do not use compressed air to clean an assembled carburetor, since the float and float valve can be damaged.

Reassembly

Reverse the disassembly procedure to reassemble the carburetor. Always use new gaskets upon reassembly.

CARBURETOR ADJUSTMENT

Carburetor adjustment is not normally required except for occasional attention to idle speed, or at time of carburetor overhaul.

Float Level

The machine was delivered with the float level adjusted correctly. Amal carburetors do not require float adjustment. Refer to *Bing Carburetors* for adjustment procedure for Bing floats.

Speed Range Adjustments

The carburetor was designed to provide the proper mixture under all operating conditions. Little or no benefit will result from experimenting. However, unusual operating conditions such as sustained operation at high altitudes, or unusually high or low temperatures, may make modifications to the standard specifications desirable. The adjustments described in the following paragraphs should only be undertaken if the rider has definite reason to believe they are required. Make the tests and adjustments in the order specified.

Make a road test at full throttle for final determination of main jet size. Operate the motorcycle at full throttle for at least 2 minutes, then shut the engine off, release the clutch, and bring the bike to a stop.

If the engine performance is erratic at ¾ to full throttle, even in 3rd or 4th gears, with a hollow sound to the exhaust and possibly excessive smoke, then the main jet is probably too large. If the engine runs better by closing the throttle slightly, then the main jet is too small. The engine will run evenly and regularly at full throttle if the main jet is of the correct size.

After each such test, remove and examine the spark plug. The insulator should have a light tan color. If the insulator has black sooty deposits, the mixture is too rich. If there are signs of intense heat, such as a blistered white appearance, mixture is too lean.

As a general rule, main jet size should be reduced approximately 5% for each 3,000 feet (1,000 meters) above sea level.

Table 2 lists symptoms caused by rich and lean mixtures.

Table 2   RICH/LEAN MIXTURE SYMPTOMS

Condition	Symptom
Rich Mixture	Rough idle Black exhaust smoke Hard starting, especially when hot "Blubbering" under acceleration Black deposits in exhaust pipe Gas-fouled spark plug Poor gas mileage Engine performs worse as it warms up
Lean Mixture	Backfiring Rough idle Overheating Hesitation upon acceleration Engine speed varies at fixed throttle Loss of power White color on spark plug insulator Poor acceleration

Adjust the pilot air screw as follows.

1. Turn the pilot air screw in until it seats lightly, then back it out about 1½ turns.

2. Start the engine and warm it to normal operating temperature.

3. Turn the idle speed screw in until the engine runs slower and begins to falter.

4. Adjust the pilot air screw as required to make the engine run smoothly.

5. Repeat Steps 3 and 4 to achieve the lowest stable idle speed.

Next, determine proper throttle valve cutaway size. With the engine running at idle, open the throttle. If the engine does not accelerate smoothly from idle, turn the pilot air screw in (clockwise) slightly to richen the mixture. If the condition still exists, return the air screw to its original position and replace the throttle valve with one which has a smaller cutaway. If engine operation suffers by turning the air screw, replace the throttle valve with one having a larger cutaway.

For operation at ¼ to ¾ throttle opening, adjustment is made with the jet needle. Operate the engine at ½ throttle in a manner similar to that for full throttle test described earlier. To enrich the mixture, place the jet needle clip in a lower groove. Conversely, placing the clip in a higher groove leans the mixture.

A summary of carburetor adjustments is given in **Table 3**.

Table 3   CARBURETOR ADJUSTMENTS

Throttle Opening	Adjustment	If too rich	If too lean
0 - ⅛	Air screw	Turn out	Turn in
⅛ - ¼	Throttle valve cutaway	Use larger cutaway	Use smaller cutaway
¼ - ¾	Jet needle	Raise clip	Lower clip
¾ - full	Main jet	Use smaller number	Use larger number

CARBURETOR MODIFICATION

The following paragraphs describe various components of the carburetor which may be changed to modify performance characteristics.

Throttle Valve

The throttle valve cutaway controls airflow at small throttle openings. Cutaway sizes are numbered. Larger numbers permit more air to flow at a given throttle opening and result in a leaner mixture. Conversely, smaller numbers result in a richer mixture.

Jet Needle

The jet needle, together with the needle jet, controls the mixture at medium speeds. As the throttle valve rises to increase airflow through the carburetor, the jet needle rises with it. The tapered portion of the jet needle rises from the needle jet and allows more fuel to flow, thereby providing the engine with the proper mixture at up to about ¾ throttle opening. The grooves at the top of the jet needle permit adjustment of the mixture ratio in the medium speed range.

Needle Jet

The needle jet operates with the jet needle. Several holes are drilled through the side of the needle jet. These meter the airflow from the air jet. Air from the air jet is bled into the needle jet to assist in atomization of the fuel.

Main Jet

The main jet controls the mixture at full throttle, and has some effect at lesser throttle openings. Each main jet is stamped with a number. Fuel flow is approximately proportional to the number. Larger numbers provide a richer mixture.

MISCELLANEOUS CARBURETOR PROBLEMS

Water in the carburetor float bowl and sticking carburetor slide valves can result from careless washing of the motorcycle. To remedy the problem, remove and clean the carburetor bowl, main jet, and any other affected parts. Be sure to cover air intake when washing the motorcycle.

Be sure that the ring nut on the top of the carburetor is secure. Also be sure that the carburetor mounting bolts are tight.

If gasoline leaks past the float bowl gasket, high speed fuel starvation may occur. Varnish deposits on the outside of the float bowl are evidence of this condition.

Dirt in the fuel may lodge in the float valve and cause an overrich mixture. As a temporary measure, tap the carburetor lightly with any convenient tool to dislodge the dirt. Clean the fuel tank, petcock, fuel line, and carburetor at the first opportunity, should this occur.

CHAPTER FIVE

CHASSIS SERVICE

FRAME

Montesa frames are made of welded steel tubing. Service is limited to inspection for bending of frame members and cracked welds. Examine the frame carefully if the bike has suffered a collision or hard spill.

HANDLEBAR

The handlebar is made from solid drawn steel tubing. Clutch, throttle, and front brake controls are mounted on the handlebar.

Some machines are equipped with a scale (**Figure 1**) so handlebar position may be read.

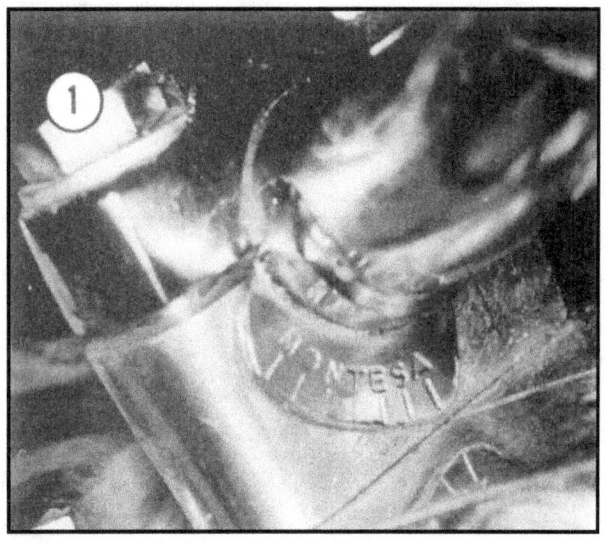

The throttle grips on some models are equipped with adjustable stops. To adjust the throttle stop, open the throttle fully, then turn the adjusting screw in (**Figure 2**) until it just bottoms. Hold the screw in this position, then tighten the locknut.

Examine the handlebar for cracking or bending. Minor bends may be straightened. Replace the handlebar if any cracks exist, or if there is serious bending.

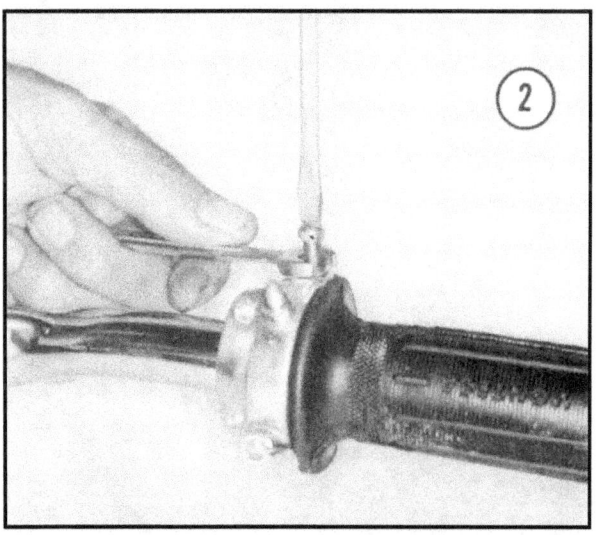

FRONT FORKS

Front forks feature oil damping and internal springs. Damping characteristics may be changed readily by changing oil viscosity.

Fork Removal

Fork removal is similar for all models. The following steps are set forth as a guide:

1. Remove the front axle nut (**Figure 3**), or on some models, both front axle clamp bolts.

2. Remove upper (**Figure 4**) and lower (**Figure 5**) brake torque link bolts.

3. Disconnect the front brake cable at the front brake.
4. Raise the front end of the machine and support it on a box or other suitable support under the engine.
5. Remove the front fender.
6. Pull out the front axle, then remove the front wheel.
7. Place a suitable container under the fork legs, then remove the drain plug from the lower end of the fork tube.
8. Loosen lower and upper fork tube clamp bolts (**Figure 6**).
9. Remove handlebar assembly (**Figure 7**).
10. Remove the fork tube head bolt (**Figure 8**).
11. Pull the fork tube downward to remove it from the steering head.

Fork Disassembly

1. Remove the front axle clamp bolt (**Figure 9**).
2. Remove the fork plunger retaining bolt (**Figure 10**). On some older models, the plunger is retained by the drain bolt.

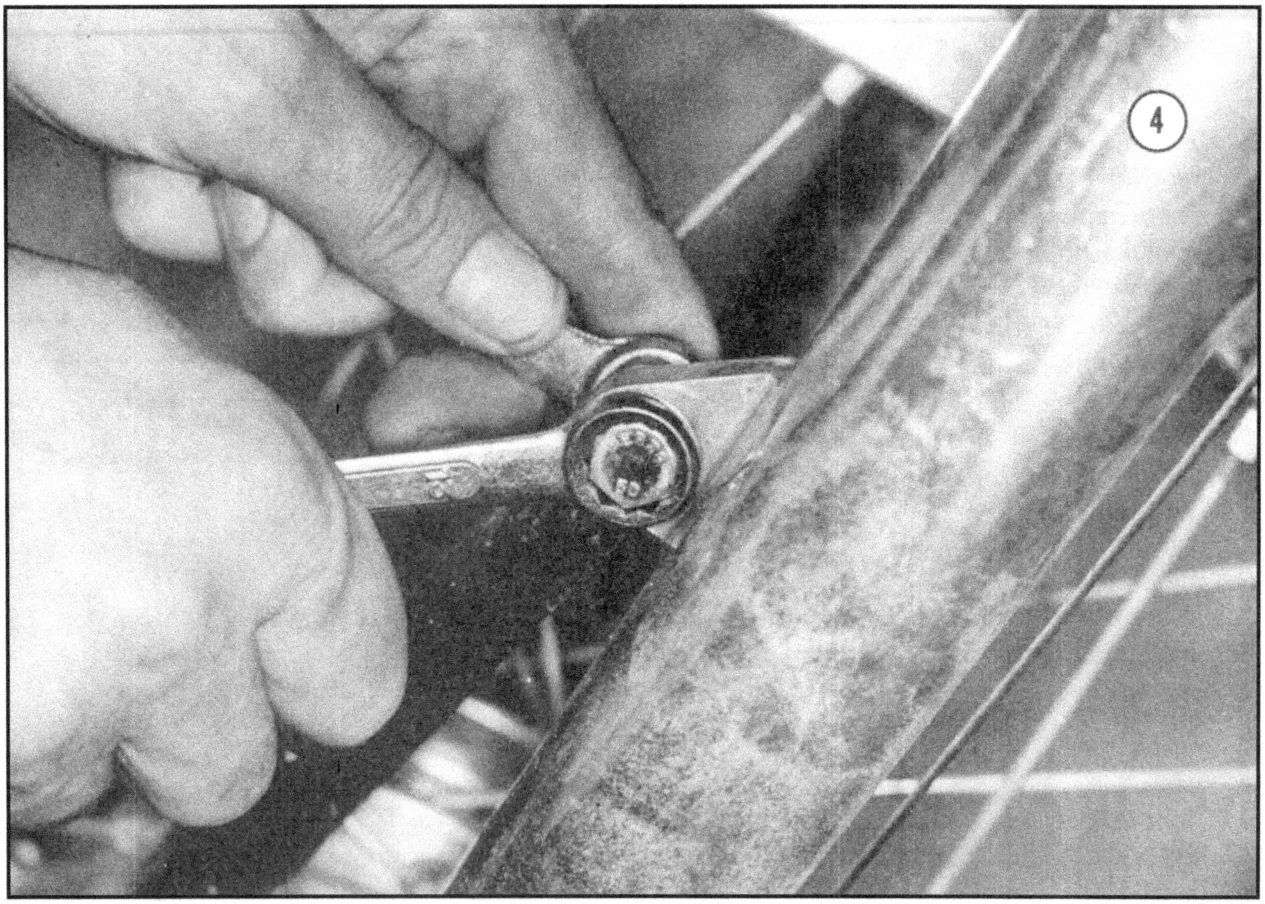

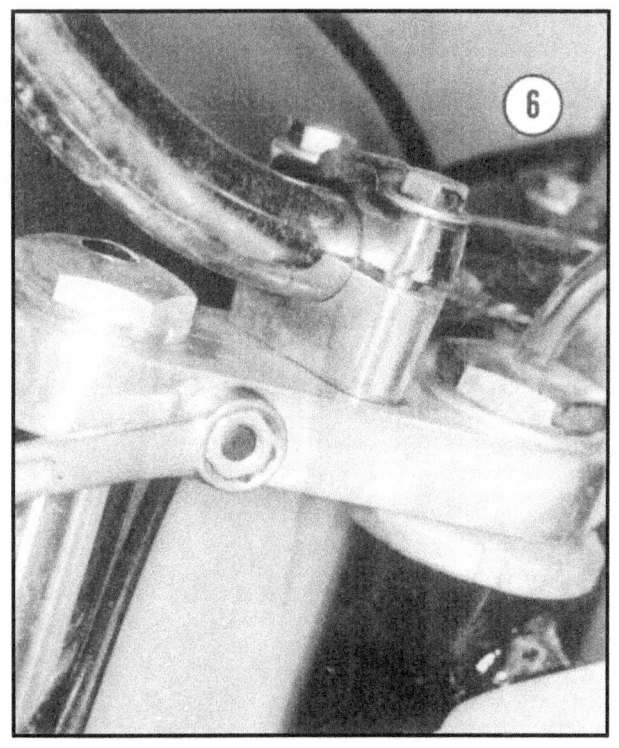
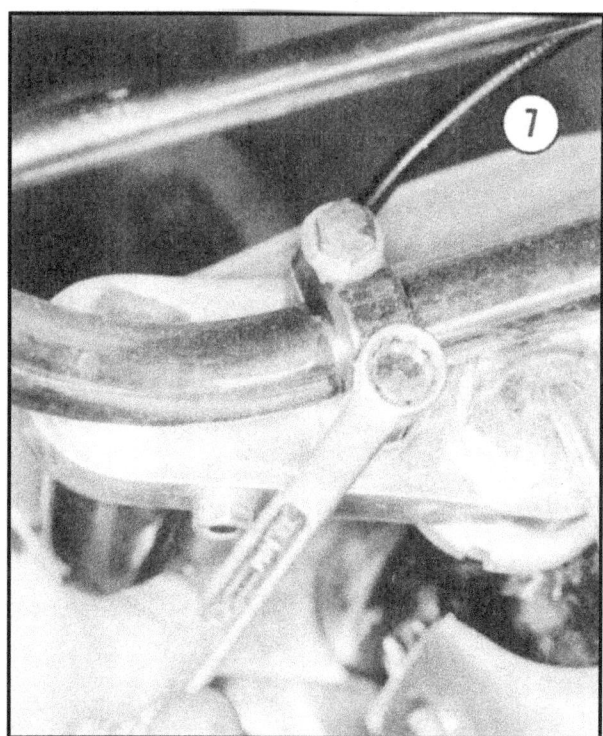

8

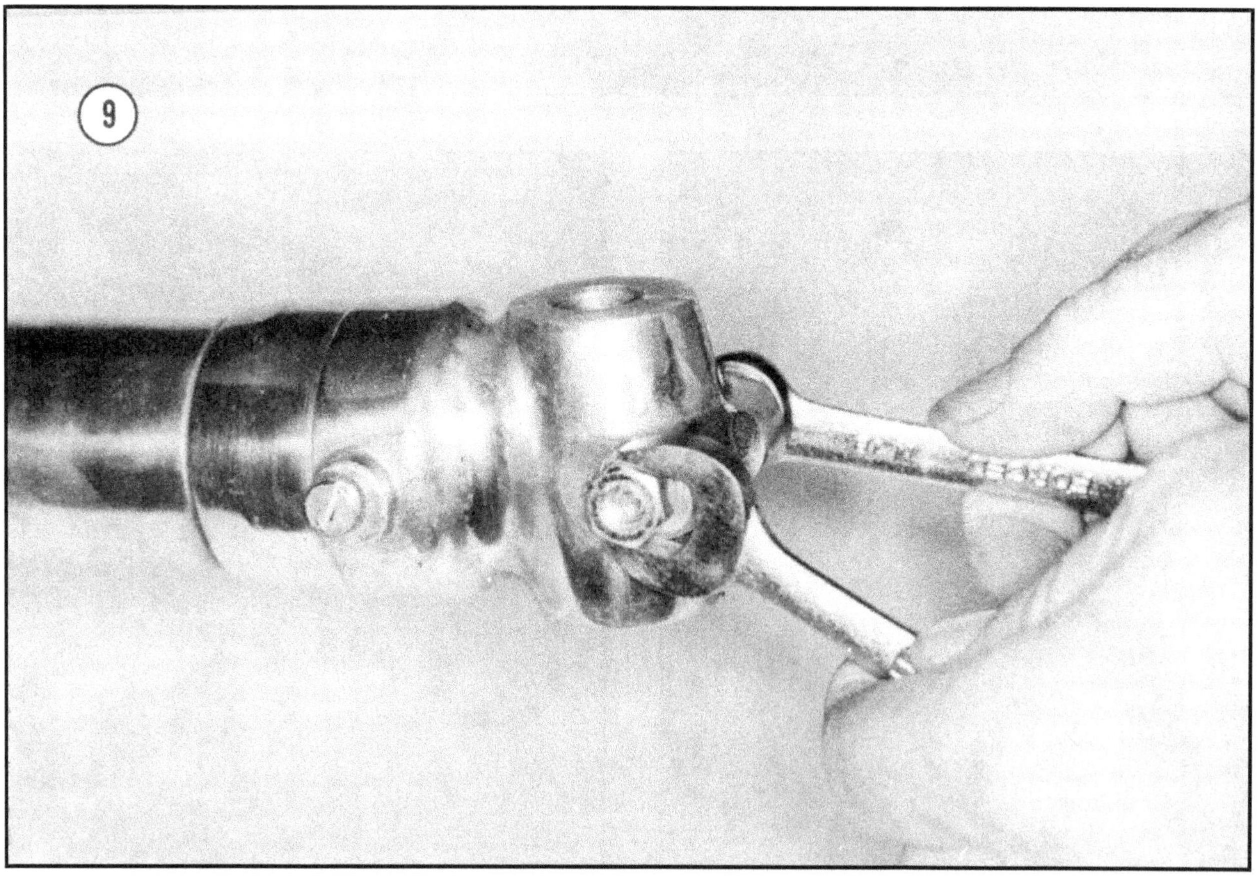

9

96

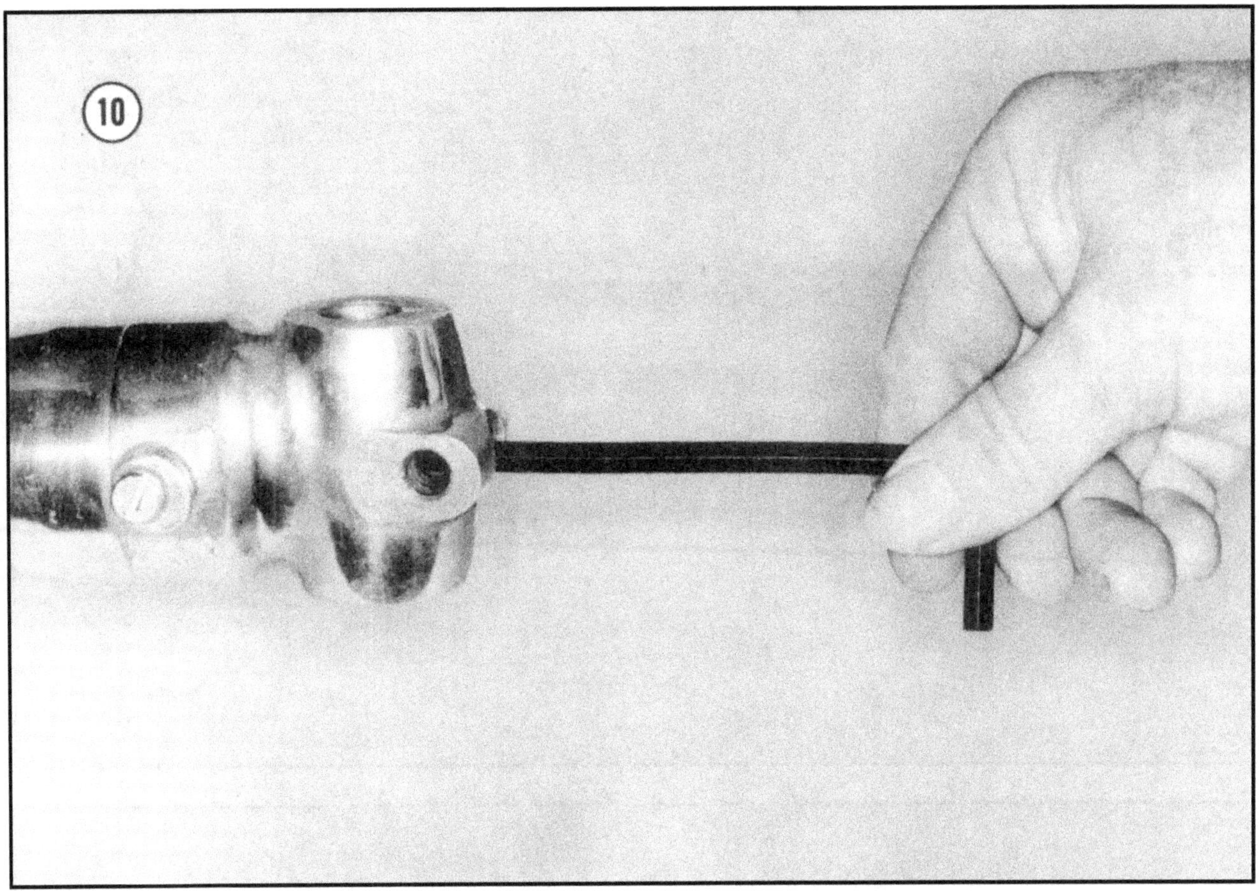

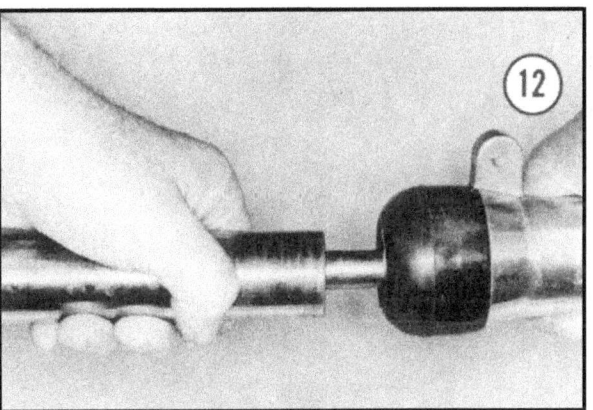

3. Invert the tube to remove the fork spring (**Figure 11**).

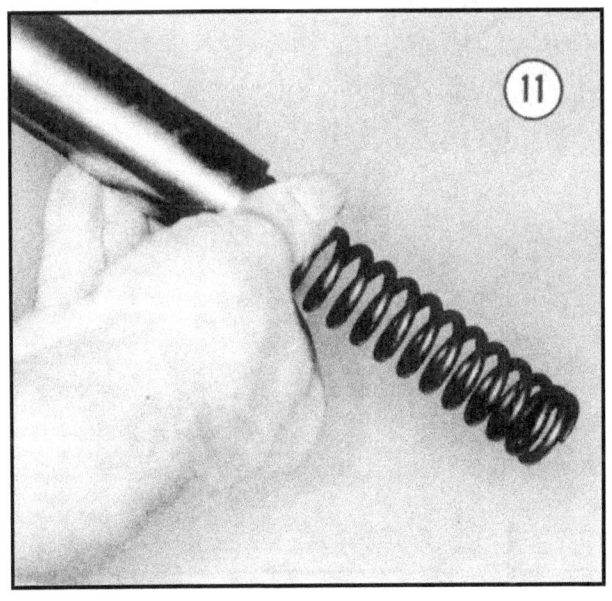

4. Pull the inner and outer fork tubes apart (**Figure 12**).

5. Remove the snap ring (**Figure 13**), then pull out the plunger assembly (**Figure 14**).

6. Pull off the dust cover (**Figure 15**) from the outer tube.

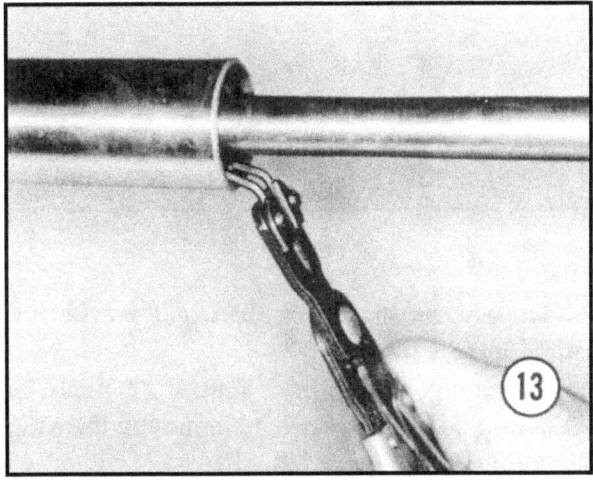

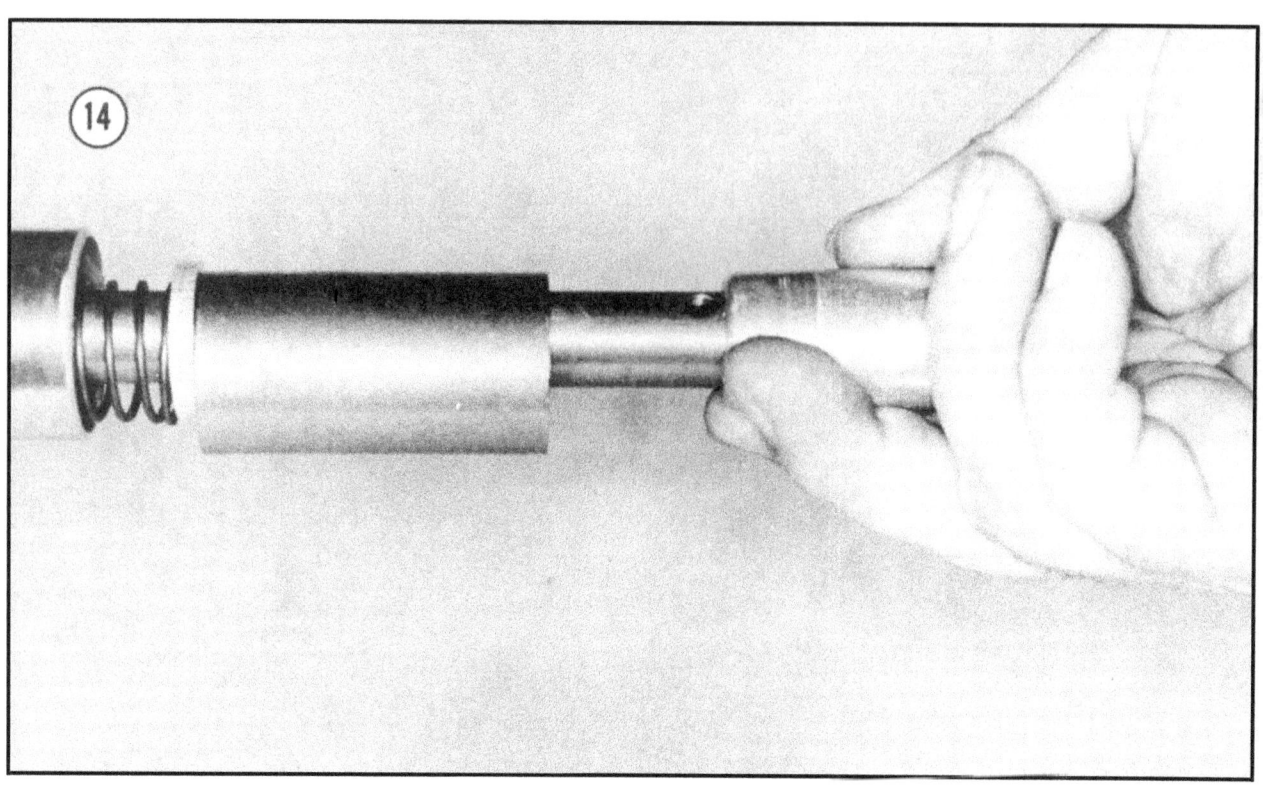

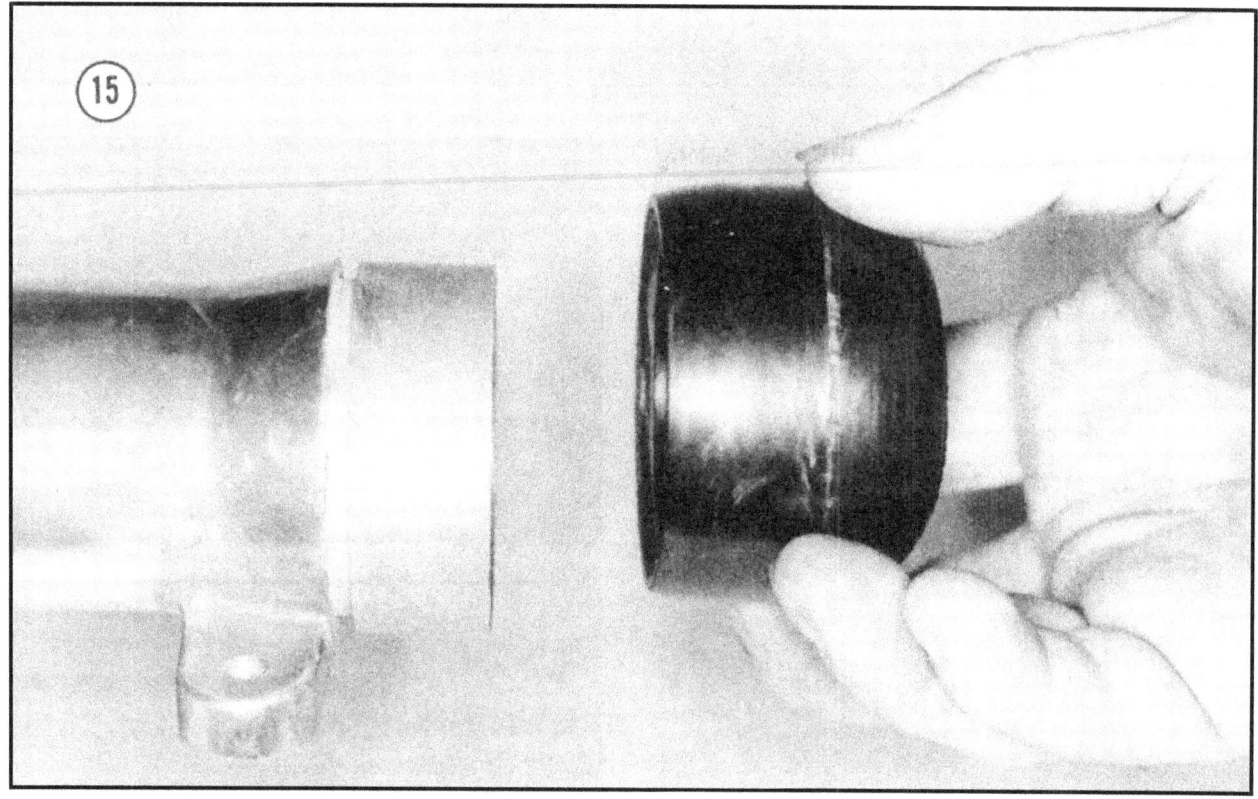

7. Remove the snap ring, then pull out the oil seal (**Figure 16**).

8. The plunger assembly (**Figure 17**) may be disassembled, if necessary, by removing the snap ring at one end (**Figure 18**).

Inspection

1. Assemble the inner and outer tubes, then slide them together. Check for looseness, noise, or binding. It's sometimes possible to straighten a bent fork tube, but better to replace it.

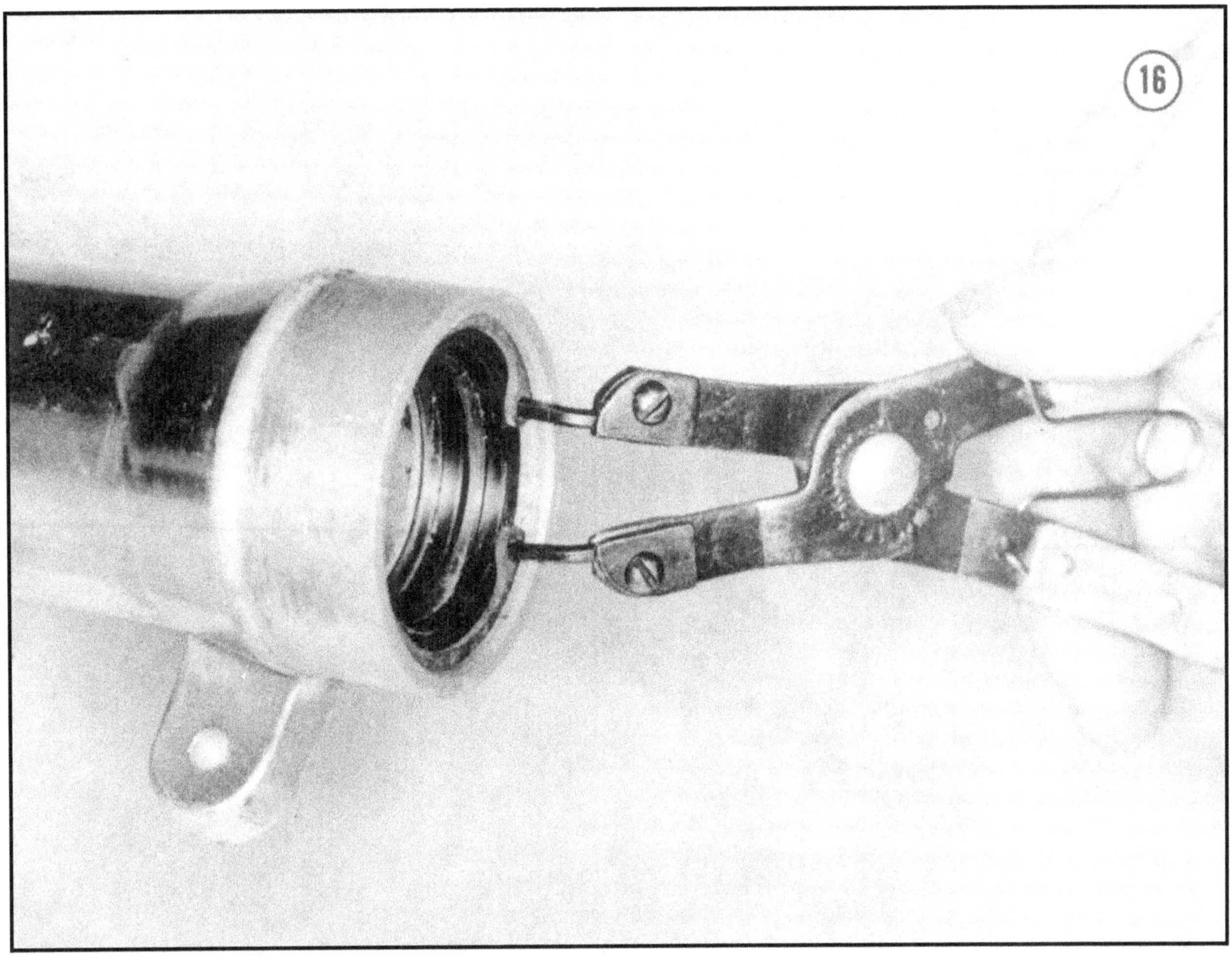

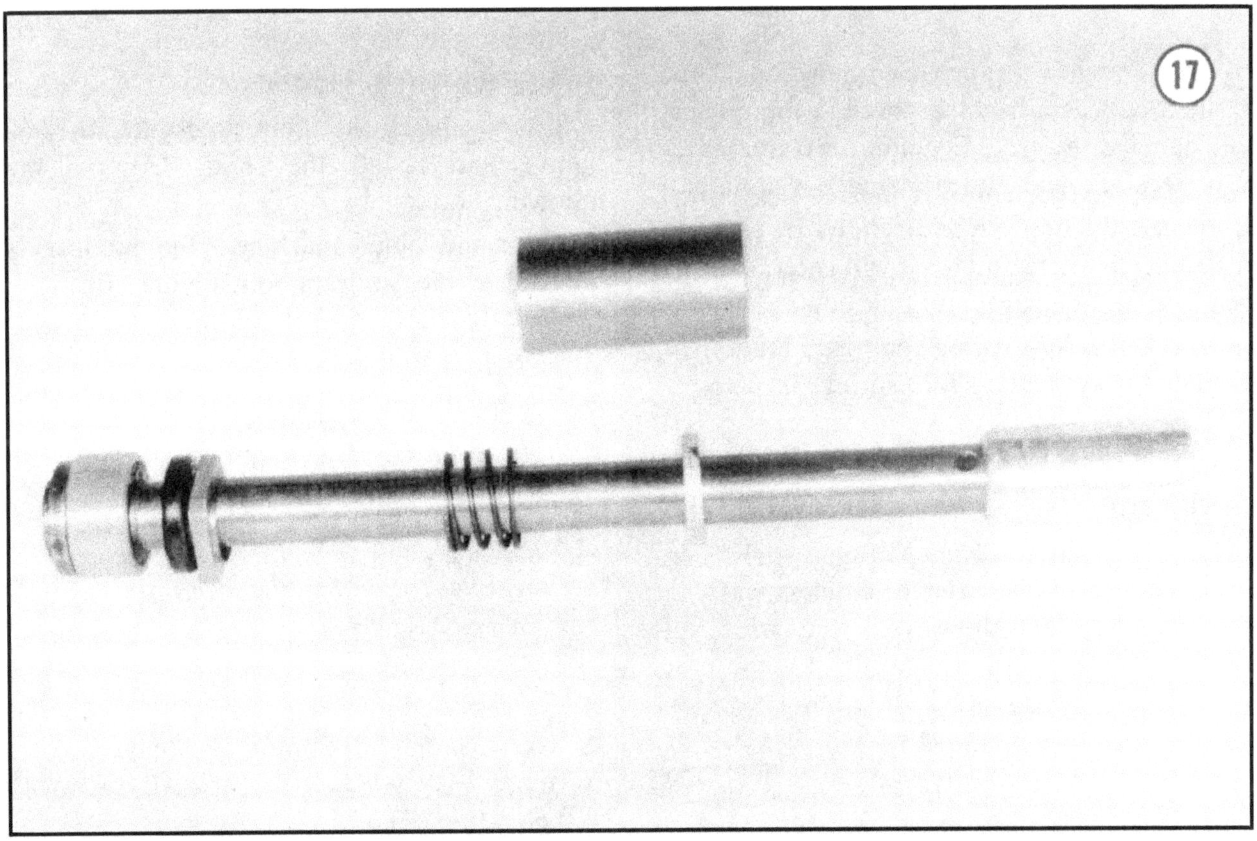

16

17

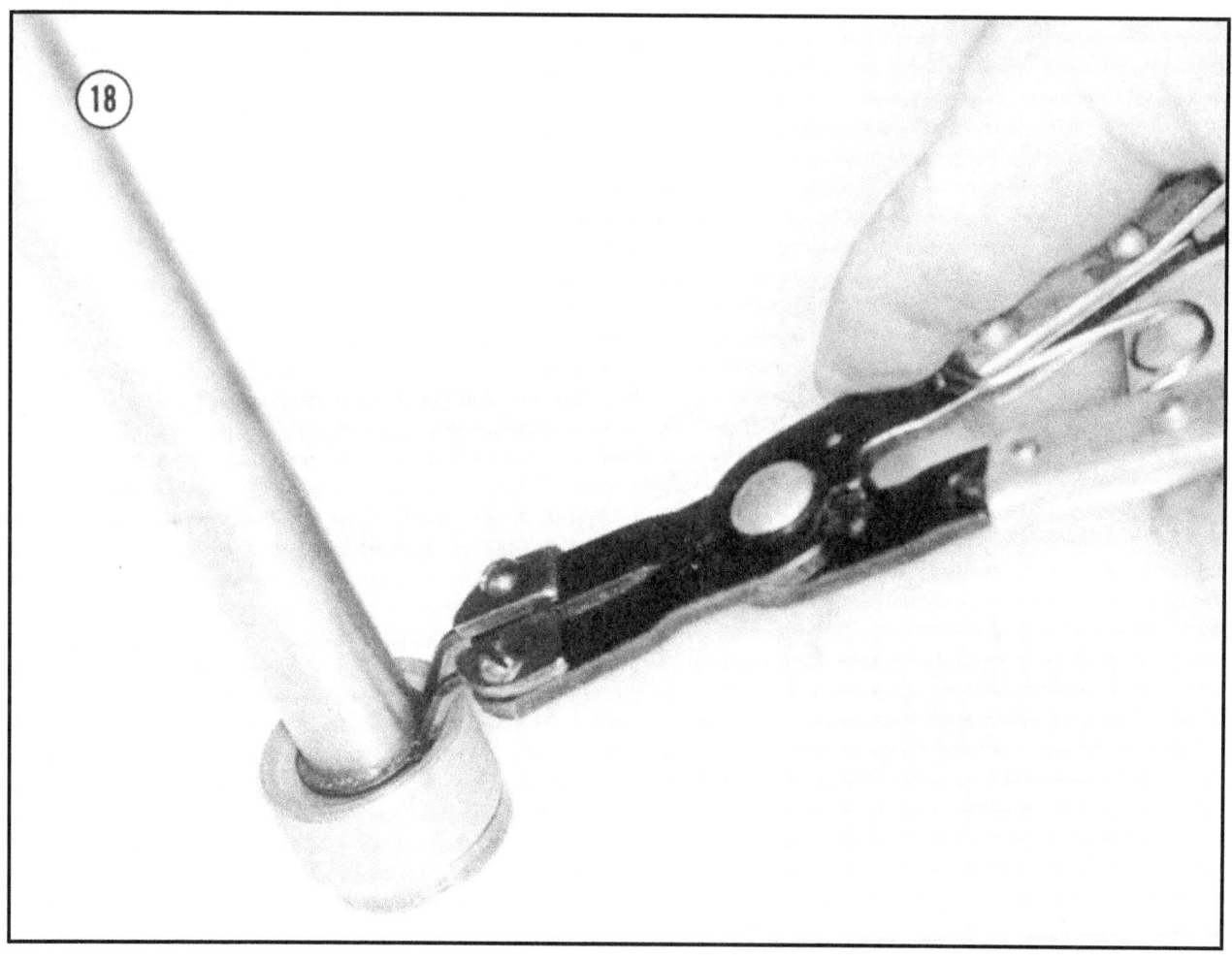

2. Any scratches or roughness on the inner tube in the area where it passes through the oil seal will damage the seal. Examine this area carefully. Replace inner tube if damage is apparent.

3. Inspect the dust cover carefully. If it's worn or damaged, foreign material will enter, causing wear, oil seal damage, and fluid loss.

4. Check the fork spring for wear, cracks, or fatigue. Always replace fork springs in pairs.

Check Valve

The check valve (**Figure 19**) may stick open or closed as a result of dirt or careless washing of the motorcycle. If the valve is stuck open, oil will spray out onto the rider. Oil will leak past the seal if the valve is stuck closed. Disassemble and clean the valve in the case of sticking. Cover the screw with a small piece of masking tape when the bike is washed.

Reassembly and Installation

Reverse the disassembly procedure to reassemble and install the forks. Observe the following notes:

1. On some older machines, the plunger is retained by the oil drain bolt (**Figure 20**).

> CAUTION
> *A serious accident may result if the oil drain bolt is not inserted through the hole in the fork plunger. Make absolutely certain that this type fork is assembled with the drain bolt through the plunger hole.*

2. Use new oil seals upon reassembly.

3. Refill the fork legs with oil in the quantities shown in **Table 1**.

Table 1 FORK LEG OIL QUANTITY

Model	Ounces	(Cubic Centimeters)
Cota 123	5	(150)
Cota 123 Trail	5	(150)
Cappra 125 VA	7.4	(220)
Enduro 250	7.6	(220)
Rapita 250	7.6	(220)
Cappra 250 V-75	6.5	(190)
All others	6.5	(190)

WHEELS AND TIRES

Various sizes of wheels and tires are fitted to Montesa bikes. Consult the specifications, Chapter Eight, to determine sizes for each model.

Rims

The wheel rim supports the tire and provides rigidity to the wheel assembly. A rim band protects the inner tube from abrasion.

Spokes

The spokes support the weight of the motorcycle and the rider, and transmit tractive and braking forces.

Check the spokes periodically for looseness or binding. A bent or otherwise faulty spoke will adversely affect neighboring spokes, and should therefore be replaced immediately. To remove the spoke, completely unscrew the threaded portion, then remove the bent end from the hub.

Spokes tend to loosen as the machine is used. Retighten each spoke one turn, beginning with those on one side of the hub, then those on the other side. Tighten the spokes on a new machine after the first 50 miles of operation, then at 50-mile intervals until they no longer loosen.

If the machine is subjected to particularly severe service, as in off-road or competition riding, check the spokes frequently.

Wheel Balance

An unbalanced wheel is unsafe. Depending on the degree of unbalance and the speed of the motorcycle, the rider may experience anything from a mild vibration to a violent shimmy and possibly even loss of control. Balance weights are applied to the spokes on the light side of the wheel to correct imbalance.

Before you attempt to balance the wheel, check to be sure that the wheel bearings are in good condition and properly lubricated, and that the brakes do not drag. The wheel must rotate freely. With the wheel raised, spin it slowly and allow it to come to rest by itself. Add balance weights to the spokes on the light side as required, so that the wheel comes to rest at a different position each time it is spun. Balance weights are available in measures of ⅓, ⅔, and one ounce (10, 20, and 30 grams). Remove the drive chain when you balance the rear wheel.

Wheel Inspection

1. Support each wheel shaft in a lathe, V-blocks, or other suitable centering device as shown in **Figure 21**. Rotate the shaft through a complete revolution. Straighten or replace the shaft if it is bent more than 0.028 in. (0.7mm).

2. Check the inner and outer races of the wheel bearings for cracks, galling, or pitting. Rotate the bearings by hand and check for roughness. Replace the bearings if they are worn or damaged.

3. Inspect the oil seal for wear or damage. Replace the oil seal if there is any doubt about its condition.

4. Check rims for bending or distortion.

Checking Wheel Runout

To measure runout of the wheel rim, support the wheel so it's free to rotate. Position a dial indicator as shown in **Figure 22**. Observe the dial indicator as you rotate the wheel through a complete revolution. The runout limit for all models is 0.12 in. (3.0mm). Excessive runout may be caused by a bent rim or loose spokes. Repair or replace as required.

BRAKES

Each brake consists of a brake pedal or lever, cable, brake panel assembly, and drum. The brake panel assembly includes the cam lever, cam shaft, brake shoes, retracting springs, and brake panel body. Some front brakes are of the dual leading shoe type. Rear brakes have one

19

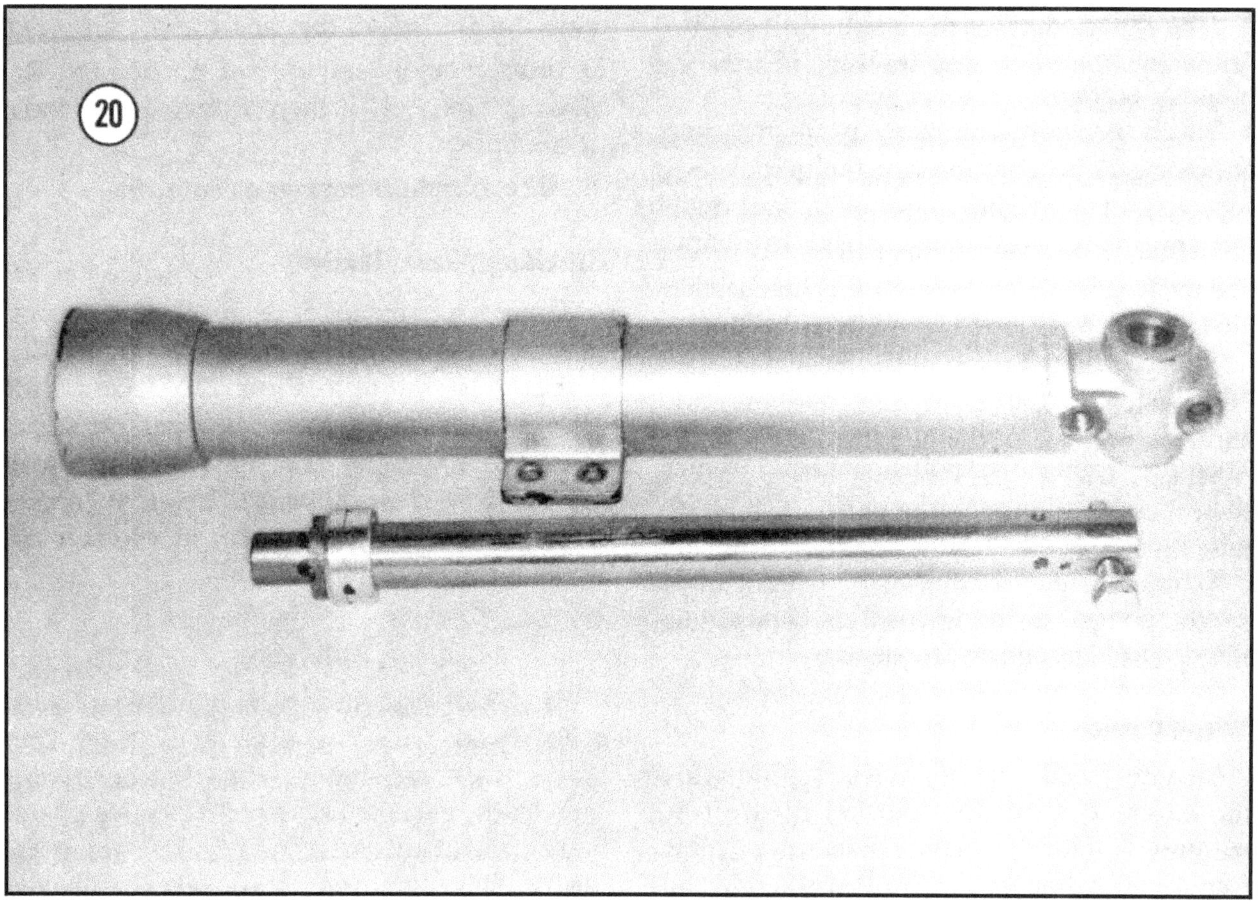

20

102

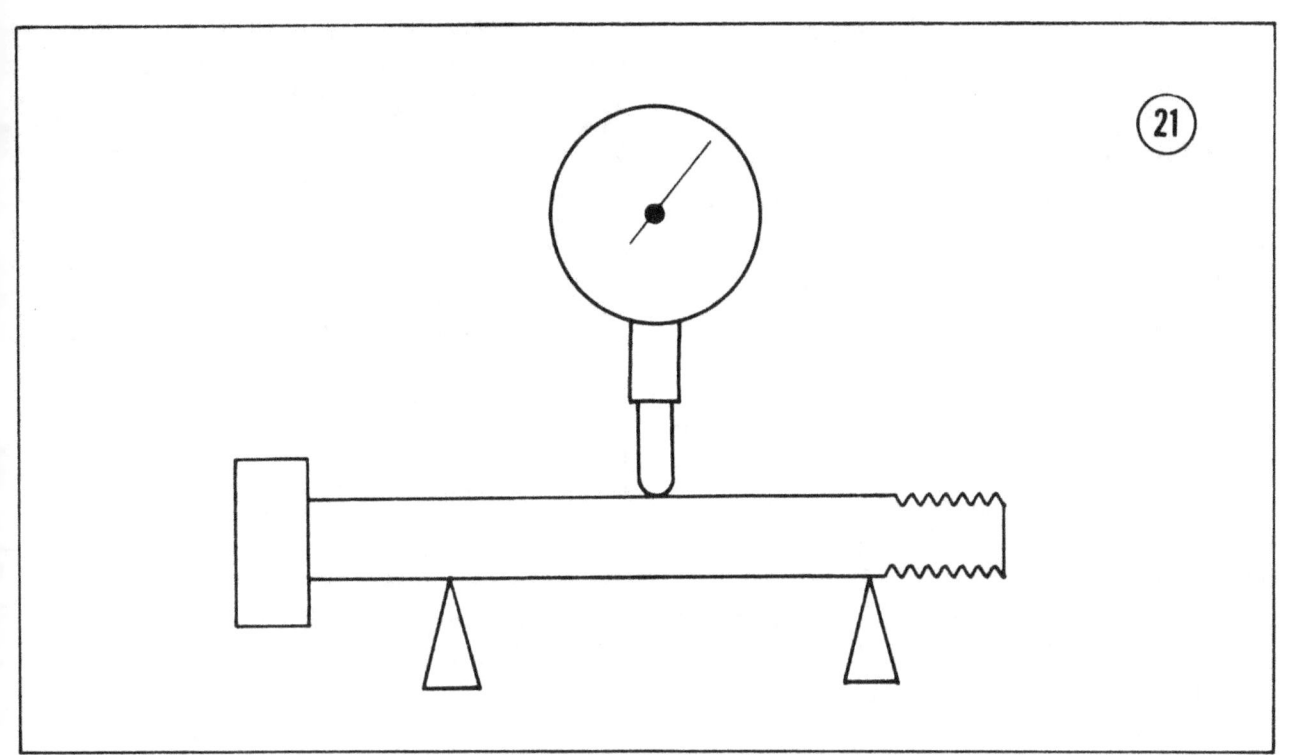

WHEEL RUNOUT

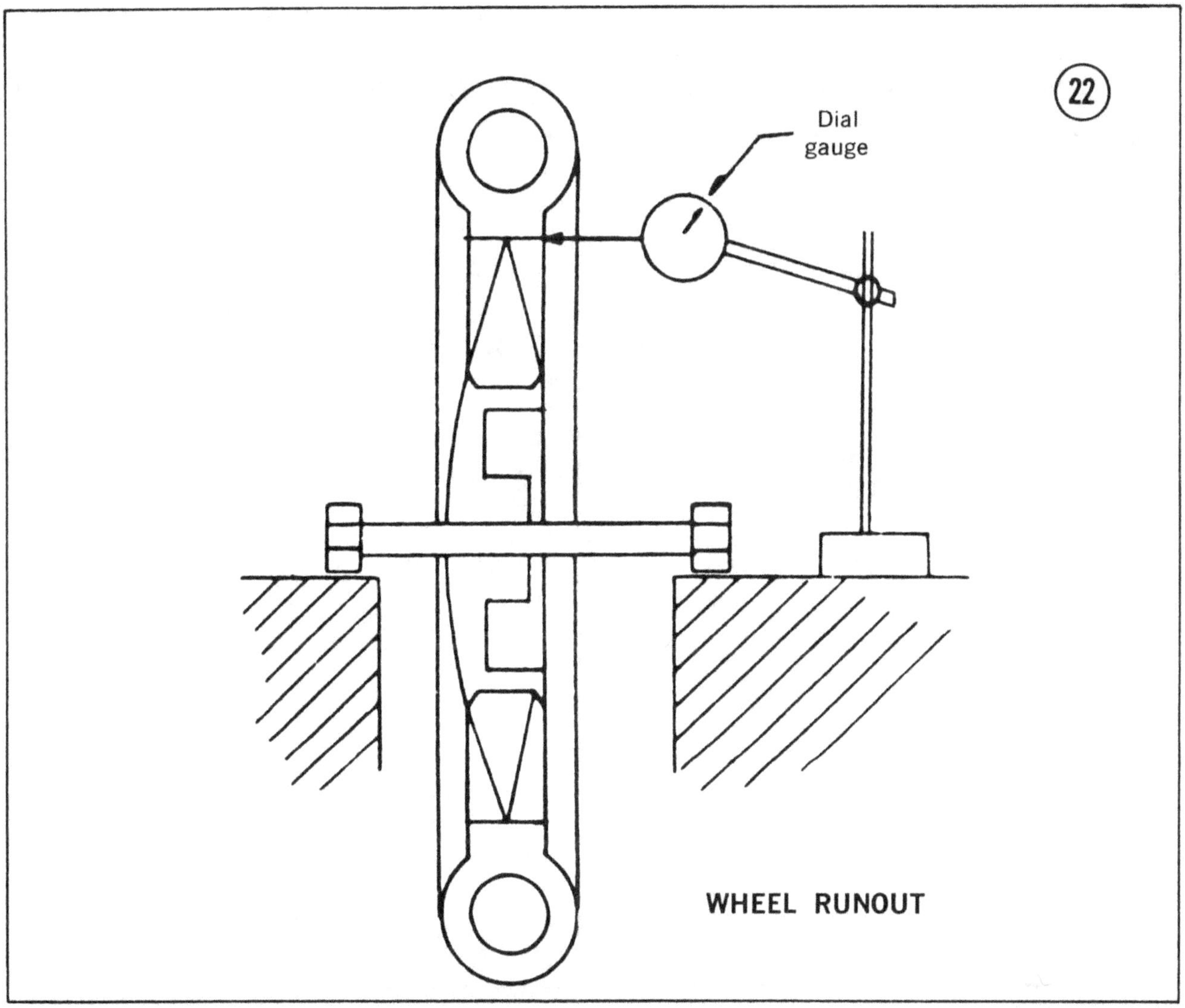

leading and one trailing shoe. **Figure 23** illustrates a typical brake assembly.

Brake Inspection

Examine the inner surface of the brake drum for wear or deep grooves. Any groove deep enough to catch a fingernail is enough to impair braking efficiency.

Examine the brake lining for oil, grease, or other foreign material. Replace oil soaked lining immediately. Dirt imbedded in the lining may be removed with a wire brush. Measure the thickness of the brake lining at its thinnest part. Replace both shoes when any portion of the lining is worn to about 0.12 in. (3mm).

If the brake shoe return spring is worn or stretched, the brake shoes will not retract fully and the brakes may drag. Replace the spring if it is stretched.

Brake Adjustment

Adjust rear brakes with the adjustment nut at the rear wheel (**Figure 24**). Front brakes, except the dual leading shoe type, are adjusted at the front brake hand lever.

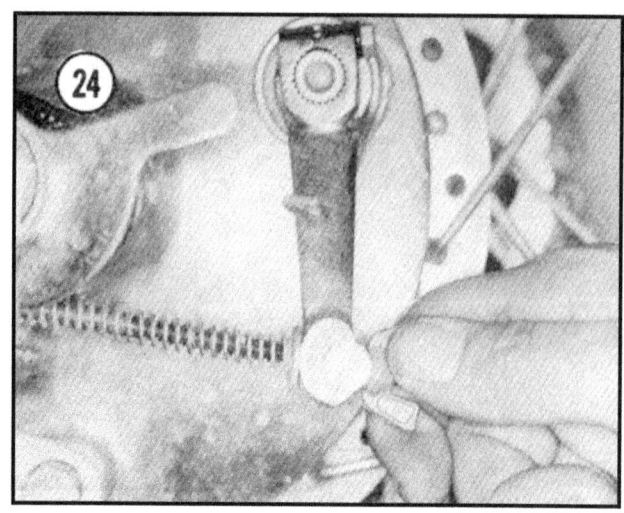

To adjust dual leading shoe brakes, proceed as follows:

1. Raise and support the front of the machine so the front wheel is free to rotate.

2. Loosen the locknut, then turn the brake cam lever connecting link enough to shorten it by about 0.25 in. (6mm). This procedure backs off

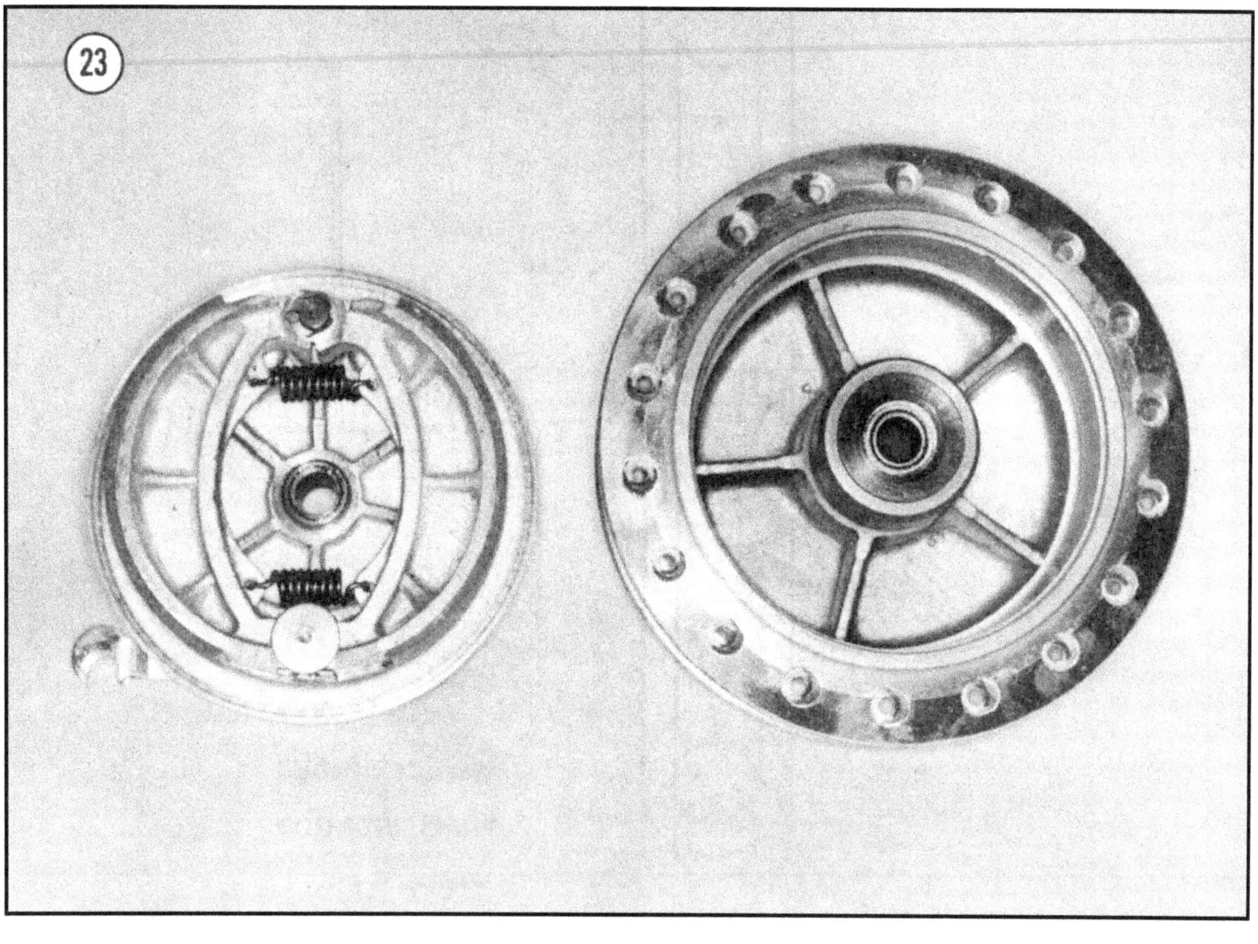

the second shoe so that it will not operate when the first shoe is adjusted.

3. Turn the adjusting nut at the front brake hand lever until the front wheel just begins to drag.

4. Turn the connecting link so that the second brake shoe makes light contact with the drum. Brake drag will increase slightly at this point. Tighten the locknut.

5. Readjust front brake hand lever as desired.

SHOCK ABSORBERS

The major parts of the shock absorber are a spring and hydraulic damping mechanism encased within the inner and outer shells. The shock absorbers may be adjusted to suit various riding conditions. Adjust both sides equally.

To remove the shock absorbers, remove the mounting bolts. Do not damage the rubber bushings as you remove and replace the bolts.

Some of the newer Montesa motorcycles, including the Cappra 250 V-75, are fitted with a special gas-filled Betor shock absorber. The procedure for removing the spring to check the shock absorber action is the same for any of the shock absorbers on any Montesa motorcycle. The gas pressure in the gas-filled Betors should, however, be measured and adjusted so the unit retains its damping qualities. Any shock absorber must be removed from the machine and its spring preload ring turned to give the maximum amount of spring length before removing the spring to check the damping action of the shock absorber.

1. Clamp the shock absorber in a vise with the pressure chamber cap facing upward.

2. Pry the rubber bumper stop down the shaft about 3 inches (**Figure 25**).

3. Use two 18 in. long wrenches to grip the coils of the spring and the shaft to compress the spring about an inch (**Figure 26**).

4. The spring retaining collar can then be pulled down and off the shaft. Gently release the pressure on the spring after the collar (**Figure 27**) has been removed.

5. Pry the metal cover from the top of the pressure chamber (**Figure 28**). Remove the valve cap (**Figure 29**).

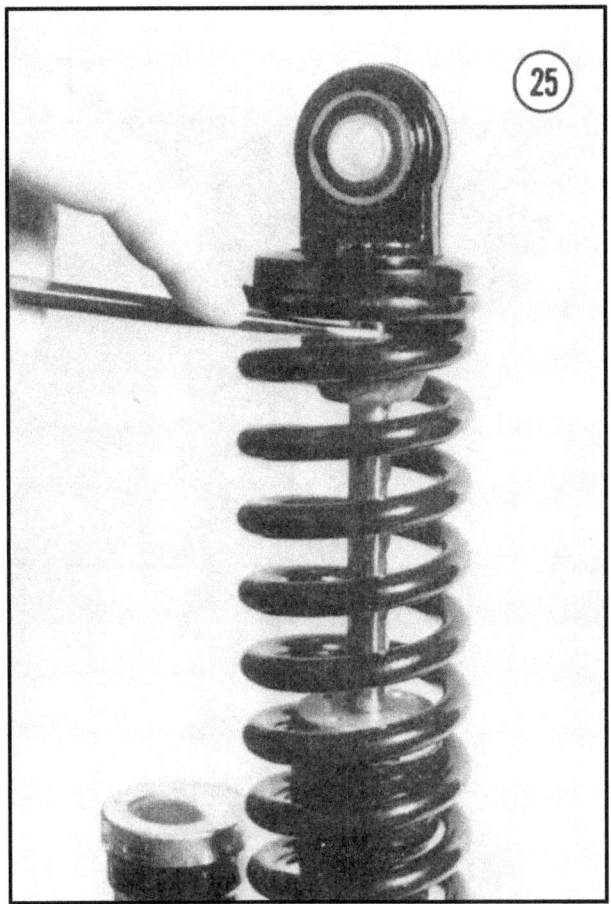

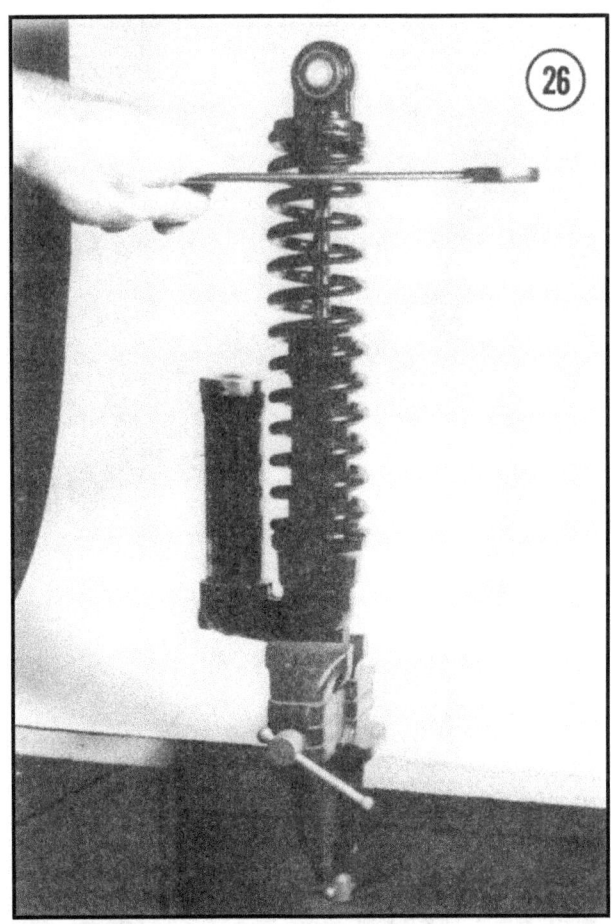

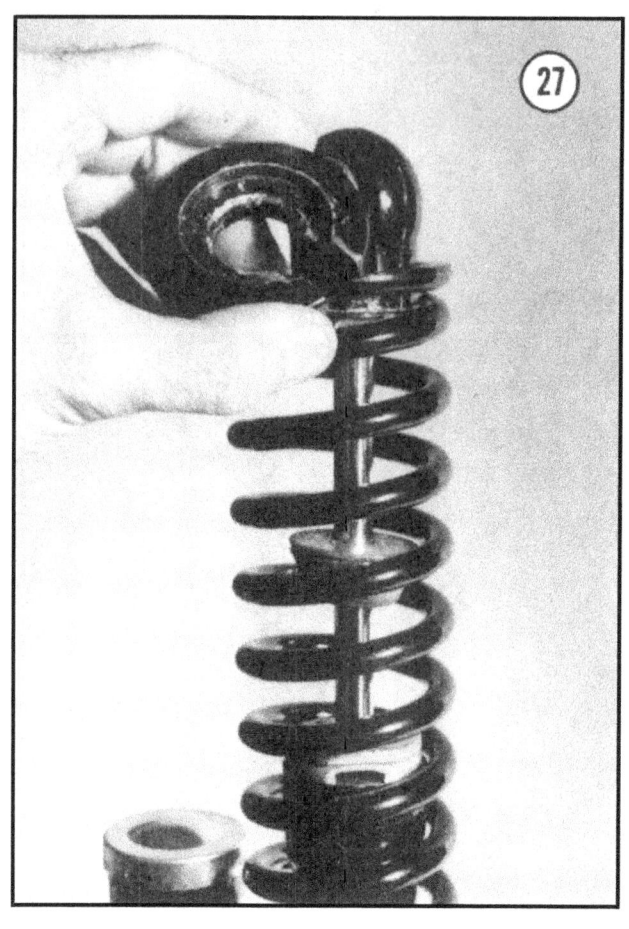

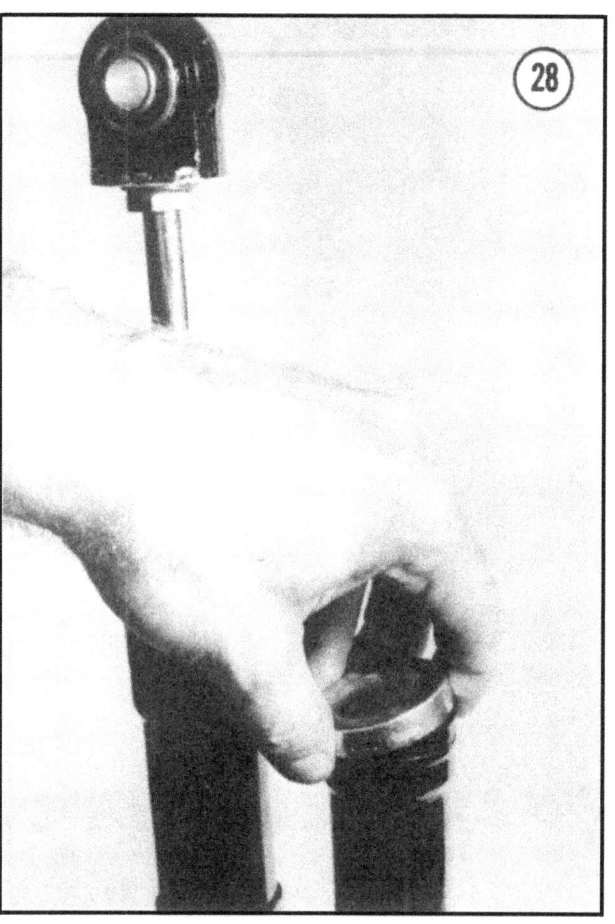

6. Depress the shock absorber completely (**Figure 30**). The damper rod should return to its fully extended position (*only* with the gas-filled Betors) if the gas pressure is correct. Check the pressure with a truck tire inflation gauge; it should be between 88 and 95 psi. Use nitrogen to repressurize the chamber if at all possible or dry air (**Figure 31**).

7. Check the damping force by attempting to compress and extend the units quickly. If there is no marked difference between the effort required to operate the unit quickly or slowly, or if there are any oil leaks, replace the shock absorber.

SWINGING ARM

The swinging arm, together with its shock absorbers, make up the rear suspension. Shimmy, wander, and wheel hop are common symptoms of worn swinging arm bushings.

To replace swinging arm bushings, proceed as follows:

1. Remove the rear wheel.
2. Remove the pivot shaft and the lower shock absorber mounting bolts.
3. Push out the old bushings.
4. Insert the metal bushing (**Figure 32**) first, from the inside.
5. Insert the rubber bushing (**Figure 33**). Brake fluid is a suitable rubber lubricant.

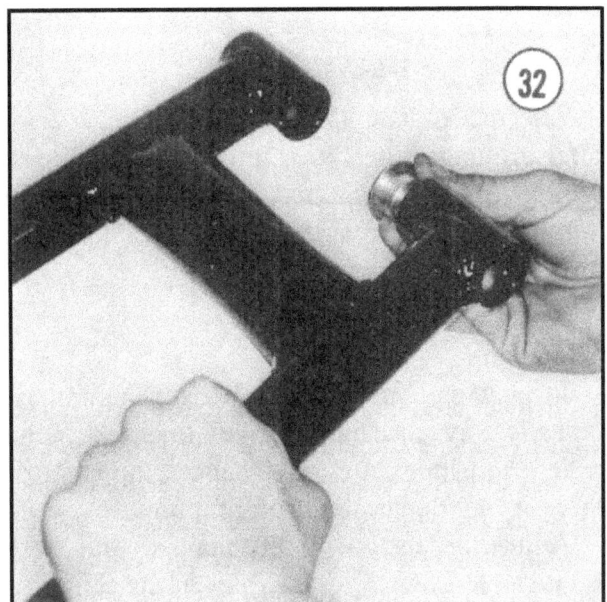

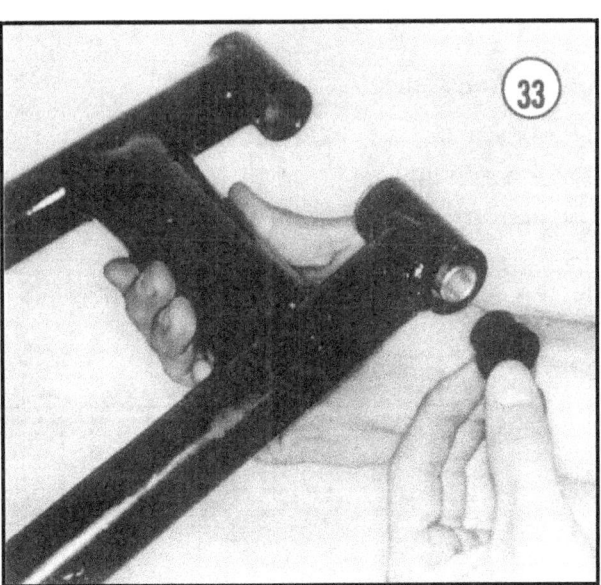

Check for bending of the pivot shaft. Replace pivot shaft if bent more than 0.02 in. (0.5mm).

If either of the arms is bent, the rear wheel will be out of alignment. Examine the weld carefully. Replace the entire swinging arm assembly if the weld is cracked.

EXHAUST SYSTEM

Carbon deposits within the exhaust pipe and muffler cause the engine to lose power. Clean the carbon from the baffle tube with a wire brush. If the deposits are too heavy to remove with a brush, heat the baffle tube with a torch and tap the tube lightly. Clean the carbon from the exhaust pipe by running a used drive chain through the pipe.

DRIVE CHAIN

The drive chain (**Figure 34**) becomes worn after prolonged use. Wear in the pins, bushings, and rollers causes the chain to stretch. Sliding between the roller surface and sprocket teeth also contributes to wear.

Inspection

Inspect and lubricate the drive chain periodically. Pay particular attention to cracks in the rollers and link plates, and replace the chain if there is any doubt about its condition.

Adjust the free-play in the chain so that there is one inch (25mm) vertical play in the center of the chain run with the machine on the ground and a rider in position.

Chain Adjustment

1. Loosen the rear axle nut (**Figure 35**).
2. Loosen the rear brake torque link nut (**Figure 36**).

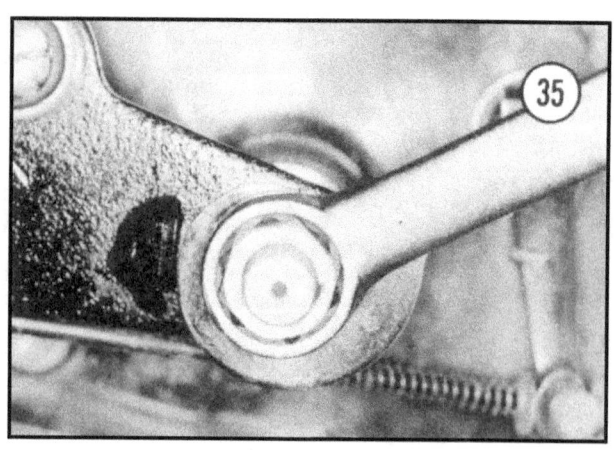

3. Turn each chain adjuster (**Figure 37**) as required to adjust the chain.
4. Sight along the chain from the rear to be sure that it runs true over the rear sprocket. Turn one or the other chain adjuster as required for chain alignment.
5. Tighten the torque link and axle nuts.

If the chain has become so worn that adjustment is not possible, use a chain breaker to shorten the chain by one link.

Install the master link so that the clip opening faces opposite to the direction of chain movement (**Figure 38**). Failure to do so may result in loss of the clip and resultant chain breakage.

REAR SPROCKET

Check the rear sprocket for wear or damaged teeth. Keep all sprocket bolts tight (**Figures 39 and 40**).

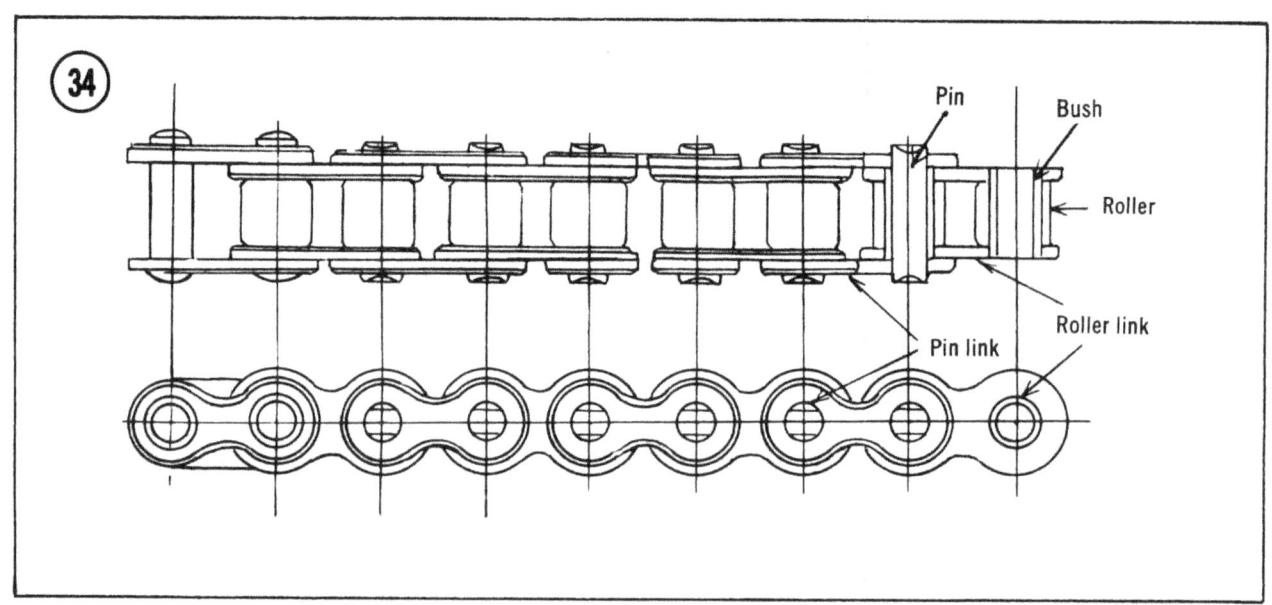

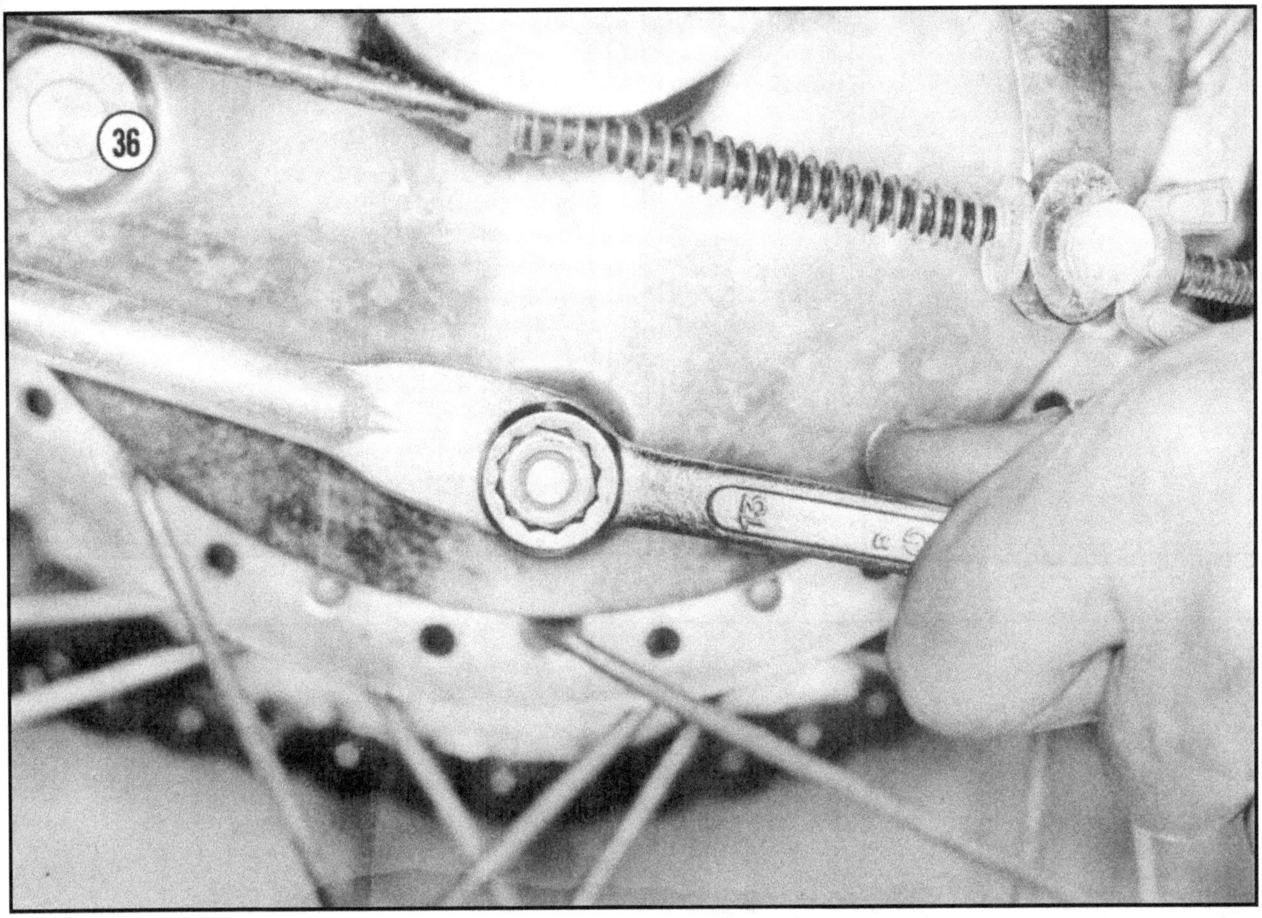

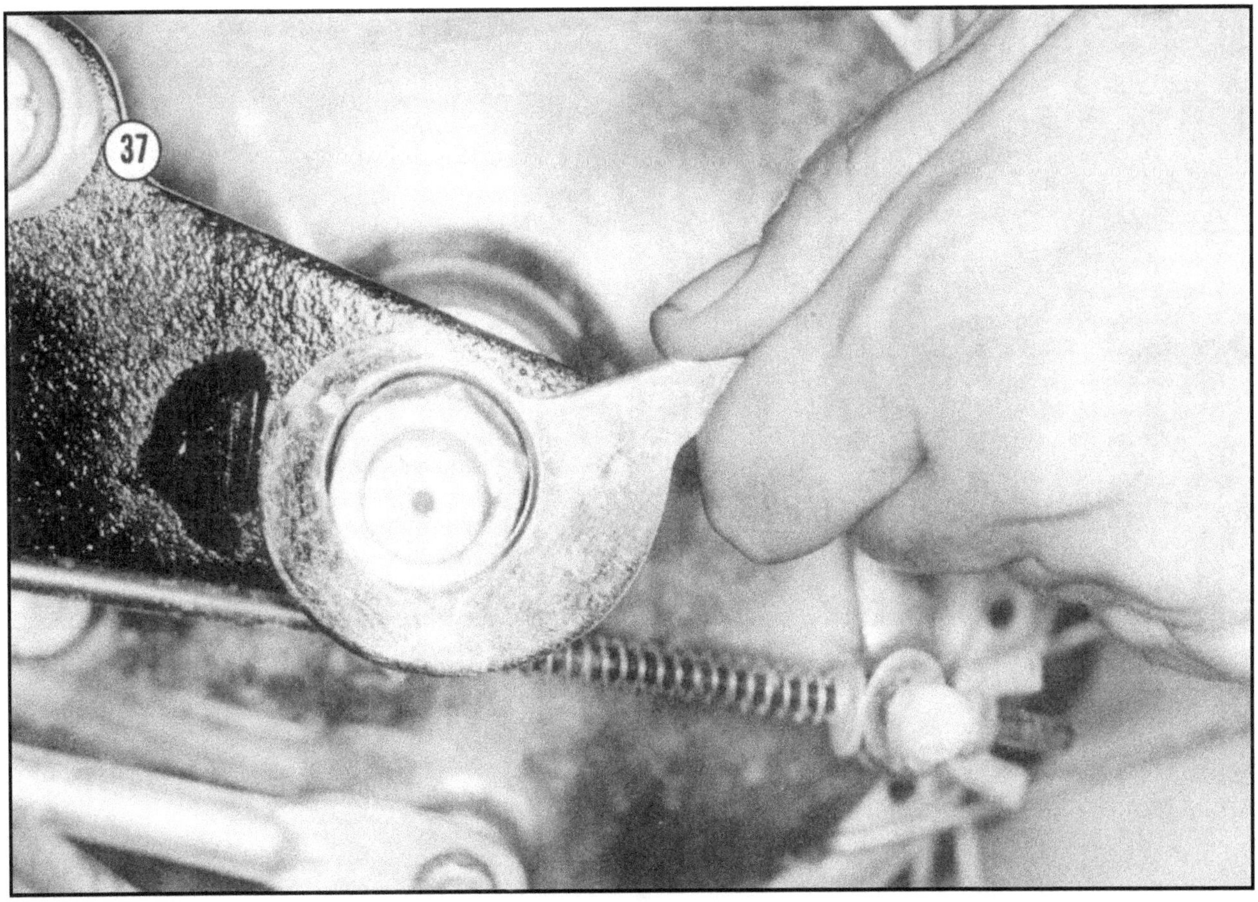

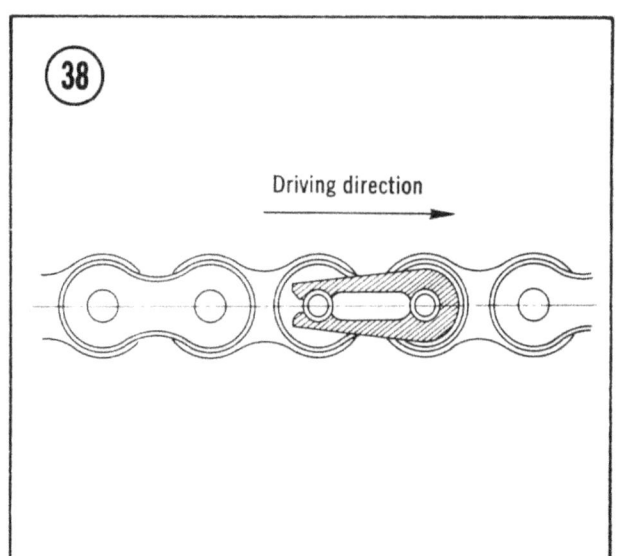

Driving direction

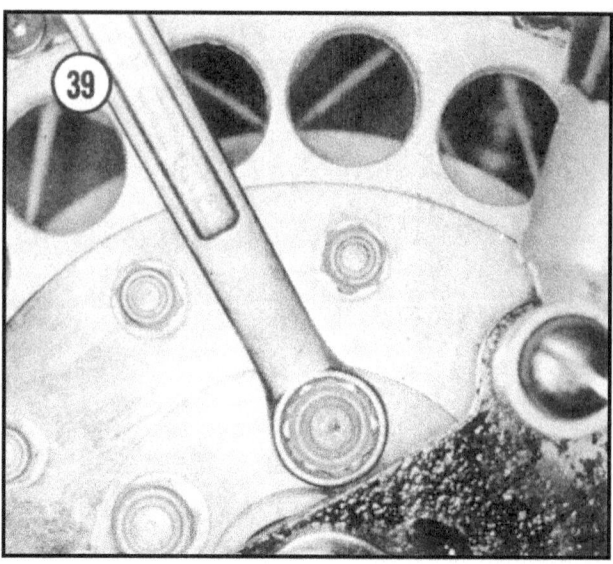

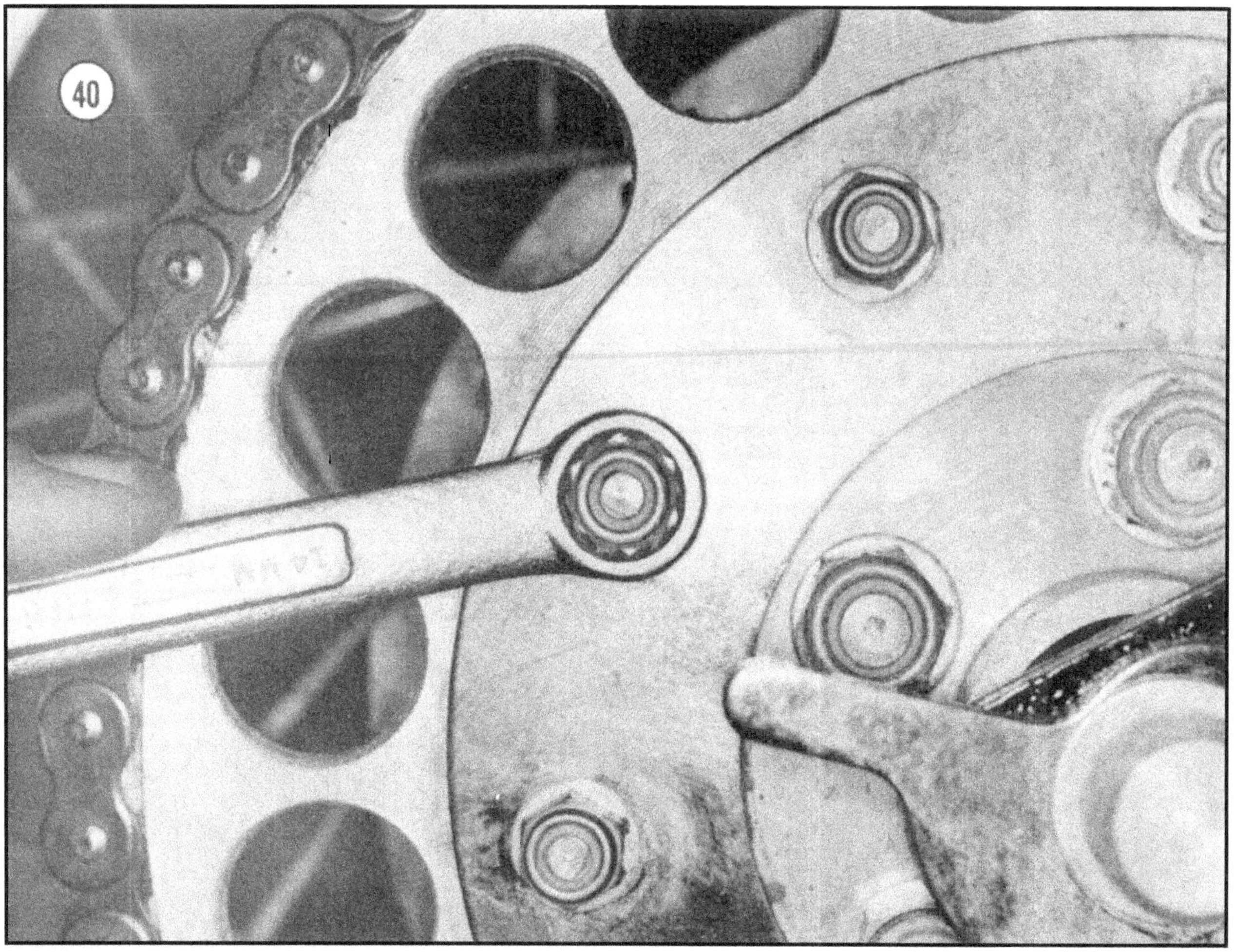

CHAPTER SIX

PERIODIC SERVICE AND MAINTENANCE

For the utmost in safety, performance, and useful life from your Montesa, it is necessary to make periodic inspections and adjustments. It frequently happens that minor problems found during such inspections are simple and inexpensive to correct at the time, but could lead to major problems later.

The following table is a suggested maintenance schedule to keep your Montesa in smooth running condition. The procedures for performing these services are described in the applicable chapters.

Maintenance Item	Miles		
	Initial 500	1000	2000
Change oil	X		X
Check spark plug	X		X
Ignition timing	X		X
Adjust clutch	X		X
Adjust carburetor	X		X
Clean air cleaner			X
Clean exhaust system			X
Adjust brakes	X	X	
Clean brakes		X	
Inspect chain	X		X
Check spokes		X	
Tighten all fastenings	X		X
Clean fuel strainer		X	
Remove carbon			X
Check battery	X	X	
Check electrical equipment	X	X	

CHAPTER SEVEN

TROUBLESHOOTING

Diagnosing motorcycle ills is relatively simple if you use orderly procedures and keep a few basic principles in mind.

Never assume anything. Don't overlook the obvious. If you are riding along and the bike suddenly quits, check the easiest, most accessible problem spots first. Is there gasoline in the tank? Is the gas petcock in the ON or RESERVE position? Has a spark plug wire fallen off? Check the ignition switch. Sometimes the weight of keys on a key ring may turn the ignition off suddenly.

If nothing obvious turns up in a cursory check, look a little further. Learning to recognize and describe symptoms will make repairs easier for you or a mechanic at the shop. Describe problems accurately and fully. Saying that "it won't run" isn't the same as saying "it quit on the highway at high speed and wouldn't start," or that "it sat in my garage for 3 months and then wouldn't start."

Gather as many symptoms together as possible to aid in diagnosis. Note whether the engine lost power gradually or all at once, what color smoke (if any) came from the exhaust, and so on. Remember that the more complicated a machine is, the easier it is to troubleshoot because symptoms point to specific problems.

You don't need fancy equipment or complicated test gear to determine whether repairs can be attempted at home. A few simple checks could save a large repair bill and time lost while the bike sits in a dealer's service department. On the other hand, be realistic and don't attempt repairs beyond your abilities. Service departments tend to charge heavily for putting together a disassembled engine that may have been abused. Some won't even take on such a job—so use common sense, and don't get in over your head.

OPERATING REQUIREMENTS

An engine needs 3 basics to run properly: correct gas/air mixture, compression, and a spark at the right time. If one or more are missing, the engine won't run. The electrical system is the weakest link of the three. More problems result from electrical breakdowns than from any other source. Keep that in mind before you begin tampering with carburetor adjustments and the like.

If a bike has been sitting for any length of time and refuses to start, check the battery if the machine is so equipped, for a charged condition first, and then look to the gasoline delivery system. This includes the tank, fuel petcocks, lines, and the carburetor. Rust may have formed in the tank, obstructing fuel flow. Gasoline deposits may have gummed up carburetor jets and air passages. Gasoline tends to lose its potency after standing for long periods. Condensation may contaminate it with water. Drain old gas and try starting with a fresh tankful.

Compression, or the lack of it, usually enters the picture only in the case of older machines. Worn or broken pistons, rings, and cylinder bores could prevent starting. Generally, a gradual power loss and harder and harder starting will be readily apparent in this case.

STARTING DIFFICULTIES

Check gas flow first. Remove the gas cap and look into the tank. If gas is present, pull off a fuel line at the carburetor and see if gas flows freely. If none comes out, the fuel tap may be shut off, blocked by rust or foreign matter, or the fuel line may be stopped up or kinked. If the carburetor is getting usable fuel, turn to the electrical system next.

Check that the battery is charged by turning on the lights or by beeping the horn. Refer to your owner's manual for starting procedures with a dead battery. Have the battery recharged if necessary.

Pull off the spark plug cap, remove the spark plug, and reconnect the cap. Lay the plug against the cylinder head so its base makes a good connection, and turn the engine over with the kickstarter. A fat, blue spark should jump across the electrodes. If there is no spark, or a weak one, you have electrical system trouble. Check for a defective plug by replacing it with a known good one. Don't assume a plug is good just because it's new.

Once the plug has been cleared of guilt, but there's still no spark, start backtracking through the system. If the contact at the end of the spark plug wire can be exposed, it can be held about 1/8 inch from the head while the engine is turned over to check for a spark. Remember to hold the wire only by its insulation to avoid a nasty shock. If the plug wires are dirty, greasy, or wet, wrap a rag around them so you don't get shocked. If you do feel a shock or see sparks along the wire, clean or replace the wire and/or its connections.

If there's no spark at the plug wire, look for loose connections at the coil and battery. If all seems in order there, check next for oil or dirty contact points. Clean points with electrical contact cleaner, or a strip of paper. On battery ignition models, with the ignition switch turned on, open and close the points manually with a screwdriver.

No spark at the points with this test indicates a failure in the ignition system. Refer to Chapter Three (*Electrical System*) for checkout procedures for the entire system and individual components. Refer to the same chapter for checking and setting ignition timing.

Note that spark plugs of an incorrect heat range (too cold) may cause hard starting. Set gap to specifications. If you have just ridden through a puddle or washed the bike and it won't start, dry off plugs and plug wire. Water may have entered the carburetor and fouled the fuel under these conditions, but a wet plug and wire are the more likely problem.

If a healthy spark occurs at the right time, and there is adequate gas flow to the carburetor, check the carburetor itself. Make sure all jets and air passages are clean, check float level, and adjust if necessary. Shake the float to check for gasoline inside it, and replace or repair as indicated. Check that the carburetor is mounted snugly, and no air is leaking past the mounting flange. Check for a clogged air filter.

Compression may be checked in the field by turning the kickstarter by hand and noting that an adequate resistance is felt, or by removing the spark plug and placing a finger over the plug hole and feeling for pressure.

POOR IDLING

Poor idling may be caused by incorrect carburetor adjustment, incorrect timing, or ignition system defects. Check the gas cap vent for an obstruction. Also check for loose carburetor mounting bolts or a poor carburetor flange gasket.

MISFIRING

Misfiring can be caused by a weak spark or dirty plugs. Check for fuel contamination. Run the machine at night or in a darkened garage to check for spark leaks along the plug wires and under the spark plug cap. If misfiring occurs only at certain throttle settings, refer to the carburetor chapter for the specific carburetor circuits involved. Misfiring under heavy load, as when climbing hills or accelerating, is usually caused by bad spark plugs.

FLAT SPOTS

If the engine seems to die momentarily when the throttle is opened and then recovers, check for a dirty main jet in the carburetor, water in the fuel, or an excessively lean mixture.

POWER LOSS

Poor condition of rings, pistons, or cylinders will cause a lack of power and speed. Ignition timing should be checked.

OVERHEATING

If the engine seems to run too hot all the time, be sure you are not idling it for long periods. Air-cooled engines are not designed to operate at a standstill for any length of time. Heavy stop and go traffic is hard on a motorcycle engine. Spark plugs of the wrong heat range can burn pistons. An excessively lean gas mixture may cause overheating. Check ignition timing. Don't ride in too high a gear. Broken or worn rings may permit compression gases to leak past them, heating heads and cylinders excessively. Check oil level and use the proper grade lubricants.

BACKFIRING

Check that the timing is not advanced too far. Check fuel for contamination.

ENGINE NOISES

Experience is needed to diagnose accurately in this area. Noises are hard to differentiate and harder yet to describe. Deep knocking noises usually mean main bearing failure. A slapping noise generally comes from loose pistons. A light knocking noise during acceleration may be a bad connecting rod bearing. Pinging, which sounds like marbles being shaken in a tin can, is caused by ignition advanced too far or gasoline with too low an octane rating. Pinging should be corrected immediately or piston damage will result. Compression leaks at the head/cylinder joint will sound like a rapid on and off squeal.

PISTON SEIZURE

Piston seizure is caused by incorrect piston clearances when fitted, fitting rings with improper end gap, too thin an oil being used, incorrect spark plug heat range, or incorrect ignition timing. Overheating from any cause may result in seizure.

EXCESSIVE VIBRATION

Excessive vibration may be caused by loose motor mounts, worn engine or transmission bearings, loose wheels, worn swinging arm bushings, a generally poor running engine, broken or cracked frame, or one that has been damaged in a collision. See also *Poor Handling*.

CLUTCH SLIP OR DRAG

Clutch slip may be due to worn plates, improper adjustment, or glazed plates. A dragging clutch could result from damaged or bent plates, improper adjustment, or uneven clutch spring pressure.

POOR HANDLING

Poor handling may be caused by improper tire pressures, a damaged frame or swinging arm, worn shocks or front forks, weak fork springs, a bent or broken steering stem, misaligned wheels, loose or missing spokes, worn tires, bent handlebars, worn wheel bearings, or dragging brakes.

BRAKE PROBLEMS

Sticking brakes may be caused by broken or weak return springs, improper cable or rod adjustment, or dry pivot and cam bushings. Grabbing brakes may be caused by greasy linings (which must be replaced). Brake grab may also be due to out-of-round drums or linings which have broken loose from the brake shoes. Glazed linings will cause loss of stopping power.

LIGHTING PROBLEMS

Bulbs which continuously burn out may be caused by excessive vibration, loose connections that permit sudden current surges, poor battery connections, or installation of the wrong type bulb.

A dead battery or one which discharges quickly may be caused by a faulty generator or rectifier. Check for loose or corroded terminals. Shorted battery cells or broken terminals will keep a battery from charging. Low water level will decrease a battery's capacity. A battery left uncharged after installation will sulphate, rendering it useless.

A majority of light and horn or other electrical accessory problems are caused by loose or corroded ground connections. Check those first, and then substitute known good units for easier troubleshooting.

TROUBLESHOOTING GUIDE

The "quick reference" guide (next page) summarizes the troubleshooting process. Use it to outline possible problem areas, then refer to the specific chapter or section involved.

TROUBLESHOOTING GUIDE

LOSS OF POWER

Cause	Things to Check	Cause	Things to check
Poor compression	Piston rings and cylinder Head gaskets Crankcase leaks	Improper mixture	Dirty air cleaner Restricted fuel flow Gas cap vent holes
Overheated engine	Lubricating oil supply Clogged cooling fins Ignition timing Slipping clutch Carbon in combustion chamber	Miscellaneous	Dragging brakes Tight wheel bearings Defective chain Clogged exhaust system

GEARSHIFTING DIFFICULTIES

Cause	Things to check	Cause	Things to check
Clutch	Adjustment Springs Friction plates Steel plates Oil quantity	Transmission	Oil quantity Oil grade Return spring or pin Change lever or spring Drum position plate Change drum Change forks

STEERING PROBLEMS

Problem	Things to check	Problem	Things to check
Hard steering	Tire pressure Steering damper adjustment Steering stem head Steering head bearings	Pulls to one side (cont.)	Defective swinging arm Defective steering head
Pulls to one side	Unbalanced shock absorbers Drive chain adjustment Front/rear wheel alignment Unbalanced tires	Shimmy	Drive chain adjustment Loose or missing spokes Deformed rims Worn wheel bearings Wheel balance

BRAKE TROUBLES

Problem	Things to check	Problem	Things to check
Poor brakes	Brake adjustment Oil or water on brake linings Loose linkage or cables	Noisy brakes	Worn or scratched lining Scratched brake drums Dirt in brakes
		Unadjustable brakes	Worn linings Worn drums Worn brake cams

CHAPTER EIGHT

SPECIFICATIONS

This chapter contains specifications and performance figures for various Montesa models. The tables are arranged in order of increasing engine size. Since there are differences between various models of the same engine size, be sure to consult the correct table for your motorcycle.

Specifications, COTA 123

ENGINE
  Bore and stroke (millimeters) 54.0 x 54.0
  Displacement (cubic centimeters) 123.6
  Compression ratio 12 to 1
  Horsepower 13 at 7,000 rpm

FUEL SYSTEM
  Carburetor: Amal 25mm

IGNITION SYSTEM
  Type: Magneto
  Spark plug: Champion N-4

TRANSMISSION
  Gear ratios
    1st 2.615 to 1
    2nd 2.133 to 1
    3rd 1.611 to 1
    4th 1.200 to 1
    5th 0.880 to 1
    6th 0.678 to 1

TIRE SIZE
  Front 2.50 - 20
  Rear   3.75 - 17

Specifications, CAPPRA 125 VA

ENGINE
  Bore and stroke (millimeters) 54 x 54
  Displacement (cubic centimeters) 123.7
  Compression ratio 14 to 1
  Horsepower NA

FUEL SYSTEM
  Carburetor: Bing 32mm

IGNITION SYSTEM
  Type: Electronic
  Spark plug: Bosch 370

TRANSMISSION
  Gear ratios
    1st 2.215 to 1
    2nd 1.764 to 1
    3rd 1.421 to 1
    4th 1.142 to 1
    5th 0.956 to 1
    6th 0.807 to 1

TIRE SIZE
  Front 3.00 - 21
  Rear 4.00 - 18

Specifications, COTA 123 TRAIL

ENGINE
  Bore and stroke (millimeters) 54 x 54
  Displacement (cubic centimeters) 123.6
  Compression ratio 12 to 1
  Horsepower 13 at 7,000 rpm

FUEL SYSTEM
  Carburetor: Amal 25mm

IGNITION SYSTEM
  Type: Magneto
  Spark plug: Champion N-4

TRANSMISSION
  Gear ratios
    1st 2.615 to 1
    2nd 2.133 to 1
    3rd 1.611 to 1
    4th 1.200 to 1
    5th 0.880 to 1
    6th 0.678 to 1

TIRE SIZE
  Front 2.50 - 20
  Rear 3.75 - 17

Specifications, COTA 172

ENGINE
  Bore and stroke (millimeters) 60.93 x 54
  Displacement (cubic centimeters) 157.5
  Compression ratio 11.5 to 1
  Horsepower NA

FUEL SYSTEM
  Carburetor: Amal 20mm

IGNITION SYSTEM
  Type: Magneto
  Spark plug: Champion N-4

TRANSMISSION
  Gear ratios
    1st 2.615 to 1
    2nd 2.133 to 1
    3rd 1.611 to 1
    4th 1.200 to 1
    5th 0.880 to 1
    6th 0.678 to 1

TIRE SIZE
  Front 2.75 - 21
  Rear 4.00 - 18

Specifications, CAPPRA 125-MX

ENGINE
  Bore and stroke (millimeters) 51.5 x 60
  Displacement (cubic centimeters) 124.98
  Compression ratio 14 to 1
  Horsepower 21 at 8,000 rpm

FUEL SYSTEM
  Carburetor: Amal 27mm

IGNITION SYSTEM
  Type: Electronic
  Spark plug: Champion L-57R

TRANSMISSION
  Gear Ratios
    1st 1.846 to 1
    2nd 1.467 to 1
    3rd 1.176 to 1
    4th 0.9474 to 1

TIRE SIZE
  Front 3.00 - 18
  Rear   4.00 - 18

Specifications, IMPALA - CROSS 175

ENGINE
  Bore and stroke (millimeters) 60.9 x 60
  Displacement (cubic centimeters) 174.7
  Compression ratio 14 to 1
  Horsepower 17 at 7,500 rpm

FUEL SYSTEM
  Carburetor: Amal 27mm

IGNITION SYSTEM
  Type: Magneto
  Spark plug: Champion L-56 or L-57

TRANSMISSION
  Gear ratios
    1st 1.86 to 1
    2nd 1.36 to 1
    3rd 1.15 to 1
    4th 0.95 to 1

TIRE SIZE
  Front 3.00 - 19
  Rear   3.50 - 19

Specifications, ENDURO

ENGINE
  Bore and stroke (millimeters) 60.9 x 60
  Displacement (cubic centimeters) 174.7
  Compression ratio 12 to 1
  Horsepower 16 at 6,500 rpm

FUEL SYSTEM
  Carburetor: IRZ 22mm

IGNITION SYSTEM
  Type: Magneto
  Spark plug: Champion L-5

TRANSMISSION
  Gear ratios
    1st 2.30 to 1
    2nd 1.38 to 1
    3rd 1.04 to 1
    4th 0.72 to 1

TIRE SIZE
  Front 2.75 - 19
  Rear   3.00 - 19

Specifications, IMPALA - SPORT

ENGINE
  Bore and stroke (millimeters) 60.9 x 60
  Displacement (cubic centimeters) 174.7
  Compression ratio 12 to 1
  Horsepower 18 at 7,000 rpm

FUEL SYSTEM
  Carburetor: Amal 25mm

IGNITION SYSTEM
  Type: Magneto
  Spark plug: Champion L-5

TRANSMISSION
  Gear ratios
    1st 2.07 to 1
    2nd 1.38 to 1
    3rd 1.04 to 1
    4th 0.87 to 1

TIRE SIZE
  Front 2.50 - 19
  Rear   2.75 - 19

Specifications, IMPALA

ENGINE

Bore and stroke (millimeters) 60.9 x 60
Displacement (cubic centimeters) 174.7
Compression ratio 8.5 to 1
Horsepower 10.5 at 5,500 rpm

FUEL SYSTEM

Carburetor: IRZ 22mm

IGNITION SYSTEM

Type: Magneto
Spark plug: Champion L-86

TRANSMISSION

Gear ratios
   1st 2.30 to 1
   2nd 1.38 to 1
   3rd 1.04 to 1
   4th 0.79 to 1

TIRE SIZE

Front 2.75 - 19
Rear 2.75 - 19

Specifications, KENYA

ENGINE

Bore and stroke (millimeters) 60.9 x 60
Displacement (cubic centimeters) 174.7
Compression ratio 8.5 to 1
Horsepower 12 at 5,500 rpm

FUEL SYSTEM

Carburetor: Amal 22mm

IGNITION SYSTEM

Type: Magneto
Spark plug: Champion L-86

TRANSMISSION

Gear ratios
   1st 2.30 to 1
   2nd 1.38 to 1
   3rd 1.04 to 1
   4th 0.79 to 1

TIRE SIZE

Front 2.50 - 17
Rear 3.00 - 17

Specifications, COMMANDO 175

ENGINE

Bore and stroke (millimeters) 60.9 x 60
Displacement (cubic centimeters) 174.7
Compression ratio 8.5 to 1
Horsepower 9 at 5,500 rpm

FUEL SYSTEM

Carburetor: Amal 18mm

IGNITION SYSTEM

Type: Magneto
Spark plug: Champion L-86

TRANSMISSION

Gear ratios
   1st 2.30 to 1
   2nd 1.38 to 1
   3rd 1.04 to 1
   4th 0.79 to 1

TIRE SIZE

Front 2.75 - 18
Rear 2.75 - 18

Specifications, 250 TRAILS

ENGINE

Bore and stroke (millimeters) 72.5 x 60
Displacement (cubic centimeters) 247.69
Compression ratio 9 to 1
Horsepower 19 at 7,000 rpm

FUEL SYSTEM

Carburetor: IRZ 24mm

IGNITION SYSTEM

Type: Magneto
Spark plug: Champion L-86

TRANSMISSION

Gear ratios
   1st 2.58 to 1
   2nd 2.07 to 1
   3rd 1.68 to 1
   4th 0.72 to 1

TIRE SIZE

Front 3.00 - 21
Rear 4.00 - 18

Specifications, IMPALA - CROSS 250

ENGINE
  Bore and stroke (millimeters) 72.5 x 60
  Displacement (cubic centimeters) 247.69
  Compression ratio 12 to 1
  Horsepower 23.1 at 8,000 rpm

FUEL SYSTEM
  Carburetor: Amal 27mm

IGNITION SYSTEM
  Type: Magneto
  Spark plug: Champion L-58R or L-57R

TRANSMISSION
  Gear ratios
    1st 1.86 to 1
    2nd 1.38 to 1
    3rd 1.15 to 1
    4th 0.95 to 1

TIRE SIZE
  Front 3.00 - 19
  Rear   4.00 - 18

Specifications, COTA 247 TRAIL

ENGINE
  Bore and stroke (millimeters) 72.5 x 60
  Displacement (cubic centimeters) 247.69
  Compression ratio 9.75 to 1
  Horsepower 19 at 6,500 rpm

FUEL SYSTEM
  Carburetor: Amal 27mm

IGNITION SYSTEM
  Type: Magneto
  Spark plug: Champion L-10

TRANSMISSION
  Gear ratios
    1st 2.60 to 1
    2nd 2.08 to 1
    3rd 1.64 to 1
    4th 1.05 to 1
    5th 0.71 to 1

TIRE SIZE
  Front 3.00 - 21
  Rear   4.00 - 18

Specifications, SPORT 250
(From Serial No. 15M0001)

ENGINE
  Bore and stroke (millimeters) 72.5 x 60
  Displacement (cubic centimeters) 247.69
  Compression ratio 10.5 to 1
  Horsepower 26 at 7,500 rpm

FUEL SYSTEM
  Carburetor: Amal 30mm

IGNITION SYSTEM
  Type: Magneto
  Spark plug: Champion L-5

TRANSMISSION
  Gear ratios
    1st 2.30 to 1
    2nd 1.38 to 1
    3rd 1.04 to 1
    4th 0.86 to 1

TIRE SIZE
  Front 2.50 - 19
  Rear   2.25 - 19

Specifications, LA CROSS 66/67

ENGINE
  Bore and stroke (millimeters) 72.5 x 60
  Displacement (cubic centimeters) 247.69
  Compression ratio 13 to 1
  Horsepower 30 at 7,000 rpm

FUEL SYSTEM
  Carburetor: Amal 30mm

IGNITION SYSTEM
  Type: Magneto
  Spark plug: Champion L-58R or L-57R

TRANSMISSION
  Gear ratios
    1st 2.07 or 1.86 to 1
    2nd 1.38 to 1
    3rd 1.15 to 1
    4th 0.95 to 1

TIRE SIZE
  Front 3.50 - 19
  Rear   4.00 - 18

Specifications, SCORPION 250

ENGINE
  Bore and stroke (millimeters) 72.5 x 60
  Displacement (cubic centimeters) 247.69
  Compression ratio 9 to 1
  Horsepower 21 at 7,000 rpm

FUEL SYSTEM
  Carburetor: Amal 30mm

IGNITION SYSTEM
  Type: Magneto
  Spark plug: Champion L-5

TRANSMISSION
  Gear ratios
    1st 2.30 to 1
    2nd 1.38 to 1
    3rd 1.04 to 1
    4th 0.79 to 1

TIRE SIZE
  Front 3.00-21
  Rear   4.00-18

Specifications, CAPPRA 250

ENGINE
  Bore and stroke (millimeters) 72.5 x 60
  Displacement (cubic centimeters) 247.69
  Compression ratio 13 to 1
  Horsepower 30 at 6,500 rpm

FUEL SYSTEM
  Carburetor: Amal 32mm

IGNITION SYSTEM
  Type: Magneto
  Spark plug: Champion L-58R or L-57R

TRANSMISSION
  Gear ratios
    1st 1.77 to 1
    2nd 1.46 to 1
    3rd 1.17 to 1
    4th 0.94 to 1

TIRE SIZE
  Front 3.00 - 21
  Rear   4.00 - 18

Specifications, SPORT 250
(From Serial No. 25M0001)

ENGINE
  Bore and stroke (millimeters) 72.5 x 60
  Displacement (cubic centimeters) 247.69
  Compression ratio 10.5 to 1
  Horsepower 26 at 7,500 rpm

FUEL SYSTEM
  Carburetor: Amal 30mm

IGNITION SYSTEM
  Type: Magneto
  Spark plug: Champion L-5

TRANSMISSION
  Gear ratios
    1st 2.30 to 1
    2nd 1.38 to 1
    3rd 1.04 to 1
    4th 0.86 to 1

TIRE SIZE
  Front 3.25 - 19
  Rear   3.50 - 19

Specifications, COTA 247

ENGINE
  Bore and stroke (millimeters) 72.5 x 60
  Displacement (cubic centimeters) 247.69
  Compression ratio 9.75 to 1
  Horsepower 19 at 6,500 rpm

FUEL SYSTEM
  Carburetor: Amal 27mm

IGNITION SYSTEM
  Type: Magneto
  Spark plug: Champion L-10

TRANSMISSION
  Gear ratios
    1st 2.60 to 1
    2nd 2.08 to 1
    3rd 1.64 to 1
    4th 1.05 to 1
    5th 0.71 to 1

TIRE SIZE
  Front 3.00 - 21
  Rear   4.00 - 18

Specifications, KING SCORPION

ENGINE
  Bore and stroke (millimeters) 72.5 x 60
  Displacement (cubic centimeters) 247.69
  Compression ratio 10 to 1
  Horsepower 22.8 at 6,500 rpm

FUEL SYSTEM
  Carburetor: Amal 27mm

IGNITION SYSTEM
  Type: Electronic
  Spark plug: Champion L-5

TRANSMISSION
  Gear ratios
    1st 2.272 to 1
    2nd 1.571 to 1
    3rd 1.176 to 1
    4th 0.894 to 1
    5th 0.714 to 1

TIRE SIZE
  Front 3.00 - 21
  Rear   4.00 - 18

Specifications, CAPPRA 250-FIVE

ENGINE
  Bore and stroke (millimeters) 72.5 x 60
  Displacement (cubic centimeters) 247.69
  Compression ratio 13 to 1
  Horsepower 33 at 6,500 rpm

FUEL SYSTEM
  Carburetor: Amal 32mm

IGNITION SYSTEM
  Type: Magneto
  Spark plug: Champion N-58R

TRANSMISSION
  Gear ratios
    1st 2.00 to 1
    2nd 1.46 to 1
    3rd 1.17 to 1
    4th 0.94 to 1
    5th 0.85 to 1

TIRE SIZE
  Front 3.00 - 18
  Rear   4.00 - 18

Specifications, KING SCORPION AUTOMIX

ENGINE
  Bore and stroke (millimeters) 70.0 x 64
  Displacement (cubic centimeters) 246.3
  Compression ratio 10 to 1

FUEL SYSTEM
  Carburetor: Bing 32mm

IGNITION SYSTEM
  Type: Electronic
  Spark plug: Champion N-3

TRANSMISSION
  Gear ratios
    1st 2.600 to 1
    2nd 1.615 to 1
    3rd 1.117 to 1
    4th 0.833 to 1
    5th 0.681 to 1

TIRE SIZE
  Front 3.00 - 21
  Rear   4.00 - 18

Specifications, CAPPRA 250-GP

ENGINE
  Bore and stroke (millimeters) 72.5 x 60
  Displacement (cubic centimeters) 247.69
  Compression ratio 13 to 1
  Horsepower 32 at 6,500 rpm

FUEL SYSTEM
  Carburetor: Amal 32mm

IGNITION SYSTEM
  Type: Magneto
  Spark plug: Champion L-58R or L-57R

TRANSMISSION
  Gear ratios
    1st 1.84 to 1
    2nd 1.46 to 1
    3rd 1.17 to 1
    4th 0.94 to 1

TIRE SIZE
  Front 3.00 - 21
  Rear   4.00 - 18

Specifications, CAPPRA 250-MX

ENGINE
  Bore and stroke (millimeters) 72.5 x 60
  Displacement (cubic centimeters) 247.69
  Compression ratio 13 to 1
  Horsepower 35 at 7,000 rpm

FUEL SYSTEM
  Carburetor: Amal 32mm

IGNITION SYSTEM
  Type: Electronic
  Spark plug: Champion L-57R

TRANSMISSION
  Gear ratios
    1st 1.846 to 1
    2nd 1.467 to 1
    3rd 1.176 to 1
    4th 0.9474 to 1
    5th 0.8000 to 1

TIRE SIZE
  Front 3.00 - 21
  Rear   4.00 - 18

Specifications, ENDURO 250

ENGINE
  Bore and stroke (millimeters) 70 x 64
  Displacement (cubic centimeters) 246.3
  Compression ratio 12 to 1
  Horsepower NA

FUEL SYSTEM
  Carburetor: Amal Mk II 32mm

IGNITION SYSTEM
  Type: Electronic
  Spark plug: Champion N-3

TRANSMISSION
  Gear ratios
    1st 2.600 to 1
    2nd 1.615 to 1
    3rd 1.117 to 1
    4th 0.833 to 1
    5th 0.681 to 1

TIRE SIZE
  Front 3.00 - 21
  Rear   4.50 - 18

Specifications, CAPPRA 250 VR

ENGINE
  Bore and stroke (millimeters) 70 x 64
  Displacement (cubic centimeters) 246.3
  Compression ratio 12 to 1

FUEL SYSTEM
  Carburetor: Bing 34mm

IGNITION SYSTEM
  Type: Electronic
  Spark plug: Champion N-60R

TRANSMISSION
  Gear ratios
    1st 1.846 to 1
    2nd 1.466 to 1
    3rd 1.176 to 1
    4th 0.947 to 1
    5th 0.800 to 1

TIRE SIZE
  Front 3.00 - 21
  Rear   4.50 - 18

Specifications, RAPITA 250

ENGINE
  Bore and stroke (millimeters) 70 x 64
  Displacement (cubic centimeters) 246.3
  Compression ratio 12 to 1
  Horsepower NA

FUEL SYSTEM
  Carburetor: Amal Mk II 32mm

IGNITION SYSTEM
  Type: Electronic
  Spark plug: Champion N-3

TRANSMISSION
  Gear ratios
    1st 2.600 to 1
    2nd 1.615 to 1
    3rd 1.117 to 1
    4th 0.833 to 1
    5th 0.681 to 1

TIRE SIZE
  Front 3.25 - 19
  Rear   3.50 - 18

Specifications, CAPPRA 250 V-75

ENGINE
  Bore and stroke (millimeters) 70 x 64
  Displacement (cubic centimeters) 246.3
  Compression ratio 12 to 1
  Horsepower NA

FUEL SYSTEM
  Carburetor: Bing 34mm

IGNITION SYSTEM
  Type: Electronic
  Spark plug: Champion N-57R

TRANSMISSION
  Gear ratios
    1st 1.846 to 1
    2nd 1.466 to 1
    3rd 1.176 to 1
    4th 0.947 to 1
    5th 0.800 to 1

TIRE SIZE
  Front 3.00 - 21
  Rear 4.50 - 18

Specifications, CAPPRA 360-GP (From Serial No. 46M0001)

ENGINE
  Bore and stroke (millimeters) 78 x 73.5
  Displacement (cubic centimeters) 351.2
  Compression 11 to 1
  Horsepower 38 at 6,500 rpm

FUEL SYSTEM
  Carburetor: Amal 32mm

IGNITION SYSTEM
  Type: Magneto
  Spark plug: Champion N-58R

TRANSMISSION
  Gear ratios
    1st 1.77 to 1
    2nd 1.46 to 1
    3rd 1.17 to 1
    4th 0.94 to 1

TIRE SIZE
  Front 3.00 - 21
  Rear 4.00 - 18

Specifications, CAPPRA 360-GP (From Serial No. 36M0300)

ENGINE
  Bore and stroke (millimeters) 78 x 73.5
  Displacement (cubic centimeters) 351.2
  Compression ratio 12.75 to 1
  Horsepower 39.5 at 6,500 rpm

FUEL SYSTEM
  Carburetor: Amal 32mm

IGNITION SYSTEM
  Type: Magneto
  Spark plug: Champion N-58R

TRANSMISSION
  Gear ratios
    1st 1.77 to 1
    2nd 1.46 to 1
    3rd 1.17 to 1
    4th 0.94 to 1

TIRE SIZE
  Front 3.00 - 21
  Rear 4.00 - 18

Specifications, CAPPRA 360-GP (From Serial No. 46M0600)

ENGINE
  Bore and stroke (millimeters) 78 x 73.5
  Displacement (cubic centimeters) 351.2
  Compression ratio 11 to 1
  Horsepower 38 at 6,500 rpm

FUEL SYSTEM
  Carburetor: Amal 32mm

IGNITION SYSTEM
  Type: Magneto
  Spark plug: Champion N-57R

TRANSMISSION
  Gear ratios
    1st 2.00 to 1
    2nd 1.46 to 1
    3rd 1.17 to 1
    4th 0.94 to 1

TIRE SIZE
  Front 3.50 - 19
  Rear 4.00 - 18

Specifications, CAPPRA 360-DS

ENGINE
    Bore and stroke (millimeters) 78 x 73.5
    Displacement (cubic centimeters) 351.2
    Compression ratio 12.75 to 1
    Horsepower 39.5 at 6,500 rpm

FUEL SYSTEM
    Carburetor: Amal 32mm

IGNITION SYSTEM
    Type: Magneto
    Spark plug: Champion N-58R

TRANSMISSION
    Gear ratios
        1st 2.00 to 1
        2nd 1.46 to 1
        3rd 1.17 to 1
        4th 0.94 to 1

TIRE SIZE
    Front 3.25 - 19
    Rear   4.00 - 18

INDEX

A

Air cleaner 5
Automix pump 49

B

Battery 64-65
Bearings 45-48
Brake light switch 65
Brakes
    Adjustment 104-105
    Description 101-104
    Inspection 104
    Troubleshooting 114, 116
Breaker points, magneto ignition system ...51-53

C

Carbon removal (combustion chamber) 5-6
Carburetor, Amal concentric
    Disassembly 76-80
    Inspection 80-81
    Reassembly 81
Carburetor, Amal Mark II
    Disassembly 86-89
    Inspection 89-91
    Reassembly 91
Carburetor, Amal monobloc
    Disassembly 72-75
    Inspection 75-76
    Reassembly 76
Carburetor, Bing
    Disassembly 81-82
    Inspection 82-86
    Reassembly 86
Carburetor, general
    Description 66
    Float level adjustment 91
    Float mechanism 67
    Main fuel system 71-72
    Modifications 92
    Overhaul frequency 72
    Pilot system 67-70
    Problems, miscellaneous 92
    Speed range adjustments 91-92
    Tickler system 72
Chassis
    Brakes 101-105
    Drive chain 108
    Exhaust system 108
    Forks, front 93-100
    Frame 93
    Handlebar 93
    Shock absorbers 105-106
    Sprocket, rear 108
    Swinging arm 106-107
    Wheels and tires 101
Clutch
    Adjustment 22
    Disc replacement 21-22
    Inspection 19
    Oil changing 6
    Removal 18
    Slip or drag 114
Condenser, magneto ignition system 57
Crankcase covers 14
Crankcase halves
    Disassembly 31-33
    Inspection 33
    Reassembly 33-34
Crankshaft
    Bearings 45-48
    Inspection 43-44
    Oil seals 48-49
    Overhaul 44-45
    Removal 43
Cylinder and cylinder head
    Bore diameter 10
    Carbon removal 7, 8
    Cylinder head removal and installation ... 7
    Cylinder inspection and installation 8
    Cylinder removal 7-8
    Sleeve replacement 8-11

D

Drive chain 108

E

Electrical system
    Battery 64-65
    Electronic ignition system 59-63
    Lights 65
    Magneto ignition system 51-59
    Rectifier 63
    Spark plug 63-64
Electronic ignition system
    Cautions 63
    Description and operation 59-60
    Ignition timing 60-61
    Maintenance 60
    Troubleshooting 62-63
Engine
    Air cleaner 5
    Automix pump 49

Bearings 45-48
Carbon removal 5-6
Crankcase covers 14
Crankcase halves 31-34
Crankshaft 43-45
Cylinder and cylinder head 7-11
Disassembly, preparation for 6-7
Engine sprocket 14-15
Magneto 15-17
Oil change 6
Oil seals 48-49
Operating requirements 112-113
Piston, pin and rings 11-13
Principles of operation 4-5
Exhaust system 108

F

Fork, front
   Check valve 100
   Disassembly 94-98
   Inspection 98-100
   Reassembly and installation 100
   Removal 94
Frame 93

G

Gearshifting difficulties 116
General information 1-3

H

Handlebar 93
Headlight 65

I

Idling, poor 113
Ignition system (see Magneto ignition system or Electronic ignition system)

K

Kickstarter
   Type 1 .... 29, 34-43
   Type 2 29-31

L

Lights 65

M

Magneto
   Auxiliary flywheel 16
   Installation 16
   Removal 15-16

Magneto ignition system
   Breaker point installation 52
   Breaker point maintenance 51-52
   Condenser 57
   Ignition coil 56-57
   Ignition timing 54-56
   Magneto operation 51
   Magneto troubleshooting 57-59
   Point gap adjustment 52-54
Maintenance, periodic 111
Misfiring 113-114

O

Oil change 6
Oil pump, Automix 49
Oil seals 48-49
Overheating 114

P

Piston, pin, and rings
   Pin 11
   Piston clearance 13
   Piston installation 13
   Piston seizure 114
   Ring replacement 12-13
Primary drive gear
   Inspection and installation 23
   Removal 22-23

R

Rectifier 63

S

Safety hints 2
Service hints 1
Shift mechanism (see page 23 for discussion of types)
   Adustment, Type 1 26
   Disassembly, Type 1 23
   Disassembly, Type 2 26-28
   Inspection, Type 1 24
   Inspection, Type 2 28
   Reassembly, Type 1 24-26
   Reassembly, Type 2 28
Shock absorbers 105-106
Spark plug 63-64
Specifications
   Cappra 125-MX 119
   Cappra 125 VA 118
   Cappra 250 122
   Cappra 250-Five 123
   Cappra 250-GP 123

Cappra 250-MX 124
Cappra 250 VR 124
Cappra 250 V-75 125
Cappra 360-DS 126
Cappra 360-GP (from serial
   No. 36M0300) 125
Cappra 360-GP (from serial
   No. 46M0001) 125
Cappra 360-GP (from serial
   No. 46M0600) 125
Commando 175 120
Cota 123 118
Cota 123 Trail 118
Cota 172 118
Cota 247 122
Cota 247 Trail 121
Enduro 119
Enduro 250 124
Impala 120
Impala - Cross 175 119
Impala - Cross 250 121
Impala - Sport 119
Kenya 120
King Scorpion 123
King Scorpion Automix 123
La Cross 66/67 121
Rapita 250 124
Scorpion 250 122
Sport 250 (from serial No. 15M0001) ... 121
Sport 250 (from serial No. 25M0001) ... 122
250 Trails 120
Spokes 101
Sprocket, rear 108
Starting difficulties 113
Steering problems 116
Supplies, expendable 2
Swinging arm 106-107

T

Tools 1-2
Transmission
   Bearings 45
   Disassembly, 5-speed 34
   Disassembly, 6-speed 38
   End play adjustment 40-43
   Inspection, 5-speed 34
   Inspection, 6-speed 38-40
   Oil changing 6
   Reassembly, 5-speed 34-38
   Reassembly, 6-speed 40
Troubleshooting
   Backfiring 114
   Brake problems 114
   Clutch slip or drag 114
   Engine noises 114
   Engine operating requirements ... 113
   Flat spots 114
   Gearshifting difficulties 116
   General information 112
   Handling, poor 114
   Idling, poor 113
   Lighting problems 115
   Misfiring 113-114
   Overheating 114
   Piston seizure 114
   Power loss 114
   Starting difficulties 113
   Steering problems 116
   Troubleshooting summary 116
   Vibration, excessive.............. 114

W

Wheels and tires 101

VELOCEPRESS MANUALS – MOTORCYCLE BY MAKE

AJS 1932-1948 SINGLES & TWINS 250cc THRU 1000cc (BOOK OF)
AJS 1945-1960 SINGLES 350cc & 500cc MODELS 16 & 18 (BOOK OF)
AJS 1955-1965 SINGLES 350cc & 500cc (BOOK OF)
AJS 1957-1966 FACTORY WSM - ALL SINGLES & TWINS
AJS 1959-1969 FACTORY WSM G80CS G85CS & P11 OFF ROAD
AJS 1968-1974 STORMER FACTORY WSM & PARTS LIST
ARIEL UP TO 1932 (BOOK OF)
ARIEL 1932-1939 PREWAR MODELS (BOOK OF)
ARIEL 1933-1951 (WORKSHOP MANUAL)
ARIEL 1939-1960 4 STROKE SINGLES (BOOK OF)
ARIEL 1958-1964 LEADER & ARROW FACTORY WSM & PARTS LIST
ARIEL 1958-1964 LEADER & ARROW (BOOK OF)
BMW R26 R27 (1956-1967) FACTORY WORKSHOP MANUAL
BMW R50 R50S R60 R69S (1955-1969) FACTORY WORKSHOP MANUAL
BMW R50/5 R60/5 R75/5 (1969-1973) FACTORY WORKSHOP MANUAL
BRIDGESTONE 90 SERIES FACTORY WSM & PARTS CATALOGUE
BRIDGESTONE 175 SERIES FACTORY WSM & PARTS CATALOGUE
BRIDGESTONE 350 SERIES FACTORY WSM & PARTS CATALOGUES
BSA SERVICE SHEETS MASTER CATALOGUE ALL MODELS 1945-1967
BSA BANTAM D1 TO D7 1948-1966 FACTORY SERVICE SHEETS MANUAL
BSA BANTAM ALL MODELS FROM 1948 ONWARDS (BOOK OF)
BSA BANTAM D14 FACTORY SERVICE MANUAL
BSA DANDY FACTORY WORKSHOP MANUAL (COMPILATION)
BSA SINGLES & V-TWINS UP TO 1926 inc. 1927 SUPPLEMENT (BOOK OF)
BSA SINGLES & V-TWINS UP TO 1930 (BOOK OF)
BSA SINGLES & V-TWINS UP TO 1935 (BOOK OF)
BSA SINGLES & V-TWINS 1936-1939 (BOOK OF)
BSA C10, C11 & C12 1945-1958 FACTORY SERVICE SHEETS MANUAL
BSA OHV & SV SINGLES 250-600cc 1945-1959 (BOOK OF)
BSA C15 & B40 1958-1967 FACTORY SERVICE SHEETS MANUAL
BSA OHV & SV SINGLES 250cc (ONLY) 1954-1970 (BOOK OF)
BSA B31, B32, B33 & B34 1945-60 FACTORY SERVICE SHEETS MANUAL
BSA OHV SINGLES 350 & 500cc 1955-1967 (BOOK OF)
BSA M20, M21 & M33 1945-1963 FACTORY SERVICE SHEETS MANUAL
BSA TWINS A7 & A10 1948-1962 FACTORY SERVICE SHEETS MANUAL
BSA TWINS A7 & A10 1948-1962 (BOOK OF)
BSA TWINS A50 & A65 1962-1965 FACTORY WORKSHOP MANUAL
BSA TWINS A50 & A65 1962-1969 (SECOND BOOK OF)
BULTACO 125cc to 37cc SINGLES 1968-1979 WORKSHOP MANUAL
CZ 125cc to 380cc SINGLES 1967-1974 WORKSHOP MANUAL
DOUGLAS 1929-1939 PREWAR ALL MODELS (BOOK OF)
DOUGLAS 1948-1957 POSTWAR ALL MODELS FACTORY SHOP MANUAL
DUCATI 160cc, 250cc & 350cc OHC MODELS FACTORY SHOP MANUAL
HODAKA 90cc,100cc & 125cc SINGLES 1964-1978 WORKSHOP MANUAL
HONDA 50cc ALL MODELS UP TO 1970 INC MONKEY & TRAIL (BOOK OF)
HONDA 90cc ALL MODELS UP TO 1966 (BOOK OF)
HONDA TWINS & SINGLES 50cc THRU 305cc 1960-1966 (BOOK OF)
HONDA TWINS ALL MODELS 125cc THRU 450cc UP TO 1968 (BOOK OF)
HONDA C100 50cc SUPER CUB O.H.C. 1959-1962 FACTORY WSM
HONDA C110 50cc SPORT CUB O.H.C. 1960-1962 FACTORY WSM
HONDA 50-65-70-90cc O.H.C. SINGLES 1959-1983 WSM
HONDA 100-125cc SINGLES CB/CD/CL/SL/TL 1970-1984 FACTORY WSM
HONDA 125-150cc TWINS C/CS/CB/CA 1959-1966 FACTORY WSM
HONDA 125-160-175-200cc TWINS 1965-1978 WORKSHOP MANUAL
HONDA 250-305cc TWINS C/CS/CB 1961-1968 FACTORY WSM
HOHDA 250-350cc TWINS CB/CL/SL 1968-1973 FACTORY WSM
HONDA 250-360cc TWINS CB/CL/CJ 1974-1977 FACTORY WSM
HONDA 350F & 400F 4-CYLINDER 1972-1977 FACTORY WSM
HONDA 450cc TWINS CB/CL 1965-1974 K0 to K7 WORKSHOP MANUAL
HONDA 500cc & 550cc 4-CYL 1971-1978 FACTORY WORKSHOP MANUAL
HONDA 750cc SHOC 4-CYL 1969-1978 K0~K8 WORKSHOP MANUAL
HUSQVARNA 125cc to 450cc SINGLES 1965-1975 WORKSHOP MANUAL
INDIAN PONYBIKE, BOY RACER & PAPOOSE ILL PARTS LIST & SALES LIT

J.A.P. ENGINES 1927-1952 & MOTORCYCLES 1934-1952 (BOOK OF)
MAICO 250cc to 501cc 1968-1978 WORKSHOP MANUAL
MATCHLESS 1931-1939 ALL MODELS 250cc THRU 990cc (BOOK OF)
MATCHLESS 1945-1956 350 & 500cc SINGLES (BOOK OF)
MATCHLESS 1955-1966 350 & 500cc SINGLES (BOOK OF)
MATCHLESS 1957-1966 FACTORY WSM - ALL SINGLES & TWINS
MONTESA 1962-1978 125cc to 360cc ALL MODELS WORKSHOP MANUAL
NEW IMPERIAL ALL SV & OHV FROM 1935 ONWARDS (BOOK OF)
NORTON 1932-1939 PREWAR MODELS (BOOK OF)
NORTON 1932-1947 (BOOK OF)
NORTON 1938-1956 (BOOK OF)
NORTON 1945-1963 MODELS 16H, Big4, ES2, 19 & 50 WSM'S & PARTS
NORTON 1955-1963 MODELS 19, 50 & ES2 (BOOK OF)
NORTON 1948-1970 DOMINATOR TWINS FACTORY WSM'S & PARTS
NORTON 1955-1965 DOMINATOR TWINS (BOOK OF)
NORTON 1960-1970 TWIN CYLINDER FACTORY WORKSHOP MANUAL
NORTON 1970-1975 COMMANDO 850 & 750cc FACTORY WSM
NORTON 1975-1978 MK 3 COMMANDO 850 cc FACTORY WSM
PANTHER 1932-1958 LIGHTWEIGHT MODELS 250 & 350cc (BOOK OF)
PANTHER 1938-1966 HEAVYWEIGHT MODELS 600 & 650cc (BOOK OF)
PENTON-KTM-SACHS 1968-1975 100cc & 125cc WORKSHOP MANUAL
PENTON-KTM 1972-1975 175cc, 250cc & 400cc WSM & PARTS MANUALS
RALEIGH MOTORCYCLES 1919-1933 (BOOK OF)
ROYAL ENFIELD 1934-1946 SINGLES & V TWINS (BOOK OF)
ROYAL ENFIELD 1937-1953 SINGLES & V TWINS (BOOK OF)
ROYAL ENFIELD 1946-1962 SINGLES (BOOK OF)
ROYAL ENFIELD 1948-1962 350cc & 500cc PRE-UNIT BULLET WSM
ROYAL ENFIELD 1948-1963 500cc TWINS FACTORY WORKSHOP MANUAL
ROYAL ENFIELD 1952-1963 700cc TWINS FACTORY WORKSHOP MANUAL
ROYAL ENFIELD 1956-1966 250cc CRUSADER & 350cc NEW BULLET WSM
ROYAL ENFIELD 1958-1966 250cc & 350cc SINGLES (SECOND BOOK OF)
ROYAL ENFIELD 1962-1970 INTERCEPTOR WSM'S & PARTS (Compilation)
RUDGE 1933-1939 (BOOK OF)
SACHS 1968-1975 100cc & 125cc ENGINES WSM & M/CYCLE PARTS LIST
SUNBEAM 1928-1939 (BOOK OF)
SUNBEAM 1946-1957 S7 & S8 (BOOK OF)
SUZUKI 50cc & 80cc UP TO 1966 (BOOK OF)
SUZUKI T10 1963-1967 FACTORY WORKSHOP MANUAL
SUZUKI T20 & T200 1965-1969 FACTORY WORKSHOP MANUAL
SUZUKI TWINS 1962 ONWARDS 125-500cc WORKSHOP MANUAL
TRIUMPH 1935-1949 SINGLES & TWINS (BOOK OF)
TRIUMPH 1937-1961 SINGLES SV & OHV 250cc-600cc + TERRIER & CUB
TRIUMPH 1945-1955 PRE-UNIT 350cc, 500cc & 650cc TWINS WSM No.11
TRIUMPH 1945-1959 TWINS (BOOK OF)
TRIUMPH 1956-1969 TWINS (BOOK OF)
TRIUMPH 1956-1962 PRE-UNIT 500cc & 650cc TWINS WSM No.17
TRIUMPH 1957-1963 UNIT CONSTRUCTION 350-500cc WSM No.4
TRIUMPH 1963-1974 UNIT CONSTRUCTION 350-500cc FACTORY WSM
TRIUMPH 1963-1970 UNIT CONSTRUCTION 650cc FACTORY WSM
TRIUMPH 1968-1974 TRIDENT T150 & T150V FACTORY WSM
TRIUMPH 1971-1973 650cc OIL-IN-FRAME FACTORY WSM
TRIUMPH 1973-1978 750cc BONNEVILLE & TIGER FACTORY WSM
TRIUMPH 1979-1983 750cc T140, TR7 & TR65 FACTORY WSM
VELOCETTE 1925-1970 ALL SINGLES & TWINS (BOOK OF)
VELOCETTE 1933-1952 MOV-MAC-MSS RIGID FRAME FACTORY WSM
VELOCETTE 1953-1960 MAC SPRING FRAME WSM & ILL PARTS LIST
VELOCETTE 1954-1971 MSS-VENOM-THRUXTON-VIPER FACTORY WSM
VILLIERS ENGINE UP TO 1959 INC. 3 WHEELERS (BOOK OF)
VILLIERS ENGINE UP TO 1969 (BOOK OF)
VINCENT 1935-1955 (WORKSHOP MANUAL)
YAMAHA 1961-1967 YA5 & YA6 (WORKSHOP MANUAL & ILL PARTS LIST)
YAMAHA 1968-1971 DT1 & MX SERIES Inc. GYT WORKSHOP MANUAL
YAMAHA 1971-1972 JT1& JT2 (WORKSHOP MANUAL & ILL PARTS LIST)

VELOCEPRESS MANUALS – SCOOTERS BY MAKE

BSA SUNBEAM SCOOTER WORKSHOP MANUAL 1959-1965
BSA SUNBEAM SCOOTER 1959-1965 (BOOK OF)
LAMBRETTA 1947-1957 ALL 125 & 150cc MODELS (BOOK OF)
LAMBRETTA 1957-1970 LI & TV MODELS (SECOND BOOK OF)
NSU PRIMA 1956-1964 ALL MODELS (BOOK OF)
TRIUMPH TIGRESS SCOOTER WORKSHOP MANUAL 1959-1965
TRIUMPH TIGRESS SCOOTER (BOOK OF)
VESPA 1951-1961 (BOOK OF)
VESPA 1955-1963 125 & 150cc & GS MODELS (SECOND BOOK OF)
VESPA 1955-1968 GS & SS (BOOK OF)
VESPA 1963-1972 90, 125 & 150cc (THIRD BOOK OF)

VELOCEPRESS MANUALS – MOPEDS & MOTORIZED BICYCLES

CYCLEMOTOR (BOOK OF)
NSU QUICKLY 1953-1963 ALL MODELS (BOOK OF)
PUCH MAXI N & S MAINTENANCE & REPAIR (3 MANUAL COMPILATION)
RALEIGH MOPEDS 1960-1969 (BOOK OF)

VELOCEPRESS MANUALS - THREE WHEELER'S

BOND MINICAR THREE WHEELER 1948-1967 (BOOK OF)
BMW ISETTA FACTORY WORKSHOP MANUAL
BSA THREE WHEELER (BOOK OF)
RELIANT REGAL THREE WHEELER 1952-1973 (BOOK OF)
VINTAGE MORGAN THREE WHEELER (BOOK OF)

VELOCEPRESS TECHNICAL BOOKS – MOTORCYCLE

1930'S BRITISH MOTORCYCLE CARBS & ELEC COMPONENTS (BOOK OF)
1930'S BRITISH MOTORCYCLE ENGINES (OVERHAUL & MAINTENANCE)
1930'S BRITISH MOTORCYCLE GEARBOXES & CLUTCHES (BOOK OF)
CATALOG OF BRITISH MOTORCYCLES (1951 MODELS)
LUCAS ELECTRONICS BRITISH M/CYCLES REPAIR & PARTS (1950-1977)
MOTORCYCLE ENGINEERING (P.E. Irving)
MOTORCYCLE ROAD TESTS 1949-1953 (Motor Cycle Magazine UK)
SPEED AND HOW TO OBTAIN IT (Motor Cycle Magazine UK)
TUNING FOR SPEED (P.E. Irving)
WIPAC (COMBO) MANUAL NUMBER 3 + M/CYCLE & SCOOTER MANUAL

www.VelocePress.com

www.ingramcontent.com/pod-product-compliance
Lightning Source LLC
Chambersburg PA
CBHW080745300426
44114CB00019B/2651